ADVISORY COMMITTEES
IN ACTION

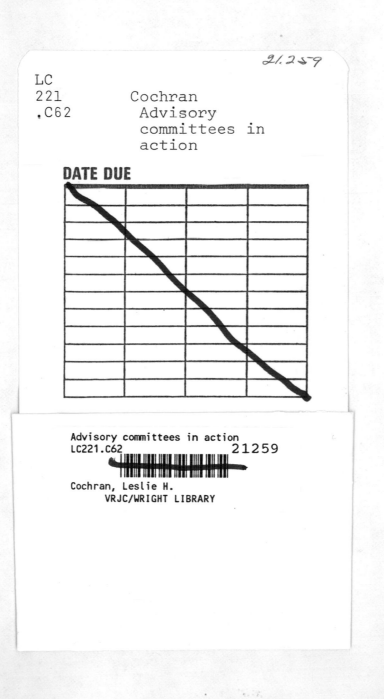

ADVISORY COMMITTEES IN ACTION

An Educational/Occupational/Community Partnership

Leslie H. Cochran
Central Michigan University

L. Allen Phelps
University of Illinois

Linda Letwin Cochran
Michigan Department of Education

Allyn and Bacon, Inc.
Boston   London   Sydney   Toronto

Library of Congress Cataloging in Publication Data

Cochran, Leslie H
   Advisory committees in action.

   Includes bibliographies and index.
   1. Citizen advisory committees in education—United
States. 2. Community and school—United States. 3. Public
relations—United States—Schools. 4. Educational surveys—
United States. I. Phelps, L. Allen, 1948– joint author.
II. Cochran, Linda Letwin, 1947– joint author. III. Title.
LC221.C62   379.73   79–15309
ISBN 0–205–06661–5

Production Editor: Robine Storm van Leeuwen
Manufacturing Buyer: Patricia Hart

Printed in the United States of America

Contents

Preface

The importance of public involvement in the educational process has been a primary tenet of American education. In practice, however, citizens have had only limited direct involvement in determining the direction of education. Even in vocational education, which has long cited the value of involvement with business and industry, there is little evidence to demonstrate the effective use of such cooperative ventures. It was not until the massive social upheaval of the 1960s that the real impact of this tenet began to appear in full force. As a partial educational response to societal problems, citizen participation emerged as a primary component in the planning and operation of all educational programs.

The movement of citizens into the mainstream of the educational process took many forms. Educators placed renewed emphasis on various community-oriented aspects of the programs and attempted to extend the school/community concept. Community-based career education programs, field-based experiences, and business- and industry-sponsored placement services were introduced. Newly formed citizen groups started to exert more pressure and influence on the formal educational structure. In addition there were legislative responses. For example, in 1972, legislation in California linked school advisory committees to the early childhood education program. In 1973, the Florida legislature mandated school advisory committees, either at the district or building level. In 1977, South Carolina followed the same pattern by passing a law requiring local school advisory committees. State and federal legislation was most prevalent in career education and vocational education, with the Education Amendments of 1976 being the most encompassing as they required advisory committees for all vocational education programs.

The advisory committee emerged as the primary mechanism to facilitate the educational/occupational/community partnership essential to relevant program development. While many programs have gained varying degrees of success without their use, programs have usually experienced broader support and effectiveness with the initiation of an advisory committee. Practical experience and recent research further emphasize the position that this significant programmatic factor cannot be left to chance. While advisory committees are an integral aspect of an effective educational program, they are especially important in career and occupational education.

Experience reveals that advisory committees are often dysfunctional and do not accomplish the purposes for which they were established due to the following reasons: (1) many administrators do not recognize the value of an active functioning advisory committee, (2) most educators do not have the time nor the expertise to communicate with advisory committees, (3) a large number of educators do not possess the ability adequately to fulfill leadership roles regarding the development and utilization of advisory committees, (4) members of advisory committees do not understand their function in the development of educational programs, and (5) both teachers and administrators are unfamiliar with their role and responsibility on an advisory committee.

Advisory Committees in Action: An Educational/Occupational/ Community Partnership was developed to deal with these problems by providing a practical orientation to the implementation of the advisory committee concept. This book is based on the premise that before advisory committees will be used effectively, educational personnel need to understand the nature and function of advisory committees, to develop basic skills in using and organizing advisory committees, and to have real examples and illustrations that may be adapted for advisory committee action. To accomplish these goals, this book is organized in three sections: Part I, Perspectives on Advisory Committees, provides an overview of the development and structure of advisory committees. Its focus is on the role and responsibility, the need for, and the degree of use of advisory committees, along with a delineation of the levels and types of advisory groups. Part II, Major Advisory Committee Functions, presents seven distinct but interrelated roles performed by advisory committees. Each function is described; and specific strategies, procedures, and illustrations are provided for initiating the basic committee activities. In addition, communication exercises are provided to assist in individual and group inservice development. Part III, Organization and Management of Advisory Committees, builds on the concepts presented in the first two sections by focusing on the establishment, operation, planning, and evaluation of advisory committees. Throughout the book, practical examples are given to assist in the implementation of an effective advisory committee.

The authors are indeed grateful to the many colleagues and leaders in the field of occupational and career education who have contributed significantly to the preparation of this book.

Several of the ideas found in Part II are based on materials collected and concepts developed in the Vocational Education Advisory Committee Project directed by Leslie H. Cochran, L. Allen Phelps, and Joseph F. Skupin and funded by the Vocational-Technical Education Service of the Michigan Department of Education. The authors are particularly grateful to the following individuals for having reviewed the manuscript and provided meaningful feedback.

Donald O. Bush   Department of Educational Administration, Central Michigan University, Mt. Pleasant, Michigan.

Richard K. Hofstrand   Department of Adult, Vocational and Technical Education, Illinois Office of Education, Springfield, Illinois

Caroline E. Hughes National Advisory Council for Vocational Education, Cushing, Oklahoma.

Thomas E. Long Division of Occupational and Vocational Studies, The Pennsylvania State University, University Park, Pennsylvania.

Bertin Michael Sauk Area Center, Crestwood, Illinois.

Robert Rose Richland Community College, Decatur, Illinois.

William Rude State Advisory Council for Vocational Education, Lansing, Michigan.

Frank S. Stillings School of Fine and Applied Arts, Central Michigan University, Mt. Pleasant, Michigan.

Jerry Wircenski Division of Occupational and Vocational Studies, The Pennsylvania State University, University Park, Pennsylvania.

A special acknowledgment is also extended to the many individuals who granted permission for the use of their material in this book.

Leslie H. Cochran
L. Allen Phelps
Linda Letwin Cochran

PART I

PERSPECTIVES ON
ADVISORY COMMITTEES

The educational role that citizens from the community play has been evolving since the early beginnings of formal education. Examples of citizen involvement in educational programs may be cited from the Middle Ages through the colonial period to the present day. While the term advisory committee has been used widely throughout the twentieth century, it was not until the time of the massive social upheavals following World War II that advisory committees emerged as a dominant force in the educational system.

This section provides an overview of the developmental process with an emphasis on the current context in which advisory committees are called upon to operate. In Chapter 1, the term advisory committee is defined, and through the definition the reader gains a better understanding of the current role and responsibility of advisory committees, the need for such committees, and the degree to which they are used. Chapter 2 presents the overall structure for advisory committee action, delineates the various roles of advisory committees, and highlights differences between committees operating at the national, state, regional, and local levels. This chapter places emphasis on describing the types of advisory committees in the local community and providing specific illustrations of different forms of committees.

Examples drawn from career education and occupational education are provided throughout the section to stress the importance of advisory committees in a relevant educational process. This section also examines current legislation to determine what responsibility has been mandated with regard to advisory committees. At the conclusion of each chapter, a list of suggested activities is provided for those individuals interested in learning more about the development or structure of advisory committees.

1 The development of advisory committees

Citizen participation in education is not one but many topics. The phrase citizen participation encompasses a wide range of ideas, programs, issues, and mechanisms that have impact on nearly every phase of the educational system. The widespread use of terms similar to the term citizen participation reflects a significant increase in activity and discussion concerning the roles of students, parents, and other citizens in determining the shape of educational programs. While career-related and occupational education programs have a long history of involvement with the community, this national trend has placed new emphasis on various cooperative arrangements between the school and business, industry, labor, and other segments of the community. The advisory committee has emerged as the primary mechanism in the community to provide citizens with an opportunity to discuss issues, analyze inputs, and provide recommendations that affect the policies, content, and future directions of the total educational program. The outcomes of this rational process are the programs that evolve and the direct benefits that are realized by students.

To provide a complete perspective of the advisory committee and its role in the total educational system, this chapter is divided into four major sections. The first section explains the concept and the purpose of the advisory committee; the second describes the overall evolution of advisory committees; the third presents the need for and the rationale supporting advisory committees; and the fourth provides a summary of research on the utilization and effectiveness of advisory committees.

THE ADVISORY COMMITTEE

It has been widely acclaimed by practitioners, researchers, and state and national leaders that the development and improvement of quality educational programs is highly dependent on maintaining a close working relationship among education, industry, business, and labor. This philosophy, which permeates all of public education, has been a guiding concept since the early development of vocational education and has provided the basic framework for all current career-related programs.

Within the category of career and occupational education, the use of field trips, of speakers from business and industry, and of industrial supplies and materials has facilitated this cooperative venture. The development of equipment loan programs, of education coordinators within industry, and of teacher exchange programs with business and industry flows from this cooperative framework. Cooperative education and work-study programs fit totally within this concept. Each of these arrangements has its own advantages and represents an attempt to extend the communication link between the school and the community.

The most widely recognized, accepted, and used approach to enhance educational/occupational/community interaction, however, is the advisory committee, which is established to maintain contact between formalized education and the community it serves. The advisory committee's prime function is to assist schools in providing education that will be of value to students upon their entry into adult society and the world of work. The advisory committee thereby serves as a formal mechanism for providing collective advice, recommendations, and service to the school or unit, its students, teachers, administrators, and other constituents.

A working definition

It is difficult to provide a specific and concise definition for advisory committees because they are formed to fulfill the necessary functions and demands that evolve from a particular level or situation. The direction taken by one advisory committee may vary considerably from that taken by another. For example, one committee may focus its attention on a continual evaluation of current practices to determine the extent to which goals are being achieved; another may address issues related to the purposes of courses of study and special services provided for students. The committee may place emphasis on questions related to long-term program planning and its effect on curriculum, equipment, and facilities. On occasion, the committee may be concerned only with program inauguration; or, it may advise on general topics involved in a particular field, occupation, or special phase of a program on a long-term basis. In still other situations, the role of the advisory committee may vary depending on whether it has a national, state, regional, or local focus.

Within the context of these variations, however, a definition is required to make the concept operational and to provide commonality of purpose. *An advisory committee is a group composed primarily of individuals outside the educational profession who are selected from segments of the community collectively to advise educational personnel regarding one or more educational programs or aspects of a program.*

Each word or phrase in this definition may be interpreted differently as the specific situation may dictate. The term *group,* for example, may range from seven to eleven individuals at the local level, fifteen to twenty at the state or regional level, and as many as twenty-five to thirty at the national level. Its composition may also vary depending on the committee focus and the type of individuals required to provide the necessary representation. *Composed primarily of individuals outside the educational profession* is a phrase which provides a common core for all advisory committees. Two-thirds to three-fourths of those on the committee come from parts of the community outside the educational profession. The phrase *who are selected* does not have any specialized meaning, but it should be emphasized that advisory committee members are selected and appointed by educational personnel. *Segments of the community* is another phrase that is very likely to take on different meanings. To illustrate, the community may be defined as a school district, city or part of a large urban area, county, region, state, or another geographic group. Likewise, a segment may refer to individuals with specialized knowledge, those representing certain industries, those with a common interest (such as the handicapped), or those concerned about a specific program. Another phrase which is common to all advisory committees is *collectively to advise educational personnel.* This is the focal point of all action because the committee's primary role is that of providing input in the form of advice or recommendations. This process is the same whether the educational personnel are in the school system, a government agency, or a business/industry training program. The final phrase, *one or more educational programs or aspects of a program,* presents numerous opportunities for deviation: it may include the entire program, one specific occupation, an occupational cluster, or a particular function such as placement.

It is possible, of course, to adapt or modify the words within this definition, but the core elements are always present. This is illustrated by the State of Illinois Board of Vocational Education and Rehabilitation [71:2] definition:

> An advisory council is a group of persons selected to collectively advise regarding career education efforts within the community. Members are predominantly from outside the field of education and are selected because of specialized knowledge.

The Department of Education in Nevada [120:2] answered the question as to what an advisory committee is by stating that

> A Vocational Education Advisory Committee is a group of people, from the work force but predominately from outside of the field of education, who advise educators on establishment and maintenance of vocational education programs to meet the needs of individuals and the community.

The State Advisory Committee for Vocational Education in Kansas [79:1] stressed the importance of this communications link and noted that

> An advisory committee may be defined as a group of persons outside the education profession, made up of representative laypersons, recognized and respected in their own fields of work, who advise and assist educational personnel regarding the building and maintaining of sound vocational education programs, based on the real needs for a community, region, state or nation.

Basic committee purpose

The function of the advisory committee naturally varies depending on how its definition is interpreted. Also, the type of committee formed along with its goals and purposes (described in Chapter 2) and the various functions assumed by the committee (described in Chapters 3–9) shape the efforts of the committee. It must be stressed from the outset, however, that *the primary purpose of an advisory committee is just that—one of providing advice. The committee has no administrative or legislative authority, nor does it in any way take away rights and/or privileges of the school staff.* As emphasized in the *Guide for Establishment and Conduct of Local Advisory Committees for Vocational Agriculture Departments**:

> First of all, it should be clearly understood that the creation and establishing of an advisory body is to assist the vocational agriculture teacher, the administration and the school board in carrying out the objectives of the agriculture program. *It is strictly advisory in its capacity and has no administrative authority.* This philosophy must be clearly understood if the committee is to function properly. Formation of advisory committees is not intended to usurp the prerogative of the Board of Education or its administrative staff.

While their purpose is clear, it should also be pointed out that the committee is composed of individuals with special skills or knowledge who provide assistance for the benefit of students in the program. The committee should not be used as a sounding board for complaints, nor should it be used as a club to settle personal problems with school administrators. As cited by Brodinsky [25:3], there are five major ways in which an advisory committee can be misused:

1. *Free labor:* "If we had a community advisory council, maybe it could dig up the facts we need."
2. *Rubber stamp:* "I'll bet a bottom dollar we could set up an advisory council to O.K. our new policies on smoking to get the parents to accept them too."
3. *Shock absorber:* "We've taken enough abuse on that issue. Let the community advisory council get some of the flak."
4. *Front-man promoter:* "We got cut down again on those sex education courses. Don't you think a citizens advisory council could push them through next year?"
5. *S.O.S. team:* "We aren't getting anywhere with the fiscal people, and now we're in a head-on fight with the teachers. Don't you think a community advisory council could . . . ."

EVOLUTION OF ADVISORY COMMITTEES

While advisory committees are certainly not new, their use has expanded dramatically in recent years. This growth, however, has been more than

---

*San Luis Obispo, Calif.: California State Polytechnic College, Vocational Education Productions, undated, p. 5. Used with permission.

a multiplying of numbers for it has been accompanied by major changes in purpose, role, function, and emphasis. As the vocational education programs have shifted from a narrow, single-purpose mission to a broad, technical-occupational-career orientation, so has the character of advisory committees changed. Historically, citizen committees served as the forerunners of several segments of the present educational system. For example, the use of experienced laity in the early apprenticeship programs developed by the guilds during the Middle Ages formed the base for advisory committees. Through close supervision, the guilds were responsible for high work standards, the creation of well-wrought and artistic productions, and the development of a system of vocational education for the working people.

Similarly, colonial officials in New England insisted that everyone should be able to read and write. When experience proved that parents were not equally diligent or able to teach their children, officials were quick to decree that the "chosen men" in every town be charged with the responsibility for "the redress of this evil." As communities grew and government became more complex, local leaders began to rely heavily on appointed committees of fellow citizens to review proposals, make recommendations, and report back to them. These groups dealt mainly with school- or academically related problems and provided impetus for the formation of other community school organizations, such as the Parent Teachers Association (PTA).

Inception of advisory committees

The earliest proponents of vocational education recognized the need to establish a close working relationship with their counterparts in business, industry, and agriculture. They recognized that the involvement of employers, employees, and community leaders was essential to ensure that the programs met local employment needs, that individuals in the community would not feel disassociated from the program, and that program relevance was maintained. Emphasis in these early efforts tended to focus on local surveys of employment needs and informal efforts involving local employers to create a feeling that it was a joint program rather than something totally initiated and run by school personnel.

School-initiated advisory committees have been present in public education for most of this century. Committees in agricultural education, for example, have been traced to 1911. In 1913, a law passed in Indiana contained a provision which stated:

> Boards of education or township trustees administering vocational departments for industrial, agricultural, or domestic science education, shall, under a scheme to be approved by the state board of education, appoint an advisory committee composed of members representing local trades, industries and occupations. It shall be the duty of the advisory committee to counsel with and advise the board and other school officials having the management and supervision of such schools or departments. [9:10]

In recognition of the interdependence of industry and education, U.S. Office of Education rules and regulations as far back as 1922 pointed to cooperation with industry as one of the duties of supervisors of trade and industrial education.

Intervening years

While the need for and the value of advisory committees were a part of the early philosophy of vocational education, in practice they tended to be used only sparingly. Despite the passage of the Smith Hughes Act in 1917, the practices of the 1920s, 1930s, and 1940s suggest that little advantage was taken of the potential bridge between educators and their counterparts in the world of work. One may only speculate as to the reason for the increased use of advisory committees following the mid- and late 1950s. Some have advanced the theory that the pressures and emergency demands of World War II created a revitalization of citizen interest in schools and thus in the utilization of advisory committees. While the events surrounding World War II may have served as a catalyst, several social conditions and movements may be used to illustrate why the following decades were to witness a dramatic increase in emphasis on the uses of advisory committees.

Public control of education. With public education firmly entrenched in the United States, the early and middle decades of the twentieth century became a time when the philosophies of Dewey, Piaget, Mann, and others were being applied. The public had an obligation to become intelligent about public education if it was to be involved in its control. As a result there was increased pressure to involve citizens in educational decision making. Small, districtwide groups, elected from local neighborhoods, began to replace the larger school boards, and various reforms were made to take partisan politics and patronage out of education. The public, however, was for the most part kept at arms length as civic-minded leaders were called upon to rally support for school policies.

Shifts in value structures. During this time major shifts in basic values were also taking place. The growth and development of large cities made it more difficult for individuals to influence school policies. The experiences of the Depression and the establishment of new social programs created new sets of issues and concerns. Many of these programs, such as Head Start and Follow Through, required community representation in their planning and execution. The work ethic came under attack. The multidimensional nature of society led to clashes in viewpoints concerning racial, economic, and social issues. The rapidity of change became an alarming factor, especially as segments of the population attempted to influence every phase of society including education. As an example, the urban poor became participants in educational politics, using aggressive modes of participation—protests, boycotts, mass rallies, marches, and militant confrontations. From an educational point of view, the point of challenge became community control of the schools.

Growth in technology and the educational enterprise. As a compounding factor, the nation moved rapidly from a society with an agricultural/industry base to a highly technological society embarking on the Space Age. Knowledge began to increase in geometric proportions. Automation, mass production, and obsolescence of skills became major issues and left vocational educators bewildered with how to maintain curriculum relevancy. The educational enterprise became so immense and complex that it gave the appearance of existing for its own sake. The mounting volume of business details led to increased specialization and to the virtual control of many school systems by highly trained professionals. In an attempt to counterbalance these forces, numerous community-based responses were made with particular support coming from two foundations. On a national scale, the Charles Stewart Mott Foundation funded community/school programs that made extensive utilization of the advisory committee as the primary communications link between the school and the community. Particularly notable was the Mott Foundation's Project SNAP, which provided direct financial support to local advisory committees. The Rockefeller Foundation, also, invested more than four million dollars in school advisory committee projects in several cities, including Los Angeles, New Orleans, Oakland, Memphis, Miami, Minneapolis, and Newark [47].

Expressions of citizen involvement and participation. With the rapid transitions in almost every segment of life, citizens began to question basic policies and practices. Equality of rights and the quality of life became paramount social issues. Mass media provided avenues for the increasingly active society to express its feelings. With this came a drive to "get involved" and "do it yourself." Citizens began to question decisions that were made without their involvement and that directly or indirectly affected their lives. As a result, the sixties stand as a decade of challenge to established patterns of authority, leaving unsolved most of the issues underlying the years of unrest and activism. One important legacy of this period is the legitimacy of public involvement in the schools, which is now reflected in an array of local policies and state and federal legislation recommending or requiring advisory committees.

State and federal response to vocational education

By the midpoint of the twentieth century, it was obvious that the dramatic changes that were taking place in the role of the school in the United States called for a new relationship between vocational education and the community. The curriculum was broader, the clientele was vastly expanded, the education of all youth was a priority, and the increased costs had generated concern and widespread interest in the educational process and its results. In response, state legislators, state boards of education, and state directors of vocational education expressed increased concern in achieving a higher level of local industry/education cooperation. Some states, notably Wisconsin, Pennsylvania, and New York passed legislation mandating the establishment of local advisory committees. Most states published material suggesting what the functions of advisory committees should or could be and urged their organization and utilization [29].

By 1961, the need for review and reevaluation of vocational education was made clear as President Kennedy formed the President's Panel of Consultants of Vocational Education. The information issuing from this panel [169] and a subsequent report [170] from the National Advisory Council on Vocational Education provided the framework for the Vocational Education Act of 1963 and The Vocational Education Amendments of 1968. These pieces of legislation broadened the concept of vocational education from providing training in a few occupational categories to providing preparation in a variety of diverse occupations. They also provided for the development of special programs to meet the occupational needs of academically, economically, or otherwise disadvantaged persons.

In addition to the fact that advisory committees played a key role in the development of key legislation, the 1968 Amendments established two major benchmarks in the evolution of advisory committees. First, it provided for a permanent National Advisory Council on Vocational Education, which has subsequently had an impact on legislation and has issued numerous cogent reports recommending improvements for vocational education. Second, it mandated the creation of state advisory councils as a condition for receiving funds. As a result, many states reemphasized the use of advisory committees at the local level, as can be verified by a review of State Plans for Vocational Education. An illustration of the Amendments' impact on individual states is provided in Appendix A, which reveals how the section on advisory committees in Michigan's *Program Standards of Quality for Vocational Technical Education Programs* responded to the intent of the 1968 Amendments and the subsequent Education Amendment of 1976.

Career education expands the need

Probably no single factor has done more to stimulate the growth of advisory committees than the legislation passed in the 1960s. The career education movement, for example, brought a greatly expanded perspective to vocational education and the already broadened concepts resulting from the 1963 and 1968 legislation. It was based upon a premise of unifying the concepts of career awareness, career exploration, and career preparation within the total education/community environment. The movement focused on providing experiences for students that would familiarize them with work values and integrate these work values into their personal value systems. While building a bridge between college preparation programs and vocational education, as well as utilizing the total community in the educational process, career education presented a new focus and new sets of issues to be addressed by all advisory committees.

Career education also established the need for a new type of advisory committee, one that focused on all segments of education rather than just occupational education. For example, the rules and general powers of the Career Education Act passed in Colorado in 1975 called for a state committee composed of "the commissioner of education, the executive director of the commission on higher education, the director of occupational education, the director of community colleges and one classroom teacher involved in a career education program or one specialist involved in a career education program."

Similarly, in Michigan, the Career Education Act passed in 1974 implemented career education planning districts. These planning districts were comprised of local and intermediate school districts in geographical proximity. Approximately fifty such districts were formed across the state of Michigan. The legislation required that each of these districts be served by an advisory council and that not more than one-half of the council members represent the education profession. Specifically, the act called for representation on the council from local and intermediate boards of education, the arts, business or industry, a labor organization or employment agency, parents, teachers, counselors, and students. The function of the councils was to increase cooperation and articulation between local educational agencies. One of the coordinating activities undertaken by the council is the annual preparation of an implementation plan for career education. This plan, developed by the career education planning district council, is based on the individual plans submitted by each local educational agency within the planning district.

At the national level, the same forces were being felt. The Education Amendments of 1974 created the National Advisory Council on Career Education. In 1977, the passage of the Career Education Incentive Act [166] reaffirmed the commitment to career education as the Congress declared that

(1) a major purpose of education is to prepare every individual for a career suitable to that individual's preference,

(2) career education should be an integral part of the Nation's educational process which serves as preparation for work,

(3) career education holds promise of improving the quality of education and opening career opportunities for all students by relating education to their life aspirations, and

(4) educational agencies and institutions (including agencies and institutions of elementary and secondary education, higher education, adult education, employment training and retraining, and vocational education) should make every effort to fulfill that purpose.

In recognition of the prime importance of work in our society and in recognition of the role that the schools play in the lives of all Americans, it is the purpose of this Act to assist States and local educational agencies and institutions of postsecondary education, including collaborative arrangements with the appropriate agencies and organizations, in making education as preparation for work, and as a means of relating work values to other life roles and choices (such as family life), a major goal of all who teach and all who learn by increasing the emphasis they place on career awareness, exploration, decision-making, and planning, and to do so in a manner which will promote equal opportunity in making career choices through the elimination of bias and stereotyping in such activities, including bias and stereotyping on account of race, sex, age, economic status, or handicap.

The act further indicated that the membership on the national council would be composed of

not less than fifteen public members broadly representative of the fields of education, guidance, and counseling, the arts, the humanities, the sciences, community services, business and industry, and the general public, including (i) members of organizations of handicapped persons, minority groups knowledgeable with respect to discrimination in employment and stereotyping affecting career choices, and women who are knowledgeable with respect to sex discrimination and stereotyping, and (ii) not less than two members who shall be representative of labor and of business, respectively . . . .

Federal mandate for advisory committees

During the first seventy-five years of the twentieth century, the use of advisory committees increased on a gradual basis. The significant growth in activity in the last ten to fifteen years of this period may be projected as only the tip of the iceberg since *the passage of the Education Amendments of 1976 has established a totally new set of parameters for the use of advisory committees in vocational education. For the first time, local advisory committees were required by federal law for those districts receiving assistance under these amendments. Furthermore, state councils were required to provide technical assistance as requested to establish and operate such committees.* The specific language in respect to local advisory committees in the act was as follows:

Sec. 105 (g) (1) Each eligible recipient receiving assistance under this Act to operate vocational education programs shall establish a local advisory council to provide such agency with advice on current job needs and on the relevancy of courses being offered by such agency in meeting such needs. Such local advisory councils shall be composed of members of the general public, especially of representatives of business, industry, and labor, and such local advisory councils may be established for program areas, schools, communities, or regions, whichever the recipient determines best to meet the needs of that recipient.

(2) Each State board shall notify eligible recipients within the State of the responsibilities of such recipients under the provisions of paragraph (1), and each State advisory council shall make available to such recipients and the local advisory councils of such recipients such technical assistance as such recipients may request to establish and operate such councils. [165]

The final rules and regulations prepared by the U.S. Office of Education to implement the act, published in the *Federal Register* on October 3, 1977, [53] stated the following:

LOCAL ADVISORY COUNCILS

104.111 Establishment of local advisory councils.

(a) Each eligible recipient (that is, each local educational agency or postsecondary educational institution which receives Federal assistance under the Act) shall establish a local advisory council on vocational education.

(b) The local advisory council may be established for:

(1) Program areas:
(2) Schools;
(3) The community; or
(4) The region in which the eligible recipient is located.

(c) The local advisory council shall be composed of representatives of the general public including at least a representative of:

(1) Business;
(2) Industry; and
(3) Labor.

(d) Each eligible recipient shall establish a local advisory council which has an appropriate representation of both sexes and an appropriate representation of the racial and ethnic minorities found in the program areas, schools, community, or region which the local advisory council serves.

(e) An eligible recipient may form a local advisory council composed of representatives from several craft committees, or representatives of several school councils, having the requisite representation in paragraph (c) of this section.

104.112 Duties of local advisory councils.

(a) The local advisory council shall advise the eligible recipient on:

(1) Current job needs; and
(2) The relevance of programs (courses) being offered by the local educational agency or postsecondary educational agency in meeting current job needs.

(b) The local advisory council shall consult with the eligible recipient in developing its application to the State board.

Additional clarity on the intent of the act was also provided in the same *Federal Register* as the comments and responses from the national public hearings regarding the previously published "proposed" rules and regulations were summarized:

LOCAL ADVISORY COUNCILS

104.111 Local advisory councils—representatives of additional groups.

Comment. Many commenters suggested broadening the categories of membership required on the local advisory council so that the categories would be similar to the categories required of membership on the State advisory councils.

Others recommended the addition of representatives of specific categories. Specific categories mentioned were: categories (17), (18), and (20) described in 104.92(a) in relation to the State advisory council; women; racial, ethnic, or major language minorities; private schools; persons knowledgeable in vocational education (but not administration); manpower services; local prime sponsor councils under the authority of CETA; the State agency responsible for data collection; and community based organization. Commenters particularly recommended that the phrase "shall be composed of members of the general public" be interpreted to include appropriate representation of women and minorities.

Response. The recommendations have been accepted in part. Since one of the main purposes of the Act is "to overcome sex discrimination and sex stereotyping in vocational education" and to "furnish equal educational opportunity" (sec. 101(3)) the Commissioner will require that an appropriate representation of women and minorities be represented on the local advisory council. Therefore, a new paragraph has been added to 104.111 to read as follows:

(d) Each eligible recipient shall establish a local advisory council which has an appropriate representation of both sexes and an appropriate representation of the racial and ethnic minorities found in the program areas, schools, community, or region which the local advisory council serves.

104.111(b) *Local advisory council establishment.*

Comment. A few commenters asked whether the regulation governing the establishment of local councils precludes the possibility of LEAs establishing local advisory councils on a regional basis with other LEAs. In the same connection, some commenters asked whether one council may serve more than one eligible recipient.

Response. Section 104.111(b) of the regulations is based on section 105(g) (1) of the Act which provides in part that "local advisory councils may be established for program areas, schools, communities, or regions, whichever the recipient determines best to meet the needs of that recipient." The eligible recipient, therefore, has the option to establish a local council which also serves another eligible recipient in the same geographical region of the State. For example, an LEA and a community college in the same region may decide to establish one local council to advise both recipients. This arrangement may be highly desirable for both recipients in the event they are striving for greater articulation between secondary and postsecondary interests. Accordingly, no change is made in the regulation.

104.111(d) *Craft committees.*

Comment. A commenter pointed out that the regulation implies that only advisory councils would be required at the local educational agency or postsecondary level, despite the fact that advisory assistance through craft committees to each vocationally-funded teacher is considered essential to insure an effective instructional program.

Response. There is no intent to diminish the importance of craft committees. In fact, by making reference in the regulation to "representatives from several craft committees, . . ." the regulation assumes that craft committees are in existence and will be continued. No change is made in the regulation.

104.111(d) *General local advisory council.*

Comment. A commenter suggested that paragraph (d) of 104.111 be eliminated since it appears to be in conflict with paragraph (a) wherein eligible recipients are required to establish local advisory councils. It is contended that this paragraph, by suggesting that existing craft committees "may join together" to form an advisory council, takes away from the eligible recipient the responsibility for determining the make-up and method of establishing its council.

Response. The regulation is considered to be merely suggestive of a method of establishing the mandated local advisory council where craft committees or school councils already exist. It is intended to be supplementary to paragraph (a) rather than in conflict with it. No change is made in the regulation.

104.112 *Public meeting.*

Comment. A commenter suggested the addition of a requirement for the local advisory council to hold not less than one public meeting each year at which time the public is given an opportunity to express views concerning the programs being offered by the local educational agency and the postsecondary educational agency.

Response. While the recommendation has merit, it is not appropriate to assign additional duties to the local advisory council when there is no authority for funding. No change is made in the regulation.

104.112(b) *Local advisory council duties.*

Comment. Commenters suggested that mandating local advisory councils to "assist" the eligible recipient in developing its application goes beyond Congressional intent and would exert an undue hardship on local educational agencies. Commenters also suggested that local advisory councils be required to take an active role in the evaluation of local programs.

Response. The first recommendation is accepted. Since the Act in section 106(a)(4)(A) uses the word "consultation," the regulation is rewritten to state "consult with" in place of "assist."

With respect to the issue of whether local councils are to conduct evaluations, section 105(g)(1) provides that the local council advise the eligible recipient on the degree to which the courses being offered by the eligible recipient meet current job needs in the area. Although this activity may be viewed as a minor component of program evaluation, it should not be considered the equivalent of evaluation. Furthermore, since the Act does not provide any funding for the local councils, assigning the costly function of evaluation to the local council does not seem appropriate. However, it is expected that local councils will make extensive use of secondary data sources and any relevant evaluations that are made by other agencies. No change is made in the regulation.

The language in the 1976 legislation provides specific details that reveal obvious requirements for action. While the future role of advisory committees in the community/education partnership is clear, a series of questions remain unanswered. For example, what systems will be developed to monitor the use of advisory committees? How will the requirements be enforced? What accountability standards will be established?

What implementation requirements will be used by local, state, and/or federal units? How will the effectiveness of advisory committees be measured?

NEED FOR ADVISORY COMMITTEES

The need for advisory committees is far too great for them to be dismissed as existing only because they are required to by federal law. Programs in the schools, for example, cannot be viewed in isolation. Careful attention must be given to the concerns reflected by the school and the community the school serves. In recognizing that there are significant differences between the school and the community, the value of the advisory committee takes on new perspectives. Why should an advisory committee be established or maintained? As already mentioned, several national study groups have focused on this topic [168] [169]. In his book, Burt [29] devoted a chapter to this issue in which he documented statements from national leaders emphasizing the need for industry/ education cooperation. Several articles have also addressed this question, but most have provided only obvious answers to what impact an advisory committee has on the educational program.

Social participation

The goals of the educational programs of a school system and the nature of the community the school system serves are reflective of each other. This concept pervades all segments of the school system and provides direction for career and occupational programs. Within this context, it is the responsiblity of leaders in the program to provide appropriate channels for group and individual participation. Through the advisory committee, individuals can be involved in planning policy, giving direction, and evaluating effectiveness. The basic group principles of social interaction that can be achieved include the following:

1. People are more likely to accept a changed pattern of behavior when they, themselves, have participated in the planning.

2. People are more likely to change their behavior if they see that other people like themselves are also planning and endorsing such a change in behavior.

3. People are more likely to act upon a request if they can be persuaded to commit themselves to a positive decision at the time they hear the request.

4. The group itself can be used to stimulate consideration of the new action, to analyze the difficulties and suggest ways of overcoming them, and finally to arrive at some decision about the action being discussed.

5. If free discussion of a proposed action results in some general agreement among group members that they will participate in this action, there is a good chance that the action will be carried out.

6. A group decision can do a great deal to strengthen an individual's good intentions and change his attitudes. [148:1]

If used effectively, the advisory committee can bring about active social participation and provide a focal point where theory, policy, and the real world can interact. The student, through a variety of experiences, must learn to integrate theory, policy, and the real world. When the faculty members and administrators in the educational programs join forces with individuals from the community through an advisory committee, the student can be presented with concrete programs that bring about such an integration of theory, policy, and the real world in a meaningful manner [84].

Educational partnership

Public education is based on the premise that the school is an integral part of the community. As a social institution serving the educational needs of youth and the community, the school, through its career and occupational programs, has a mission to improve the physical, social, and economic environment of the community. In a similar fashion, individuals in the community have an obligation to supplement the professional appraisals of educational personnel by identifying needs, working out solutions, and developing meaningful educational programs. The principle that "the school belongs to the people" thus forms a sound basis for the use of advisory committees.

Vocational education programs are in a unique position because their success is openly dependent on the degree to which the needs and requirements of the community, as well as the needs and interests of the students, are met. Programs must be attuned to what the community (the employers and the general public) wants. The community, in turn, has a shared responsibility to ensure that these goals are accomplished. The advisory committee thus serves as a vehicle for educators to gain public support and understanding while at the same time providing a framework for sharing in the educational partnership essential for the viability and effectiveness of the program.

Communication process

The advisory committee also serves as a communication link between the school and the community. Two-way communication is essential so both can share in the responsibility of preparing individuals for a place in the work force and in society.

There must be a system of understanding and communication among business, industry, education, and the community to keep the programs realistic and flexible enough to meet changing needs. [14:2]

There must be two-way communication to maintain a working relationship, and thus, perform a real public service. Local advisory committees perform this significant function because their membership represents employers that are respected and recognized as authorities in their fields. [123:2]

A free flow of communication concerning vocational education from qualified lay and professional personnel can provide purposeful direction to local and state vocational education programs. Ideally, this flow of information will start at the local level, proceed through the state and national advisory councils to the Congress, and back again to the local level. [141:10]

The professional educator should be eminently qualified to perform this task because communication is the basis of all learning. Effective communication between the community and individuals representing the school can be developed and maintained only through a conscious, planned effort. Through such effort, an advisory committee can be viewed as a public relations team supporting the career and occupational programs of the school. Formal publicity and word-of-mouth support from influential community leaders can provide significant impetus for the program. The resulting increased public confidence can further improve the image of the program and strengthen the level of support of individuals throughout the community.

Leadership strategy

A seldom-mentioned reason for establishing an advisory committee is the basic leadership style that it represents. Through the participatory approach to leadership inherent in the advisory committee, school personnel are not viewed as authoritarian but are seen as team members striving to work with the community in a cohesive manner. This participatory style is contrasted with the directive leadership style in which authority is used to achieve goals and in which all action is centralized in the individual directing the activity. Figure 1–1 [33] compares some of the basic differences between directive and participative leadership styles.

How individuals in the community regard the program can be significant in determining the degree to which the program achieves its goals. It is possible, for example, for a program to be effective in many respects and yet be poorly understood by individuals in the community. Conversely, the same may be true as a program is measured by individuals within the occupational program itself. The participatory approach reflected in an advisory committee provides an avenue through which issues

FIGURE 1-1. *Selected leadership styles and traits*

Directive	Participative
Leader uses power and discipline	Leader tries to persuade, not force
Activity is leader-centered	Activity is group-centered
Leader utilizes one-way communication	Leader encourages two-way communication
Leader stays aloof from group	Leader is involved in group
Leader's role is to provide direction	Leader's role is group involvement
Leader seeks stable, predictable situations	Leader is more flexible and adaptive
Psychological result is dependency	Psychological result is participation

of this type can be discussed in a constructive manner. Participatory leadership strategy may convey to the individuals of the community that there is an interest in their ideas, it can provide an expanded leadership base, and it can demonstrate to the community that there is a goal for involvement and that there really can be an educational/occupational/community partnership.

Program considerations

The need for advisory committees can best be seen by their impact on the instructional program as expressed through benefits to the student, teacher, administrator, committee member, employer, or individual in the community. Regardless of the target group, the advisory committee is an indispensable component of the career and occupational education programs. The following is a list of possible ways in which an advisory committee can assist:

- They may obtain *advice* on course content and placement services equipment, and employment needs.
- They may make an *assessment* of the effectiveness of the program, placement services, or instructional methods employed.
- They may provide *assistance* in developing new instructional programs, identifying community resources, securing materials and equipment, or conducting occupational surveys.
- They may provide *guidance* regarding the use of specific practices, the development of new policies, or the selection of instructional materials.
- They may foster the *identification* of new occupational patterns, placement opportunities, or required employment skills.
- They may secure *support* for the establishment of a cooperative education program, a new facility, or a program review process.

UTILIZATION AND EFFECTIVENESS OF ADVISORY COMMITTEES

The amount of research pertaining to advisory committees prior to 1968 is quite limited. While there was a growing national trend for greater citizen participation and involvement in school programs during the late 1950s and early 1960s, it was not until the passage of The Vocational Education Amendments of 1968 that there was a marked increase in research on advisory committees. There have been numerous studies since then that present significant implications for how advisory committees will be used in the future.

Most of these studies focus on the nature and scope of advisory committee action at the local level, depicting the functions of advisory committees in career-related areas. Some of the studies have also tried to gain insights into how individuals regard advisory committees and into how effective advisory committees are. Other studies have attempted to define and analyze the roles of state advisory councils with regard to vocational education. As might be expected, each of these studies suggests a body of knowledge that should be considered in reviewing the utilization and effectiveness of advisory committees. Many of the findings of these studies have been incorporated in other chapters to support and substantiate positions and/or concepts.

Nature and scope of local advisory committee activity

The roles, responsibilities, and nature of advisory committee activity has received broad study by researchers in the field. The methodologies have varied considerably, but the studies have attempted to determine the activities advisory committees perform. At the community college level, for example, Olson [128] used a model based on the structure, composition, and role of an advisory committee to compare the practices in eighteen community colleges in the large metropolitan areas. The study demonstrated that only relatively minor modifications would be required to adapt the theoretical model to a practical application. In another study, McInnis [96] supported these findings by noting that a random sample of 126 members serving on advisory committees for occupational education programs in Washington community colleges indicated that there was agreement and consistency with the established guidelines of advisory committee organization and the functions they performed. Vogler [171] provided additional support for these studies as he identified thirty-two techniques that were deemed important for use by community college occupational advisory committees; these techniques were consistently measured as important by members on agribusiness and agrimechanics advisory committees.

At the secondary level, the studies have taken a slightly different direction in relationship to the activities advisory committees perform.

Bennett [20], for example, reported on two state-wide studies in Ohio and New Jersey that focused on the organizational structure and operational aspects of advisory committees. Rogan [146] conducted a similar analysis of advisory committees in Michigan. In analyzing the comments from supervisor-coordinators in randomly selected states, Nagel [103] provided a summary of the common characteristics of advisory committees and indicated that they were most directly involved in developing or revising the vocational curriculum, assisting in the placement of vocational students for on-the-job training, analyzing community needs, improving the local programs' public relations, determining local program objectives, and recommending course content and sequence. Ramey [141] supported these findings as he reported a study, based on 138 survey instruments collected in Virginia, that indicated that the activities of advisory committees could be grouped in the following order of importance:

FIGURE 1-2. *Activities of advisory committees*

Guiding Statements	Rank	Total Points Received
An occupational or vocational advisory committee is valuable to a vocational program by:		
a. providing assistance in the development of good community public relations	1	450
b. offering advice in the development of new or revised occupational course content	2	409
c. utilizing community resources to support the instructional program	3	406
d. reviewing occupational programs and providing suggestions for program improvement	4	393
e. assisting the staff in conducting occupational and/or community surveys	5	366
f. making recommendations regarding equipment and facility planning	5	366
g. assisting counselors and teachers in the placement of students	6	329
h. assisting and supporting the administration in locating, identifying, and recommending qualified instructional staff	7	246

In a similar study, Cochran, Phelps, and Skupin [38] submitted a forty-one-item questionnaire to administrators, teachers, board members, and advisory committee members in secondary and postsecondary vocational education programs throughout Michigan. These items were grouped under eight major functions in an attempt to determine the extent to which the basic functions were performed. They concluded that the amount of involvement in these functions could be summarized as follows:

Functions	Percent Involvement
Occupational Surveys	20–30
Course Content Advisement	40–60
Student Placement	15–25
Community Public Relations	10–15
Equipment and Facilities	50–60
Program Staffing	0–5
Program Review	25–35
Obtaining Community Resources	30–50

The detailed rankings of the forty-one items for secondary and post-secondary advisory committee involvement measured in this study are provided in Appendices B and C. Behymer [19], in conducting a parallel study in Missouri, sampled 572 advisory committee members and administrators from comprehensive high schools, area vocational schools, and community/junior colleges throughout the state. In respect to participation ratings, effectiveness ratings, and relative importance, it was found that program evaluation, course content, and program objectives were most important. The administrators in the study agreed with the importance of course content, but they put instructional equipment and placement of graduates in the top category. As a result, Behymer concluded that, without some intervening activity, it could not be expected that advisory committee members and administrators would assign the same rank of importance to the various advisory committee functions.

Perceptions of advisory committees

How individuals involved in an advisory committee perceive the committee's role, responsibility, and effectiveness has an important influence on the actions taken by that committee. The general atmosphere that permeates a committee can directly affect the outcomes produced by the committee. In order to better understand the internal operations of the committee, several studies have been conducted on how individuals involved in advisory committees perceive the committee's role.

For the most part, these studies reveal a wide disparity in the perceptions of the committee's role held by those serving on or associated with advisory committees. While most of the studies have identified specific areas of common perception, they have also noted areas in which significant differences in opinion exist. Based upon an eighty-item instrument, for example, Hagman [63] found that there was a significant difference in perception of thirty-eight items between educators and other committee members regarding the importance of selected factors considered in a craft/occupational advisory committee. Cochran, Phelps, and Skupin [38] substantiated this finding and noted that there were important group differences. This was illustrated by the specific differences in perception that were found between business and industry representatives and labor representatives. They also noted differences in the perception of teachers identified as serving on "effective committees" and those serving on "noneffective committees," and between administrators as represented by community college occupational deans and secondary vocational education directors.

Allen [7] also found limited agreement among the forty-seven secondary vocational education directors in North Carolina on the role of advisory committees in programming. He indicated that there was a high consensus on 63 percent of a sixty-seven-item questionnaire on programming roles and a high consensus on 20 percent of a fifteen-item questionnaire on organizational structure. In relationship to curriculum planning, however, Henning [67] found much higher levels of agreement between advisory committee members and the teaching faculty. Lahren [85] substantiated this position in respect to the curriculum area but found a lesser degree of support for other advisory committee functions.

Link [88] provided a partial explanation for these disparities in perception by reporting that members of established committees tended to have a significantly greater number of differing perceptions of the committee's roles than did those of newly created committees. He also indicated that the role of educators tended to shift significantly with the makeup of the committee and that educators tended to become more dominant when veteran (noneducator) members were removed or not present.

Evaluation of advisory committee effectiveness

A critical activity to be performed by all advisory committees is the evaluating of program effectiveness. Likewise, it is equally important that the advisory committee itself be evaluated; in fact, the evaluation of advisory committee action is essential to the total review of the educational program. While several studies have been conducted to fulfill this responsibility, the evaluation of advisory committees remains an area requiring further research.

The studies that have been completed in this area reveal advisory committee accomplishments and also point to a need for improvement. Danenburg, Keen, and Miller [46] stressed this point as they analyzed 275 questionnaires from advisory committee members and vocational and technical educators in school districts and community colleges in Florida. They concluded that there was a discrepancy between how effective the committee members perceived their committees to be and the degree to which the committees were actually performing the activities indicative of effectiveness. In another study in Michigan, 119 school superintendents, community college presidents, board members, and trustees illustrated the wide discrepancy between the degree of use of committees and the degree of their effectiveness (see Appendix D).

Land [86] supported this position by concluding from a survey of 105 advisory committee members in Utah that the degree of agreement was only 33 percent between the actual practice and the theoretical model of a committee's functions. The degree of agreement between the relative importance of functions and the theoretical model was 83 percent. McInnis [96] provided additional support in this respect at the community college level when he concluded that committees were not practicing established organizational concepts to the extent that citizens and occupational educators involved with the committee support the concepts.

The reasons for these poor evaluations of advisory committees are many. Korb [83] pointed to the lack of budget appropriations as a major factor. Douglas [50] and Sorensen [151] further identified problems that contribute to the ineffectiveness of advisory committees. Emphasis was placed on the lack of expertise in "how to establish, maintain, and operate a committee," the lack of availability of materials and guides on committee use, the lack of preparation in using advisory committees, the lack of time devoted to this "extra assignment," and the lack of knowledge concerning advisory committees.

Nature and role of state advisory councils

Prior to the passage of The Vocational Education Amendments of 1968 mandating the formation of state advisory councils for vocational education, thirty-seven states had already established such councils [9]. The operation of these councils varied considerably as a result of the loosely prescribed roles and responsibilities created by the individual states. By the early 1970s, some of these roles had been clarified, but the shifts in vocational education programs and individual state orientations still left wide variances in the operation of individual state councils. In a national survey of executive officers of state boards of vocational education, staff executives of state advisory councils on vocational education, and state advisory council members, Pitale [138] reviewed these roles and found significant differences between actual and ideal role statement perceptions. While there are differences, Jobe [78] found in surveying state directors of vocational education and chairpersons of state advisory councils on vocational education that there was general agreement on the relative importance of the nine selected functions of state advisory councils. Both groups chose evaluation of programs, services, and activities as the most important function and advising the state board in developing a state plan as the second most important function. The two groups were also in agreement in selecting the function of advising in policy matters in the administration of the state plan as the least important.

Recognizing the importance of the evaluation role, Reid [142] developed guidelines to be used by states in performing this function. Based upon data collected from advisory council executive directors in each of the fifty states, it was concluded that (1) councils had developed a satisfactory relationship with the state board and state departments of vocational education, (2) councils were using their own plan for evaluation, (3) student placement and program availability were major evaluation criteria, and (4) they perceived their role as assessing the effectiveness and accessibility of all types of public vocational education. In addition, seventeen major evaluative functions to be performed by state advisory councils were identified.

SUGGESTED ACTIVITIES

1. Develop a working definition for a local advisory committee with which you will be involved.

2. Review your state plan for vocational education or your state's guide for administration of vocational education to determine specific requirements for the use of local advisory committees.

3. Review current state legislation or state board of education policy regarding career education in your state. Is the use of advisory committees either required or strongly recommended? Are guidelines for their composition and responsibilities provided?

4. List all advisory committees currently used by your school and in one sentence identify the major purpose of each.

5. Identify the communication links that currently exist between your school and the community.

6. Determine if your state department of education has prepared a booklet or brochure regarding the use of advisory committees at the local level. If so, obtain a copy for your reference.

7. List some ways in which an advisory committee might be misused. Identify one or two ways to prevent each type of misuse.

8. Prepare a position paper regarding the need for forming a particular advisory committee. Assume this position paper is to be presented to the appropriate administrative office or board of education.

9. Review one research study on advisory committees and apply the findings to a particular situation.

10. Identify a concern or problem regarding the use of advisory committees and prepare a tentative plan or outline for conducting a research study that would address that concern or problem.

SELECTED REFERENCES

American Vocational Association. *The Advisory Committee and Vocational Education.* Washington, D.C.: American Vocational Association, 1969.

Brodinsky, Ben, ed. *Policies for Better Advisory Committees.* Waterford, Conn.: EPS/NSPA Policy Information Clearinghouse, 1972.

Burt, Samuel M. *Industry and Vocational-Technical Education.* New York: McGraw-Hill Book Co., 1967.

Cochran, Leslie H.; Phelps, L. Allen; and Skupin, Joseph F. *Needs Assessment on the Use of Vocational Advisory Committees in Michigan.* Lansing: Michigan Department of Education, 1974.

Davies, Don; Stanton, Jim; Clasby, Miriam; Zerchykov, Ross; and Powers, Brian. *Sharing the Power?* Boston: Institute for Responsive Education, 1978.

Hofstrand, Richard K., and Phipps, Lloyd J. *Advisory Councils for Education: A Handbook.* Urbana: Rurban Educational Development Laboratory, University of Illinois, 1971.

Marburger, Carl L. "The Role of the Citizen in Education." *Journal of Teacher Education* 26 (1975): 24–29.

Mial, Dorothy, and Mial, H. Curtis, eds. *Forces in Community Development.* Washington, D.C.: National Education Association, 1961.

North Carolina Department of Community Colleges. *Organization, Function, and Operation of Advisory Committees.* Raleigh, N.C.: Department of Community Colleges. 1972.

Pucinski, Roman. *The Role of State and Local Advisory Councils in Vocational Education.* Columbus: The National Center for Research in Vocational Education, The Ohio State University, 1978.

Ramey, Walter S. *A Guide for the Organization and Operation of Local Advisory Committees for Vocational Education.* Richmond: Virginia State Department of Education, 1975.

San Diego County Department of Education. *A Guide for Community School Advisory Councils.* San Diego: San Diego County Department of Education, 1975.

Sumption, Merle R., and Engstrom, Yvonne. *School-Community Relations.* New York: McGraw-Hill Book Co., 1966.

U.S. Congress, Public Law 88–210. *Vocational Education Act of 1963.* 88th Congress, 1963.

U.S. Congress, Public Law 90–576. *The Vocational Education Amendments of 1968.* 90th Congress, 1968.

U.S. Congress, Public Law 94–482. *Education Amendments of 1976.* 94th Congress, 1976.

U.S. Congress, Public Law 95–207. *Career Education Incentive Act.* 95th Congress, 1977.

U.S. Congress, Public Law 95–524. *Comprehensive Employment and Training Act Amendments of 1978.* 95th Congress, 1978.

2 The structure of advisory committees

Chapter 1 emphasized how the increase in public awareness and involvement had stressed the vitally important role of advisory committees. In addition, there is a need to be aware of some current trends that have even greater implications for the role and structure of advisory committees—namely, communities are demanding a greater voice in the decisions that result in program services; staff alignments are changing with minorities assuming more positions of authority; corporations are accepting the premise of a corporate responsibility to the community; boards and staffs are becoming more representative of the communities they serve; similar and dissimilar organizations are required to collaborate in their efforts; and organizations are required to be cognizant of racial, ethnic, and sex balance.

Each of these new directions suggest expanded parameters for advisory committee action. Three key structural elements of advisory committees are present in this chapter. First, the role and responsibilities of advisory committees are delineated to provide an overall view of the purpose of advisory groups. Second, the role of advisory councils at the national, state, and regional levels are described to provide a proper perspective for advisory committee actions. Third, the major types of advisory committees, along with specific examples, are presented to illustrate the interrelationships between committees at the local level.

ROLE OF ADVISORY COMMITTEES

Some of the outside forces are specifically focused on education in an attempt to bring about change, while the mere existence of other forces presents challenges and/or directions for advisory committee action. In response to these forces, educators have placed renewed emphasis on various community-oriented aspects of the program or have attempted to extend the community/school concept through the development of community-based career education programs, field-based experiences, business- and industry-sponsored placement services, and other approaches that tie the community and school more closely together. These same sensitivities and efforts to demonstrate accountability and responsiveness to community needs has shaped the role of advisory committees. The application of some of these concerns to occupational education was expressed by the New York State Department of Education:

> As the technology changes in the working environment, the skill requirements of workers are also changed. Accordingly, there is a need for educational agencies to develop new curriculum and properly equipped facilities to keep pace in the particular affected occupation. The educational institution needs access to information concerning the occupation to identify job potential, develop viable job descriptions, skill requirements, educational materials, equipment lists and facilities layouts. The basic source of this knowledge is the employee and employer in the occupation. Providing information to the occupational educators is one of the primary uses of consultant committees for occupations. [127:5]

The importance of clarifying the role of advisory committees in this respect cannot be overstated. To maintain and operate a successful advisory committee, its role must be clearly stated in terms that can be made operational. The General Accounting Office [40:31], in a 1974 report to Congress stressed this point by indicating the negative impact that has resulted from this lack of direction:

> Local communities have been encouraged to make use of advisory committees in planning vocational education programs, but neither OE (Office of Education) nor State agencies have provided the necessary guidance to LEAs (local education agencies) regarding the appropriate role and function for advisory committees.

The report went on to conclude that the variations in the effectiveness of local vocational advisory committees were a product of this confusion.

A description of how the advisory committee is organized provides a starting point for an analysis of what its role is and how it operates. As stated in Chapter 1, *an advisory committee is a group composed primarily of individuals outside the educational profession who are selected from segments of the community collectively to advise educational personnel regarding one or more educational programs or aspects of a program.* The committee's duties and focus must be clearly delineated as being *advisory.* The level of the committee—whether it is national, state, regional, or local—and the type of committee must be identified. Within this framework, the purposes and goals must outline the overall direction of the committee, the functions or major areas of committee action must be agreed upon, and the specific activities that may be performed by the committee must be identified.

FIGURE 2-1. Relationship between goals, functions, and activities

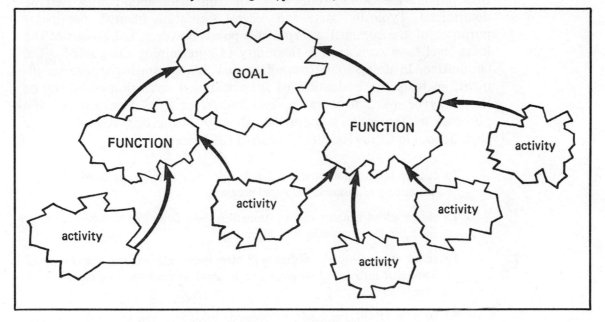

To understand how advisory committees work, examine some of the basic theories of the group dynamics process. Cartwright [34] suggests eight guiding principles to be followed if change is to be brought about within the group (either the advisory committee itself or the community):

1. If the group is to be used effectively as a medium of change, those people who are to be changed and those who are to exert influence for change must have a strong sense of belonging to the same group.

2. The more attractive the group is to its members, the greater is the influence that the group can exert on its members.

3. In attempts to change attitudes, values, or behavior, the more relevant they are to the basis of attraction to the group, the greater will be the influence that the group can exert upon them.

4. The greater the prestige of a group member in the eyes of the other members, the greater the influence he can exert.

5. Efforts to change individuals or subparts of a group which, if successful, would have the result of making them deviate from the norms of the group, will encounter strong resistance.

6. Strong pressure for changes in the group can be established by creating a shared perception by members of the need for change, thus making the source of pressure for change lie within the group.

7. Information relating to the need for change, plans for change, and consequences of change must be shared by all relevant people in the group.

8. Changes in one part of a group produce strain in other related parts which can be reduced only by eliminating the change or by bringing about readjustments in the related parts.

Purposes and goals

In reviewing the role of an advisory committee, the purposes and goals that provide the overall framework for committee action must first be determined. Typically, state and federal legislation identify the major purposes of the committee. From this point, however, individuals at the local level have considerable flexibility in determining the goals for the committee. In doing so, a committee may have a single-purpose assignment, such as the evaluation of the vocational education offerings, or they may be asked to work in several different areas. For example, the purposes of the business/industrial advisory committee at Mesa Verde High School in Citrus Heights, California [39], are

> To acquire information which will help update, modify, expand and improve the quality of Business/Industrial programs.
>
> To obtain added support and to strengthen the relationship between business, industry, the community and education.
>
> To make recommendations that will strengthen and expand the Business/Industrial instruction program and to assist in implementing these recommendations.
>
> To assist in identifying needs, determining priorities, reviewing and evaluating programs.

Regardless of the committee's assignment, however, its goals can usually be grouped under one of the following seven areas of responsibility.

Assessment and review. The advisory committee's most common goal is that of assessment and review. This is an ongoing and continuous process designed to ascertain whether or not the occupational or career education program is providing the type of education that real situations demand. It provides an opportunity for citizens in the community to assess program goals and objectives, to provide input for curriculum decisions, and to suggest improvements and additions that will enable the school to better serve the needs of the community.

All too often this evaluation tends to be off-hand, vague, and unsystematic. As a result, many committees have failed to fulfill this responsibility because their efforts were not measured effectively. The review must be based upon measurable data and objectives. The committee should also be aware that there are "fine lines" to be observed in this assessment process. For example, it is inappropriate for the committee to become involved in evaluating the methods used by teachers in the program. In regard to "how the content is taught," a clear distinction must be maintained between administrative and teacher roles and the advisory committee's responsibility for the review of instructional materials, course outlines, required standards, and the equipment and facilities used in the program. By maintaining such dialogue, program improvements can be made while at the same time crystalizing community support for the program.

Change agent. The advisory committee plays a vital role in changing the educational system. While little has been written on this role, it is clear from the stated goals of advisory committees that they can be instrumental in changing or improving the program. Whether or not this is actually stated or is simply subsumed in other goal statements is not the question. By definition, change agents are those who advance change by their presence in the system. They are often known as influentials, opinion leaders, or interventionists.

Change for the sake of change is not desirable, but change to increase a program's relevance is a key to the future. Because the segments of society are interrelated, the acceptance of change by any one social system requires other social institutions to respond. Changes in business and industry, for example, require shifts in the educational system so it can continue to prepare individuals to live and work in the community. Advisory committees can alert educators of such changes through assessment and review, direction setting, and needs determination. They can present new concepts, introduce new technologies, and reveal shifts in the community's economic and population base. In addition to serving as vanguards for change, advisory committee members can actively support new programs, express the need for new facilities, and convey to the community points of view that might not be accepted or understood if presented by educators closely associated with the "interworkings" of the school system.

Communications link. One of the primary tenets upon which advisory committees are built is that of serving as a communication link between the community and the school. Educators also use other avenues to maintain this link, but the role of the advisory committee is of paramount importance in bridging the unnecessary chasm between the school and the community.

Effective communication is a two-way process with communications both to and from the community, committee, administration, and other school personnel. The committee provides a base for the flow of ideas and suggestions concerning social and institutional trends, technical advancements, and the varied requirements of employers for specific skills and preparation. It also serves as a means to disseminate information to the entire community through such techniques as group discussions, personal contacts, presentations in the media, and other public relations strategies.

An important premise in the communication process is that the acceptance of a sound decision depends on a credible presentation of the facts. If a sound decision is communicated poorly, that decision may not be accepted. The utilization of a team approach as exemplified in advisory committee action is crucial to this role. It provides an expanded leadership and communications base for unifying and integrating various elements in the community, thereby increasing public confidence in the program offerings and administrative decisions in the school.

Direction setting. Advisory committees can also provide direction for the specific or overall program they serve. Like so many other roles performed by the committee, direction setting should be handled with great care. The committee must avoid making statements that are merely sets of rules and regulations dealing with the operation of the program. These decisions should be left to school personnel. The committee should not place itself in a crisis or conflict situation within the community, thereby losing its effectiveness and being viewed as either an arm of the school system or a community special interest group.

The committee can set direction for the program by ensuring that new programs are based on sound planning principles, that they are based on current occupational forecasts, and that an overall comprehensive and balanced program is offered. The curriculum content must be based on the needs of the occupational area rather than on a narrow focus to meet the specific needs of one employer. The committee can assist in maintaining internal consistency within the program and external consistency between the school and the world of work. It must be stressed, however, that whatever role is assumed by the committee in direction setting, the fact of having community leaders involved in this process may, in some cases, be more important than the actual recommendation that is made.

Legislative input. One of the newest goals of the advisory committee is that of providing input to state and federal legislators regarding current or pending legislation and corresponding appropriations. In the past, this role received little attention and, if carried out at all, was only accomplished on a limited individual basis. Recently, both state and federal legislation have had a direct and significant impact on the local community. This has been particularly true of education legislation and thus has accentuated the need for committee input in the formulation of legislation. This is a two-way process and one in which the advisory committee can serve a key role.

The American Vocational Association supports a national network that encourages and promotes public input into federal legislation. Many state educational organizations provide similar avenues for influencing state legislation. While these organizational systems have been developed so that educational personnel can communicate with elected officials regarding current legislation, advisory committees, as an important link in the educational/occupational/community partnership, must assume an active role in this process. For example, an advisory committee representing broad community views can demonstrate to lawmakers that career and occupational programs are supported by community, business, industry, and labor leaders. Often influence from such sources can be more beneficial than input made by educators. Advisory committee members should make an effort to stay informed regarding legislative activity; they should send letters and telegrams and should make personal contacts with key legislators at the appropriate time. Business, industry, and labor are at home in the legislative arena. Their political influence and knowledge of the legislative process must be utilized by educational personnel.

Needs determination. Advisory committees were originally used in vocational education to determine the occupational needs of the community so programs could furnish education in those fields where employment opportunities were available. Needs determination has evolved into a broad-based and complex effort by which communities and schools maintain curriculum relevance and assess and plan programs. More than any other role, the needs determination process has a direct impact on each of the other roles performed by the committee because it is an information-gathering process that forms a community base for assessing and determining community needs, interests, and resources. The committee may collect such information in a variety of ways and from a variety of sources. Certain information may come in an unstructured form, such as opinions, ideas, and concerns of individuals; other information may be obtained through more structured means, by the use of studies or surveys.

The community survey is the most common tool used in needs determination. The advisory committee may advise in this process or it may actually conduct the study. Regardless of direction, it may be involved in designing the survey, collecting information, encouraging wide community participation, analyzing the data, and/or reporting the findings and recommendations. Through such a process, the advisory committee can assist school personnel in maintaining a curriculum that has practical value and real meaning for both youth and adults in terms of conditions in the community.

Service.   While service is not typically stated as a major goal, it is a role commonly performed by advisory committees. In addition to the other roles, the expertise of the individual committee member can be used to support the program. For example, the members may show support for increased financial assistance, donate equipment and supplies, schedule field trips, speak before classes and public hearings, place students, recruit faculty members, and provide other forms of public information to the community. Since the major role of the advisory committee is to provide advice and assistance, it must take care that the service role does not erode the advice-giving and assessing roles.

Advisory committee functions

One of the assets of utilizing advisory committees as the principal vehicle in the educational/occupational/community partnership is the supportive functions they may serve. Within the context of the goals, these functions, or major areas of committee action, may be performed by different types of committees in different settings depending upon the level of activity, type of program, and the committee's assignment. These functions form the nucleus for an active program of work. The majority of an advisory committee's actions can be grouped under one or more of the following seven functions:

· curriculum content advisement
· equipment, facilities, and instructional resources review
· community resource coordination
· career guidance and placement services

- program evaluation
- community public relations
- professional development

These functions are described in detail in the chapters in Part II. In the practical setting, however, such distinctions are not easily made because the functions are totally or in part interrelated.

Advisory committee activities

The individual activities performed by a committee must fall within the scope described by its functions. If, for example, a committee is given a single-purpose assignment, then its activities must fall within this framework and support the specific function. The number of activities and their diversity are limited only by the imagination of the members on the committee and the specific needs and characteristics of the body or community they serve.

These activities are to advise, aid, arrange, assist, guide, help, provide, recommend, serve, and support. While often written in general terms, these statements provide a measurable basis for the committee to make an assessment of its own activities. This is a critical role in determining the total effectiveness of the committee (see Chapter 13). The chapters that focus on the specific functions also illustrate how such activities are interwoven within each of the major functions. To illustrate the use of activities from a general perspective, however, the following examples are provided.

The cooperative education manual used in Vermont [87:26] suggests ten activities for advisory committee action relative to cooperative work education programs:

1. Aid in publicizing and promoting cooperative vocational education programs in the community.

2. Identify areas in which cooperative vocational education programs can be expanded.

3. Help to determine criteria for the selection of training stations.

4. Review training plans.

5. Assist with the evaluation of the program.

6. Advise on program objectives and course content and provide information on job opportunities in the occupational areas included in the cooperative vocational education program.

7. Assist in obtaining jobs for graduates who have successfully completed their training.

8. Help organize community surveys by determining the data to be gathered, by supporting the need for the survey, and by helping evaluate the data.

9. Help to acquaint other citizens with the needs of the school.

10. Serve as a liaison group to help cooperative vocational education students who are interested in seeking postsecondary, college, or university education to make the transition.

The North Dakota State Board for Vocational Education* has identified fifteen activities with several subactivities:

1. Determine community needs
   a. For cooperative vocational education programs
   b. For adult classes

2. Evaluate program
   a. Advise whether or not program is providing the kind of training life situations demand
   b. Review curriculum and objectives of program
   c. Review adult classes
   d. Secure opinions from business people
   e. Review all features of the program including the various forms used

3. Assist in the preparation and selection of course material
   a. Establish need for a course
   b. Review present course outlines and texts used
   c. Suggest revisions or additions
   d. Review objectives

4. Help in securing training stations and assist in placement of graduates

5. Recommend resource personnel and guest speakers
   a. Guest speaker
   b. Instructors for adult program

6. Guide and support vocational instruction
   a. Give encouragement and stimulation
   b. Give constructive criticism enabling instructor to adjust activities

7. Assist in surveys
   a. Determine data to be gathered
   b. Suggest means for securing data
   c. Help secure certain information
   d. Assist in data interpretation

8. Help to provide continuity
   a. Maintain program of work even though there is a change in instructors

9. Provide financial and legislative support
   a. Arrange for donations (equipment, supplies, etc.)
   b. Establish scholarships, awards for honor students
   c. Support school administration for local appropriations
   d. Support state and national legislation affecting vocational education

10. Provide public relations service
    a. Interpret program in community
    b. Provide information for counselors.
    c. Arrange for exhibits at meetings and in store windows

*The Vocational Education Advisory Committee. Fargo, N.D.: North Dakota State Board for Vocational Education, undated, pp. 6–8. Used with permission.

     d. Develop plans for recognizing students, such as in store advertisements

     e. Arrange to have vocational instructor present talks before community groups

     f. Help prepare or review brochures explaining the vocational education program

     g. Advise on other forms of program promotion

11. Recommend policies for cooperative program
    a. Regulations for employment of students
    b. Type of students to be enrolled
    c. Releasing students for employment
    d. Student ratings

12. Help secure equipment, supplies and instructional material
    a. Arrange for purchase or by gift
    b. Locate instructional material from local businesses

13. Assist in vocational student organizations
    a. Suggest means of raising club funds
    b. Help secure speakers
    c. Provide financial aid for individual members to attend state or national conference
    d. Serve as judge for local awards and contests
    e. Attend installation ceremony of local officers

14. Assist in securing meeting places
    a. For adult classes
    b. For advisory committee meetings
    c. For field trips, special demonstrations

15. Help plan special events
    a. Vocational Education Week
    b. National Student Organization Week
    c. Banquet and other social activities
    d. Attend and participate in certain special events

LEVELS OF ADVISORY COUNCIL ACTIVITY

One of the overriding factors that determine the role of an advisory committee is the level at which it is called to serve. As already illustrated, this controls the goals, functions, and activities performed by the committee. There are four levels in which advisory groups are used in support of the career and occupational education programs—namely, national, state, regional, and local. The first three of these are presented in this section. A more detailed description of local advisory committees follows in the next section of this chapter.

The importance of understanding the overall framework that national, state, regional, and local advisory groups provide cannot be overlooked. There are three major reasons that might be used to illustrate why individuals, representing an advisory group at the local, state, regional, or national level, need to have a thorough understanding of how advisory bodies function at the other levels. First, there is natural interaction and practical linkage between advisory committees at various levels. For example, advisory committee input at the local level shapes the programs which, in turn, influence the development of the state plan for vocational education. It is the responsibility of the state advisory council to review the objectives of the state plan and make appropriate recommendations. There is also a similar relationship at the national level. Concepts represented in the state plans may be reflected in recommendations and new directions for future legislation and/or advisory committee action taken at the national level. Second, action taken by a local committee may directly influence a recommendation at another level. To illustrate, employment demand may be localized, extend to a regional area, or encompass the state. The data collected at the local level could have a direct impact on a recommendation at any of these levels in regard to program development or expansion. Third, a common use of terminology provides a consistent and common communications base. If, for example, committees perform similar functions in different communities but these functions are referred to by different terms, their actions may not be correctly interpreted by advisory committees in another part of the state or nation.

As a case in point, federal legislation refers to national, state, and local "councils." In practice, however, the term "council" is seldom used at the local level unless it represents a larger geographic area or community-wide group, such as a citizen's advisory council for the school system, a council for vocational education in a large city, or a career education planning district council. Even then, while these groups may be functioning at what is commonly referred to as the local level, they take on qualities more characteristic of a regional council. To maintain clarity within career and occupational education, *the term "council" is recommended for national, state, and regional advisory groups, and the term "committee" is suggested for groups organized at the local level.*

National advisory council on vocational education

Advisory councils have been used in one form or another in vocational education since the turn of the century. Various panels and advisory groups played critical roles in the legislation enacted in 1963 and 1968. Prior to this time, the use of advisory councils was sporadic. There are a few examples, however, that can be pointed to as providing significant direction for vocational education. The Federal Board for Vocational Education was originally an administrative body formed in 1917 with representatives from agriculture, manufacturing, commerce, and labor. It gradually emerged as an advisory council and functioned in this manner until it was dissolved in 1946. Several advisory groups were used in connection with the development of guiding policies for the George-Deen Act passed in 1937. Similarly, a national advisory committee was used in developing administrative policies for vocational education to implement the George-Barden Act passed in 1947.

The passage of the Vocational Education Amendments of 1968 provided the framework for the current National Advisory Council on Vocational Education (NACVE). Through its reports, recommendations, and legislative input, the council has had a significant impact on vocational education in the nation. Lund [90] highlighted some of the efforts of the council after its first four years of operation by stressing that it had been instrumental in supporting projects aimed at research efforts, trends, and legislative processes, upgrading the USOE bureau of vocational education, increasing basic grants to states, holding public hearings, sponsoring public information projects, and supporting youth organization efforts.

The Education Amendments of 1976 [165] built upon this base and detailed the existing composition and responsibilities of the National Advisory Council on Vocational Education. Some of the critical council activities in respect to programs covered by the act are to

- Advise the President, Congress, Secretary, and Commissioner [Secretary of HEW] concerning the administration and preparation of general regulations and budget requests for vocational education programs.

- Review the administration and operation of vocational education programs and make appropriate reports and recommendations.

- Identify the vocational education and employment and training needs of the Nation and assess the extent to which vocational education programs are consistent with these needs and other programs in operation.

- Conduct independent evaluations, studies, and hearings as deemed appropriate in connection with vocational education.

- Provide technical assistance and leadership to state advisory councils.

Specifically, that section of the act concerning the NACVE [165] stated:

NATIONAL ADVISORY COUNCIL ON VOCATIONAL EDUCATION

SEC. 162. (a) The National Advisory Council on Vocational Education, established pursuant to section 104(a) of the Vocational Education Act of 1963, in effect prior to the enactment of the Education Amendments of 1976, shall continue to exist during the period for which appropriations are authorized under this Act. Individuals who are members of the Council on the date of the enactment of this Act may continue to serve for the terms for which they were appointed. Members appointed to succeed such individuals shall be appointed by the President for terms of three years. The Council shall consist of twenty-one members, each of whom shall be designated as representing one of the categories set forth in the following sentence. The National Advisory Council shall include individuals—

(1) representative of labor and management, including persons who have knowledge of semiskilled, skilled, and technical employment;

(2) representative of new and emerging occupational fields;

(3) knowledgeable in the field of vocational guidance and counseling;

(4) representing the National Commission for Manpower Policy created pursuant to title V of the Comprehensive Employment and Training Act of 1973;

(5) representing nonprofit private schools;

(6) who are women with backgrounds and experiences in employment and training programs, who are knowledgeable with respect to problems of sex discrimination in job training and in employment, including women who are members of minority groups and who have, in addition to such backgrounds and experiences, special knowledge of the problems of discrimination in job training and employment against women who are members of such groups;

(7) knowledgeable about the administration of State and local vocational education programs, including members of school boards and private institutions;

(8) experienced in the education and training of handicapped persons and of persons of limited English-speaking ability (as defined in section 703(a) of the Elementary and Secondary Education Act of 1965);

(9) familiar with the special problems and needs of individuals disadvantaged by their socioeconomic backgrounds;

(10) having special knowledge of postsecondary and adult vocational education programs;

(11) familiar with the special problems of individuals in correctional institutions; and

(12) representative of the general public who are not Federal employees, including parents and students, except that they must not be representative of categories (1) through (11), and who shall constitute not less than one-third of the total membership.

The National Council shall have as a majority of its members persons who are not educators or administrators in the field of education. In appointing the National Advisory Council, the President shall insure that there is appropriate representation of both sexes, racial and ethnic minorities, and the various geographic regions of the country. The President shall select the chairman. The National Advisory Council shall meet at the call of the Chairman, but not less than four times a year.

(b) The National Advisory Council shall—

(1) advise the President, Congress, Secretary, and Commissioner concerning the administration of, preparation of general regulations and budget requests for, and operation of, vocational education programs supported with assistance under this Act;

(2) review the administration and operation of vocational education programs under this Act, and other pertinent laws affecting vocational education and manpower training (including the effectiveness of such programs in meeting the purposes for which they are established and operated), make recommendations with respect thereto, and make annual reports of its findings and recommendations (including recommendations for changes in the provisions of this Act and such other pertinent laws) to the President, Congress, Secretary, and Commissioner;

(3) make such other reports or recommendations to the President, Congress, Secretary, Commissioner, or head of any other Federal department or agency as it may deem desirable;

(4) (A) identify, after consultation with the National Commission for Manpower Policy, the vocational education and employment and training needs of the Nation and assess the extent to which vocational education, employment training, vocational rehabilitation, and other programs under this and related Acts represent a consistent, integrated, and coordinated approach to meeting such needs; and (B) comment, at least once annually, on the reports of the National Commission, which comments shall be included in one of the reports submitted by the National Advisory Council pursuant to this section and in one of the reports submitted by the National Commission pursuant to section 505 of the Comprehensive Employment and Training Act of 1973;

(5) conduct such studies, hearings, or other activities as it deems necessary to enable it to formulate appropriate recommendations;

(6) conduct independent evaluations of programs carried out under this Act and publish and distribute the results thereof; and

(7) provide technical assistance and leadership to State advisory councils established pursuant to section 105, in order to assist them in carrying out their responsibilities under this Act.

(c) There are authorized to be appropriated $450,000 for the fiscal year ending September 30, 1978, $475,000 for the fiscal year ending September 30, 1979, and $500,000 for each of the fiscal years ending prior to September 30, 1982 for the purposes of this paragraph. The Council is authorized to use the funds appropriated pursuant to the preceding sentence to carry out its functions as set forth in this section and to engage such technical assistance as may be required to assist it in performing these functions.

Other national advisory councils

The National Advisory Council for Career Education and the National Advisory Council for Vocational Education are two national groups that have a direct impact on the role of advisory committees in career and occupational education. The National Association for Industry-Education Cooperation (NAIEC) is another influential force in that it promotes increased levels of cooperation between business, industry, education, agriculture, government, and labor; formulates programs and procedures to facilitate this goal; and communicates nationally with various groups concerned about cooperative programs and projects. Some of the other national advisory councils that have an impact on career and occupational education include

Community Education Advisory Council

National Advisory Committee on the Handicapped

National Advisory Council on Adult Education

National Advisory Council on Bilingual Education

National Advisory Council on Equality of Educational Opportunity

National Advisory Council on Indian Education

National Advisory Council on the Education of Disadvantaged Children

National Advisory Council on Women's Educational Programs

State advisory councils

Several examples have already been given that illustrate action taken by individual states to establish statewide advisory groups for both career education and vocational education. These examples are, however, not indicative of all states because the degree of usage, the processes by which such groups are formed, and the uniformity of the resulting products vary considerably. A cursory review of legislation passed in states, the fact that some have state systems, and, of course, the obvious differences resulting from economic, political, and social influences provide a perspective for the differences that have evolved.

In contrast, there are two forces at work serving to lessen the differences and to provide greater uniformity in respect to vocational education programs across the nation. First, a state plan for vocational education is required by the U.S. Office of Education for compliance with the federal legislation. The plan serves as an agreement between the state and federal governments and is thus a part of the operational administrative code of the state and has the same effect as a law. Since the U.S. Office of Education releases the rules and regulations used in developing the state plans, it is easy to see how essentially the same words might be used by states to demonstrate their compliance with the act. Second, the Education Amendments of 1976 [165] specify in detail the composition and responsibilities of the state advisory council for vocational education. In this case, twenty constituencies that must be represented are identified along with four specific responsibilities given to the SACVE:

> (d) (1) Each State advisory council shall advise the State board in the development of the five-year State plan submitted under section 107 and the annual program plan and accountability report submitted under section 108 and shall advise the State board on policy matters arising out of the administration of programs under such plans and reports.
>
> (2) Each State advisory council shall also evaluate vocational education programs, services, and activities assisted under this Act, and publish and distribute the results thereof.
>
> (3) Each State advisory council shall prepare and submit to the Commissioner and to the National Advisory Council created under section 162, through the State board, an annual evaluation report, accompanied by such additional comments of the State board as the State board deems appropriate, which (A) evaluates the effectiveness of vocational education programs, services, and activities carried out in the year under review in meeting the program goals set forth in the five-year State plan submitted under section 107 and the annual program plan and accountability report submitted under section 108, including a consideration of the program evaluation reports developed by the State pursuant to section 112 and of the analysis of the distribution of Federal funds within the State submitted by the State board pursuant to section 108, and (B) recommends such changes in such programs, services, and activities as may be deemed necessary.
>
> (4) (A) Each State advisory council shall identify, after consultation with the State Manpower Services Council, the vocational education and employment and training needs of the State and assess the extent to which vocational education, employment training, vocational rehabilitation, and other programs assisted under this and related Acts represent a consistent, integrated, and coordinated approach to meeting such needs; and (B) comment, at least once annually, on the reports of the State Manpower Services Council, which comments shall be included in the annual report submitted by the State advisory council pursuant to this section and in the annual report submitted by the State council pursuant to section 107 of the Comprehensive Employment and Training Act of 1973.

Within these guidelines, individual states have implemented their own plan for the state advisory council. The three following examples are provided to illustrate different approaches to meeting this requirement. First, in Florida [57], the Vocational Education Personnel Development Advisory Council is used in an advisory capacity to the Division of Vocational Education regarding the development, implementation, and evaluation of a statewide coordinated professional preparatory and in-service training program.

A Vocational EPD Advisory Council will be appointed and composed of persons representing labor, business, and industry; local educational agencies; community colleges, State Board of Regents; State EPDA Coordinator; Certification and Program Approval, Deputy Commissioner for Special Programs, Department of Education; and the Council on Teacher Education. Members of the council will be appointed by the Commissioner who may rely on the recommendations of the Division Director. The duties of the Vocational EPD Advisory Council will include the following:

(1) Review of annual assessment of the needs for personnel development in vocational education

(2) Recommendation of priorities for meeting these needs

(3) Recommendation of procedures for coordinating programs of local, state, and federal agencies to avoid duplication and maximize training opportunities for vocational education personnel

(4) Recommendations in the selection of local educational agencies and institutions of higher learning for participation in vocational education staff development programs

(5) Recommendations in the review and evaluation of vocational staff development programs

Second, the Indiana State Advisory Council for Vocational Education [75:4–5] was established to fulfill both the federal requirements and a state legislative mandate.

Advise–the SBVTE on the development of the Indiana State Plan for administration of Vocational Education and to advise on policy matters relating to State Plan administration;

Hold Public Meetings–to provide the opportunity for individuals to express views concerning vocational education;

Evaluate–vocational education programs, services, and activities in terms of the goals and objectives contained in the State Plan;

Publish–the results of evaluations;

Prepare and Submit–an annual evaluation report to the SBVTE, U.S. Commissioner of Education, and the National Advisory Council on Vocational Education on the effectiveness of programs, services, and activities in the state; and

Recommend–such changes in programs, services, and activities as may be warranted through evaluations.

Third, the "Annual Program of Work for 1975–76" used in Tennessee by the State Advisory Council on Vocational Education* illustrates in detail the specific objectives used to meet its three primary goals.

Mission: *To advise on the development of the State Plan and administration of policy matters arising in the administration of the State Plan for Vocational Education and to evaluate programs, services, and activities assisted under the Vocational Education Amendments of 1968.*

Goal 1. *To advise the State Board on the development of the State Plan.*

Objective 1: Upon invitation to do so, the Council will assign its Executive Director responsibility for serving on a Task Force drafting the State Plan.

Objective 2: For the State Plan Committee of the Council to meet at least one time to study the proposed State Plan in detail.

Objective 3: For each Council member to review preliminary drafts of the State Plan, and to share views concerning the proposed plan at a regular meeting of the Council.

Objective 4: For the Council to develop a position concerning the proposed State Plan, the position statement to be read at the Public Hearing on the State Plan.

Goal 2. *To advise the State Board of Education on policy matters arising in the administration of the State Plan submitted pursuant to the Act and the regulations.*

Objective 1: For the Executive Committee to review State Board policies for vocational education at least once each year and to report its findings to the Council.

Objective 2: For time to be allowed on the agenda of each Council meeting for the Assistant Commissioner for Vocational Education, State Department of Education to bring matters of concern before the Council. Such opportunity will also be afforded in committee meetings.

Objective 3: For the Council to hold one joint meeting with the State Board for Vocational Education.

Objective 4: For the Executive Committee to evaluate the extent to which recommendations made in the 1974 Evaluation Report have been carried out.

Goal 3. *To evaluate vocational education programs, services and activities under the State Plan, and publish and distribute the results thereof.*

Objective 1: For the Council to adopt its major evaluation goals for the annual evaluation report not later than at its second meeting during each fiscal year.

*A paper provided by Bobby G. Derryberry, Department of Education, State of Tennessee, Nashville, March 1977. Used with permission.

Objective 2: For the Executive Director to make an analysis for the Council on the extent to which the program objectives set forth in the State Plan for Vocational Education are met.

Objective 3: For the Council to make a two-day tour of selected secondary and postsecondary vocational programs in the fall of 1975.

Objective 4: For each Council member to visit at least three secondary and one postsecondary vocational education programs.

Objective 5: For the Council to hold one meeting annually in which the public is invited to present views on vocational education programs, and to present a summary of these views in the Annual Evaluation Report.

Objective 6: For the Council to contract for a Cost Benefit Analysis on vocational education in the state to be undertaken in FY '75.

Objective 7: For the Council to contract for the development of an evaluation model for vocational education in Tennessee.

Objective 8: For the Council to work with local vocational education agencies in the establishment of an advisory committee in each local system offering vocational education.

State Manpower Services Council

As suggested in the preceding description of the State Advisory Council for Vocational Education, the State Manpower Services Council plays a dominant role in the overall coordination of employment and training needs in the state. Originally formed as a result of the Comprehensive Employment and Training Act of 1973 (CETA), the council has been expanded in membership and purpose by the Comprehensive Employment and Training Act Amendments of 1978. As such, the council must be composed of members who are representative of community-based organizations, employment services, handicapped individuals, education and training agencies and institutions, business, labor, and various state boards and advisory councils.

The function of the council is to submit recommendations regarding program plans and basic goals, policies, and procedures; to monitor and provide objective evaluations of employment and training programs; and to provide for continuing analysis of the needs for employment, training, and related services. More specifically, the act [167] specifies that the council shall

(1) review continuously the operation of programs conducted by each prime sponsor, and the availability, responsiveness, and adequacy of State services, and make recommendations to the prime sponsors to agencies providing employment and training services, to the Governor, and to the general public with respect to ways to improve the effectiveness of such programs or services;

(2) make an annual report to the Governor which shall be a public document, and issue such other studies, reports, or documents as it deems advisable to assist prime sponsors or to otherwise help carry out the purposes of this Act;

(3) (A) identify, in coordination with the State Advisory Council on Vocational Education, the employment and training and vocational education needs of the State and assess the extent to which employment and training, vocational education, vocational rehabilitation, public assistance, and other programs assisted under this and related Acts represent a consistent, integrated, and coordinated approach to meeting such needs; and (B) comment at least once annually on the reports of the State Advisory Council on Vocational Education, which comments shall be included in the annual report submitted by that Council pursuant to section 105 of the Vocational Education Act of 1963;

(4) review the comprehensive employment and training plans of prime sponsors pursuant to section 104, especially with respect to nonutilization or duplication of existing services;

(5) review plans of all State agencies providing employment, training, and related services, and provide comments and recommendations to the Governor, the State agencies and the appropriate Federal agencies on the relevancy and effectiveness of employment and training and related service delivery systems in the State; and

(6) participate in the development of the Governor's coordination and special services plan.

Regional advisory councils

The regional advisory council represents the level at which, to date, there has been the least activity. This does not imply, however, that it is not important. The regional council represents the newest level of advisory activity. It also represents a growing trend that most likely will receive more emphasis in the future because (1) population trends and employment needs can more accurately be measured over a larger geographic area, (2) many smaller communities cannot meet all needs with their immediate resources, and (3) duplication of programs can be reduced through a regional effort.

The federal legislation does not require the use of regional councils nor are they typically included in state laws. In those states where regional councils have been formed, they have emerged from one of two sources. In Louisiana, for example, advisory bodies are required for each vocational-technical region by action taken by the Louisiana State Board for Vocational Education [59]. In Kentucky [80], regional councils emerged as a result of an authoritative statement in the state plan. These committees in Kentucky are charged with the responsibility to

advise and assist those responsible for vocational education in the development and improvement of the entire vocational education program in the region. The Committee can help identify the vocational education needs of individuals and communities, help assess labor market requirements, contribute to the establishment and maintenance of realistic and relevant programs, participate in developing community understanding and support, assist in building the prestige of and respect for programs of occupational education, and help establish long-range and annual goals. This Committee shall be concerned with continuing program evaluation.

As is evident from this focus, the regional council may serve many of the same functions as those performed by state and local groups. In addition, the regional council does perform some broad-based activities that are not typically assumed by other councils or committees. This is possible since regional council members commonly also serve on a local committee or are involved in various local activities. As a result, they are in a position to provide assistance to local committee members so they can more effectively complete their tasks, to coordinate activities from several local committees in different communities, and to serve as an effective consultant/ member in the evaluation of the local advisory committee.

TYPES OF ADVISORY COMMITTEES

Although the national, state, and regional councils used in career and occupational education are a source of significant input in respect to providing open dialogue, program direction, planning, and evaluation, the local advisory committee is the foundation for the concept of advisory bodies. It is at the local level that the concepts behind the advisory process first emerged, were put into practice, and were refined.

The importance of advisory committees was recognized in the midsixties by the fact that all states recommended their use in one form or another; and most required their use either through state legislation or as a regulation in the state plan. As noted earlier, the mandating of their use by the Education Amendments of 1976 [165] presented significant implications for the future. Again, to quote the act:

(g) (1) Each eligible recipient receiving assistance under this Act to operate vocational education programs shall establish a local advisory council to provide such agency with advice on current job needs and on the relevancy of courses being offered by such agency in meeting such needs. Such local advisory councils shall be composed of members of the general public, especially of representatives of business, industry, and labor; and such local advisory councils may be established for program areas, schools, communities, or regions, whichever the recipient determines best to meet the needs of that recipient.

(2) Each State board shall notify eligible recipients within the State of the responsibilities of such recipients under the provisions of paragraph (1); and each State advisory council shall make available to such recipients and the local advisory councils of such recipients such technical assistance as such recipients may request to establish and operate such councils.

The implications of the requirement of advisory committees are far reaching. Either directly or indirectly, various monitoring mechanisms, reporting systems, and evaluative approaches will be placed into action, thereby providing greater assurances that the committee is not only in place, but that it is functioning in a manner consistent with the ascribed goals, functions, and activities. Early evidence of this trend can be obtained from a review of the 1977 state plans in which greater emphasis is placed on cooperative relationships, state and local affiliations, and various accountability measures.

While the Education Amendments of 1976 and the state plans provide a general framework for advisory committee action, specific direction is determined totally within the local community. The approach utilized, of course, may vary considerably depending upon such factors as the size and complexity of the program; the nature, size, and location of the community; the administrative and teacher commitment to advisory committees; and the leadership styles used within the committee structure. Regardless of the approach, the advisory committee needs to perform its basic functions and activities.

For comparative purposes, advisory committees can be grouped into one of the six major types:

- schoolwide advisory committee
- administrative advisory committee
- general advisory committee
- department advisory committee
- program advisory committee
- special-purpose advisory committee

Figure 2–2 illustrates a set of possible interrelationships that may exist when all six types of committee structures are operative within a community.

Schoolwide advisory committee

The schoolwide advisory committee may be formed to assist in the development of overall educational policy or long-range plans, to evaluate the goals and programs of the school, and to maintain two-way communications between the community and the school. The committee's membership is broad based and is a cross section of the community in terms of sex, race, occupation, socioeconomic status, and other locally appropriate factors. Typically, the committee includes representation from the school, business and industry, service clubs and action groups, social and governmental agencies, and other segments of the population such as senior citizens, youth, parents, and nonparents.

From a career and occupational education perspective, there are at

FIGURE 2-2. Relationship among various types of advisory committees

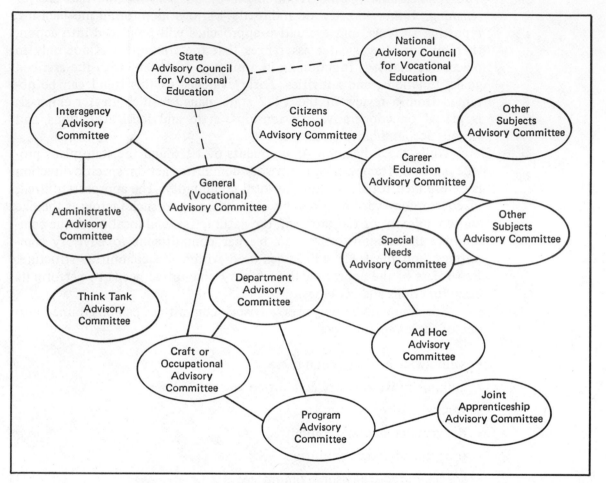

least two schoolwide committees that have the potential of interacting directly with administrators, teachers, and committee members.

First, the *citizens school advisory committee,* in dealing with schoolwide concerns and issues, may refer items to the school administration or the general advisory committee. These referrals may be sent through a member serving jointly on the two committees or directly to the committee chairperson. Similarly, data collected by vocational or occupational committees in a study to determine vocational needs may provide input for citizen committee action. The relationship between the two committees is supportive and usually limited to such areas as suggesting that studies be completed, asking for additional information, drawing points or data to the attention of the other, and recommending that consideration be given to a particular plan, proposal, or concern.

Second, the *career education advisory committee* has a much closer working relationship with individuals associated with the vocational emphasis in the school. It is usually composed of individuals in the school who represent the major program areas, such as guidance, vocational education, general education, and special education, along with individuals from business, industry, labor, and employment agencies. The primary purpose of this committee is to ensure that the programs in the school create career awareness, career orientation, career exploration, career planning, career preparation, and career placement and maximize career options and career development. As such, there is direct interaction with the general vocational advisory committee as well as with committees involved in the areas of arts, sciences, and communication.

Administrative advisory committee

The *administrative advisory committee* is organized for the specific purpose of improving administrative lines of communication between two or more schools in the community having related programs or maintaining a close working relationship. Typically, the committee deals with administrative topics, such as schedules, calendars, transportation, and processes for implementing new programs. One of the primary uses of this type of committee is to improve the working relationship between units in the community that have paralleling programs or relationships, such as area vocational schools and those schools sending students to the area vocational schools. In Missouri, for example, its prime purpose is to serve this role:

> The administrative advisory committee is appointed for the specific purpose of improving lines of communication between area vocational schools and those schools sending students to the area vocational school. This committee deals with schedules, calendars, new programs, transportation, and other items that are necessary for the administrative body to consider. [100:3]

The State Advisory Council on Vocational Education in North Carolina [125:6] suggests a slightly expanded statement of role by including evaluative and other interpretive roles:

> Advise a board on the development of its long-range and annual plan for vocational education.
>
> Advise on policy matters which affect administration of the plan.
>
> Interpret the vocational education needs of employers and employees in the area to the board and its staff.
>
> Interpret the board's policies to the community.
>
> Interpret the vocational education program to the community.
>
> Evaluate the impact of vocational education programs on the people and the community.

On occasion, the administrative committee may be referred to as a steering committee, but regardless of its name, it is used as a means for actively exchanging information, views, problems, and needs for improvement. In addition to including members who represent each of the schools involved in the program, the committee should include representatives of major occupational areas in the community as well as individuals who are knowledgeable about the community and who have specialized skills and abilities in those areas that are a focus of the committee.

General advisory committee

The general advisory committee is responsible for providing overall direction for the entire career preparation program in the community. As one of the most commonly used types of advisory committees, it is usually referred to as the *vocational education advisory committee* or, on occasion, the *occupational education advisory committee*. The primary focus of the committee is developing long-range goals and plans, studying the needs of the community, recommending programs to meet the needs, suggesting priorities to be given to these plans, and gaining support for the various career preparation programs in the community.

The composition of the committee may vary considerably, but most effective committees range in size from twelve to fifteen members. This is the committee that serves as the coordinating agent for all career preparation programs in the community. It is, therefore, most important that the committee represent the broad base within the community while, at the same time, providing representation from the department or occupational committees present in the community. In communities of moderate size, a representative from each department or program committee may serve jointly on the vocational education advisory committee. Typically, those outside of the school include representatives from employers and employees, labor organizations, chambers of commerce, governmental agencies, and others who represent the different areas covered by the program.

Some of the major activities carried out by a vocational education advisory committee may be illustrated by the guides followed by the Great Oaks Joint Vocational District in Cincinnati, Ohio [23:2–3].

1. Advise and counsel with local school authorities in determining and verifying in-school and adult vocational education program needs in the local communities.

2. Assist in the organization of occupational-craft advisory committees.

3. Provide tangible evidence that business and industry is supporting the program.

4. Make recommendations for the selection of competent consultants.

5. Provide a sounding board for advice pertaining to the operation of the overall vocational education program in the local community.

6. Become involved in public information activities that interpret the program to unions, to employers and to other interested groups and individuals.

7. Provide evaluation of the overall vocational education program, by reviewing present and past accomplishments, and forecast trends affecting training and employment.

8. Provide financial, legislative and moral support for the program.

As another example, Borgen and Davis [22:130] provided an expanded list for the general advisory committee by suggesting fourteen possible activities for action:*

1. To serve as a communication channel between the school and community groups, assisting in identification of program needs.

2. To provide close cooperation and better understanding of a particular career program between the employer, the general public, and the school.

3. To speak on behalf of community leaders in suggesting new or modified curricula.

4. To suggest related and technical information that should be considered in the development of career programs.

5. To recommend competent personnel from business and industry as potential instructors. This may be a function of the specialized committee.

6. To suggest ways for improving dissemination of program information.

7. To assist in identifying facilities for internships and on-the-job cooperative work experience. This may be a function of the specialized committee.

8. To keep the school informed of changes in labor market, specific needs, and a constant review of the curriculum in the light of current local, state, and national needs.

9. To assist the school in understanding the career program needs of the community.

10. To assist in recruiting students, providing facilities, and placing qualified graduates in appropriate positions.

11. To assist in the evaluation of the career programs and the assessment of their impact on the community.

12. To give advice on space needs for career programs.

13. To recommend ways through which occupational needs can best be met.

14. To suggest and support needed local, state, and national action to assure adequate career programs.

Department advisory committee

While the *department advisory committee* is not one of the most frequently used types of advisory committees, it may serve as an effective committee to represent such school departments as agriculture, business, home economics, health-related, industrial arts, or trade and industry within a comprehensive vocational or occupational education program. The composition of the committee follows the same areas of emphasis as the general advisory committee except that it is usually about half the size and its members represent each of the specialized interests of the de-

*Reprinted with permission from: Joseph A. Borgen and Dwight E. Davis. *Planning, Implementing, and Evaluating Career Preparation Programs.* Bloomington, Ill.: McKnight Publishing Company, 1974.

partment. For example, the suggested activities for home economics programs in California [32:6] are to

Identify areas of expansion for the Home Economics curriculum.

Assist with evaluation of the program.

Act as liaison between the community and the program.

Provide opportunity for community input.

Serve as resource people and identify community resources of a voluntary nature.

Develop ways to promote the program.

Advise in relation to program objectives, course content, and the competencies needed.

Advise on facilities and equipment.

The department advisory committee may be used as a coordinating body that unites the various occupational or craft committees within the department or as a substitute for such committees. When it serves as a coordinating group, care must be taken to ensure that the various areas are represented. The use of a department committee as a substitute for craft committees is more prevalent when the programs are relatively small in size or when it is located in a small community where the number of individuals available to serve on such a committee may be limited. In such cases, a department advisory committee may be used to serve both the home economics–related occupational programs and the consumer and homemaking education programs as noted above. As another example, in the Rich Township High School District in Illinois [126], each of the departments of business education, home economics, industrial arts, and cooperative vocational education follows a common set of guidelines:

1. Review the goals and objectives of the occupational education program.

2. Make recommendations regarding standards for instructional facilities.

3. Assist in updating of the existing philosophy of occupational education.

4. Aid in the continuous review of the content and organization of the instructional program in keeping with the occupational needs of the community.

5. Assist in locating training stations for cooperative students.

6. Assist in improvement of the student placement program.

7. Become informed of state and national legislation affecting vocational and technical education.

8. Assist in long-term program planning.

9. Assist with a continuous appraisal of occupational opportunities in the community served.

10. Assist in the identification of needed research in vocational and technical education.

11. Assist in developing a plan for educating the public about career education.

12. Study the committee's own procedures and evaluate its own work.

Program advisory committee

The advisory groups that serve a single program in a trade, occupation, or cluster of occupations are referred to as *occupational* or *craft advisory committees*. These terms are used interchangeably to denote that the committee's major activities are the identification, development, and operation of the total instructional program of a particular occupation such as data processing, horticulture, retail management, welding. As a result of the diversity of offerings, the program advisory committees represent the largest single grouping of advisory committee activity. They are composed of from five to eight members from the occupational area who possess a high level of skill as well as substantial knowledge in those areas related to the skill.

In reviewing their uses in the vocational-technical school, Basualdo [18:4] stressed that there should be a craft committee for every program in the school and noted that the committee should focus on

1. Training needs and placement opportunities in the community
2. Curriculum content and minimum standards
3. Safety rules and regulations in the trade
4. Equipment and supply standards
5. Related information required in the trade
6. Types of production work and projects to be used in the shops for training purposes
7. Publicity and public relation practices
8. Student and faculty recruiting standards
9. Counseling and guidance of students

From a more general perspective, the Midcoast Educational Development Center in Maine [44:46] identified six major areas of responsibility to guide the action of craft committees:

1. To make recommendations regarding program content and needed curriculum changes
2. To recommend equipment and facilities
3. To provide placement assistance relating to job placement and follow-up activities
4. To provide the instructor with necessary information and technical assistance
5. To assist the instructor and staff in developing performance objectives
6. To assist in craft committee and program evaluation

Special-purpose advisory committee

As a result of unique aspects of the program offerings or unusual circumstances, other types of advisory committees may be formed. These may take different forms but are grouped under a common area of special-purpose advisory committees since they are normally appointed for a short period of time and have a specific, single focus. The most common of this type is the *ad hoc advisory committee,* which may be appointed at any level in the advisory committee structure. This committee is formed in a manner similar to that of the program advisory committee because it represents a narrowed set of interests and special skills. As an illustration, an ad hoc committee may be formed to perform such tasks as conducting a feasibility study, the necessary steps to put a program into operation, or dealing with a special problem that may arise during the development or operation of the program.

Another group that is sometimes formed is the *think tank advisory committee.* The purpose of such a group is to attack an identified problem through a problem-solving approach by suggesting as many alternative solutions as possible rather than by making a specific recommendation. This committee usually ranges in size from five to fifteen and its members are simply invited to participate rather than being formally appointed. In addition to being knowledgeable on the particular topic, the members of this type of advisory committee should be especially creative, be willing to question the status quo, and have ideas to contribute.

The *interagency advisory committee* is one of the newest forms of special-purpose committees. It varies from some of the other special-purpose committees by the fact that it is used on a longer-term or standing basis. The interagency advisory committee has emerged from a need to coordinate advisory input. Such a committee might include representation from the general vocational education advisory committee, comprehensive employment and training agency advisory committee, industry-education committee, and apprenticeship committee.

A final variation of the special-purpose advisory committee is the *joint apprenticeship committee.* This committee does not follow the typical advisory committee format. It is composed jointly of employers and employees but may provide input and assistance to those in the adult and continuing education segment of the school. This committee, which performs both administrative and advisory functions, is usually organized by the Bureau of Apprenticeship and Training, U.S. Department of Labor, in locations where industrial apprenticeship programs are in operation [29].

SUGGESTED ACTIVITIES

1. After a careful review of the definition and types of advisory committees, develop operational definitions that are appropriate to your school district and region.

2. Determine the statewide network of vocational education or career education advisory committees in the state. Prepare an illustration indicating the levels of the network and the relationship of one level to another. Also, identify the role and responsibility of each.

3. Determine the membership on your state's Advisory Council for Vocational Education and what area each member represents.

4. Obtain and read recent annual reports prepared by your state's Advisory Council for Vocational Education or your state's Manpower Services Council and attend one of their public meetings.

5. Identify the goals, functions, and activities to be served by a specific advisory committee.

6. Identify a situation and outline how an advisory committee could serve as a change agent or a facilitator of two-way communications.

7. Identify alternative solutions to a common educational or procedural problem en-

countered by advisory committees. Also, identify ways in which the particular problem might be avoided in the future.

8. Attend a statewide public hearing on state vocational, career, or other related legislation such as special education, the handicapped, or CETA.

9. Determine the degree to which advisory committees have been used in the community in regard to occupational, career, or related educational programs, and identify ways in which their use could be enhanced.

10. Attend a public hearing conducted by a regional or state advisory council concerning occupational or career education, and provide input.

SELECTED REFERENCES

Allen, Fleet D. "Advisory Committee Organization, Role, and Utilization." Doctoral Dissertation, North Carolina State University at Raleigh, 1971.

Basualdo, Eugenio A. *Advisory Committees in Vocational-Technical Programs.* Memphis: State Technical Institute at Memphis, 1976.

Boyd, James E. *Organization and Effective Use of Representative Advisory Committees.* Cincinnati: Great Oaks Joint Vocational School District, 1975.

Burt, Samuel M. *Industry and Vocational-Technical Education.* New York: McGraw-Hill Book Co., 1967.

Conrad, William R., Jr., and Glenn, William E. *The Effective Voluntary Board of Directors, What It Is and How It Works.* Chicago: The Swallow Press, 1976.

Dellefield, Calvin. *Using Advisory Councils and Committees to Improve Vocational Programs for Rural Students.* Raleigh, N.C.: Center for Occupational Education, 1970.

Indiana State Advisory Council on Vocational Education. *Local Advisory Committee Handbook.* Indianapolis: Indiana State Advisory Council on Vocational Education, 1976.

Kentucky State Board of Education. *Vocational-Technical Education Regional Advisory Committees in Kentucky.* Frankfort, Ky.: State Department of Education, 1976.

King, Sam W. *Organization and Effective Use of Advisory Committees.* Washington, D.C.: GPO, 1960.

Land, Ming H. "The Status of Advisory Committees for Vocational and Technical Education in Utah with Comparison of the Structures and Functions to a Theoretical Model." Doctoral Dissertation, Utah State University, 1971.

Missouri Advisory Council on Vocational Education. *Handbook for Local Advisory Committees.* Jefferson City: Missouri Advisory Council on Vocational Education, 1977.

Nance, Everett E. *The Community Council: Its Organization and Function.* Midland, Mich.: Pendell Publishing Co., 1975.

North Dakota State Board·for Vocational Education. *The Vocational Education Advisory Committee.* Fargo: North Dakota State Advisory Council for Vocational Education, undated.

Olson, Herbert A. "The Development and Comparison of a Model Industrial Advisory Council for the Technical-Vocational Program of the Community College." Doctoral Dissertation, University of Houston, 1970.

Riendeau, Albert J. *Advisory Committees for Occupational Education: A Guide to Organization and Operation.* New York: McGraw-Hill Book Co., 1977.

Stadt, Ronald W., and Gooch, Bill G. *Cooperative Education: Vocational-Occupational-Career.* Indianapolis: The Bobbs-Merrill Co., 1977.

U.S. Congress, Public Law 93-203. *Comprehensive Employment and Training Act of 1973.* 93rd Congress, 1973.

U.S. Congress, Public Law 94-482. *Education Amendments of 1976.* 94th Congress, 1976.

U.S. Congress, Public Law 95-524. *Comprehensive Employment and Training Act Amendments of 1978.* 95th Congress, 1978.

PART II

MAJOR ADVISORY
COMMITTEE FUNCTIONS

One of the assets of utilizing advisory committees as the principal vehicle in the educational/occupational/community partnership is the many supportive roles the committee can serve. As already suggested, the primary purpose of the advisory committee is to provide advice to educational personnel in the form of giving direct advice or assistance and providing support or guidance.

Part II discusses the seven distinct but interrelated roles performed by advisory committees in contributing to the development and operation of meaningful educational programs. While each of these functions is presented in a separate chapter, such distinctions cannot be made. Furthermore, these supportive functions may be performed by different types of committees in different contexts. Depending on the type of program and the specific assignment(s) of the committee, for example, the committee may engage in numerous activities in order to fulfill its goals. These functions form the nucleus for an active program of work. Most advisory committee activity can be classified under one or more of these seven functions:

1. Curriculum content advisement
2. Equipment, facilities, and instructional resources review
3. Community resource coordination
4. Career guidance and placement services
5. Program evaluation
6. Community public relations
7. Professional development

In each chapter there is an introduction and an overview of the specific function, followed by a description of the scope of committee activities related to the function. Then there is a presentation of the basic activities associated with the function, as well as the strategies, procedures, and resource information for initiating the basic activities. Toward the end of the chapter, a case study illustrates the function in action, followed by a series of activities for those individuals interested in learning more about the function. Each chapter includes a communications exercise that can be used for individual or small-group in-service instruction.

3 The curriculum content advisement function

It is difficult to differentiate and classify advisory committee activities by singular functions, such as giving curriculum advice. For instance, in the process of providing advice, a committee may find it necessary, prior to updating the curriculum of the vocational education program, to analyze in which occupations recent graduates were placed. Because setting up a curriculum encompasses a broad range of activities and resources, there is an overlap of functions. It is difficult to separate curriculum from the community resources needed to provide instruction or the educational equipment, facilities, and instructional materials utilized. Since these program elements will be addressed in later chapters, the curriculum content advisement function described here will focus primarily on specific curriculum content as described by goals, objectives, teaching plans, and course outlines. This chapter is designed to acquaint community and educational personnel with the role and purpose of advisory committees in the area of course, curriculum, and program review.

Advisory committees have many roles in the area of curriulum. Curriculum review by an advisory committee can play an instrumental role in program improvement. While most advisory committees are not organized for the express purpose of dealing with curriculum issues, curriculum content is dealt with frequently in their reports. Most advisory groups recognize the central importance of curriculum. By dealing systematically with curriculum issues (i.e., goal setting, curriculum design, and evaluation), problems in other related areas (such as guidance and equipment and facilities) might be resolved or avoided.

Providing advice on course or program goals, objectives, and content is one of several recognized functions of advisory committees. Frequently, new advisory committee members think of curriculum content review as the *major* and sometimes the only function of such committees.

While this is seldom true in the actual operation of multipurpose, effective committees, it should be realized that providing advice regarding the curriculum is an instrumental function that usually leads to other more diversified activities. Numerous authors have recognized the importance of the curriculum content advisement function.

> In vocational education, one concern of the committees should be the establishment of practices which will keep instruction practical and functional. Committees should take an active part in helping to develop goal statements and assist in determining performance objectives since the members have the essential, specialized knowledge of work. [98:M-2]

The American Vocational Association, among other professional groups, has long supported the use of educational advisory committees and has suggested a highly functional role for advisory committees in the area of course content or curriculum advisement.

> Representatives of the fields for which instruction is to be provided must be consulted regarding the skills, instructional materials, equipment, standards for production work or service provided, and instructional content. All phases of training should be reviewed periodically in order to keep them occupationally oriented and up-to-date. [9:19-20]

SCOPE OF CURRICULUM CONTENT ADVISEMENT

Curriculum content must be viewed in a broad perspective. Depending upon the type and level of advisory committee, a variety of curricular concerns may be appropriate for the committee. Advisory committees for occupational and career education programs frequently deal with the following major concerns:

- The curriculum objectives as they relate to competencies needed for employment
- Adequacy and accuracy of career information
- Articulation of course content with prerequisite and advanced courses
- Relationship of curricular or course content to other school curriculums
- Emphasis placed on the development of human relations skills
- Emphasis placed on the development of positive attitudes toward work
- Appropriateness of curriculum content for special needs (handicapped and disadvantaged) learners
- Appropriateness of instructional materials

For a number of years diverse advisory committees have addressed questions of curriculum content at all educational levels ranging from preschool through postsecondary and higher education. Advisory committees have been frequently used in both public and private schools, industry-training programs, employment (CETA) training programs, universities, and other agencies operating educational programs. While committees have been used most frequently in advising curriculum content in vocational-technical education programs, this function has also been widespread in general secondary and university programs. In the public schools, advisory committees have also reviewed curricula in general education programs. They commonly have been formed on an ad hoc basis to study the adoption of a new textbook or assist with the development of new courses, for example those related to ecology and energy.

With the advent of career education, course content advisement is fast becoming a functional role of many advisory committees in all areas of education, not just vocational education. For example, the Career Education Incentive Act provides federal funds for establishing and operating community career education councils [166]; and the Career Education Act in Michigan has mandated the use of local career education councils. The major purpose of these councils is to increase cooperation and articulation between local educational agencies as they plan to implement a career education program. As more states and schools decide to implement career education on a full scale basis, general and vocational educators at all levels have seen the need to adapt curricula that more adequately orient and prepare individuals for career and life roles. The basis for an effective curriculum for a career education program can only emerge from a dialogue among business, industry, labor, education, and other community groups, and educational advisory committees are an effective vehicle for this continuing dialogue.

Range of responsibility

This chapter presents a broad view of the curriculum content advisement function. In actual practice, the specific responsibility given to an advisory committee will determine its scope of curriculum content advisement. For example, a (schoolwide) career education advisory committee for a K-12 school district would give advice on the full range of elementary and secondary level curricular offerings. A residential building trades advisory committee (program advisory committee) in the same school district would focus more specifically on the instructional content within an individual course. Advisory committee leaders should keep this potential range of curriculum content advisement in mind. It is difficult to target curriculum review activities appropriately. However, it is essential to do so in order to develop reasonable recommendations for program, curriculum, and/or course revision or expansion.

Curriculum development or revision

Advisory committees can be used effectively in either curriculum *development* or curriculum *revision* activities. In curriculum development the committee is concerned with new programs and curriculum. For example, a committee could be charged with assisting teachers at a new area vocational school with developing student performance objectives and course content outlines. In curriculum revision the emphasis is on modification, refinement, and improvement of an existing curriculum, program, or course. For example, the committee could revise mathematics courses to include more information on metrics.

Sometimes the committee may be involved in both development and revision. An advisory committee may recommend the addition of a particular unit of content (revision) and may subsequently be involved in the review of (and possibly the development of) new instructional outlines or materials to complete the task.

The relevancy and recency of curriculum is an ongoing concern. Educators, business leaders, and the lay public alike are continually seeking improvements in educational programs to better meet the needs of individuals entering or reentering a rapidly changing society. To this end, advisory committees for most programs are engaged in a continuing cycle of curriculum revision and development or redevelopment. Most educational philosophers contend that this cycle is a fundamentally healthy process for educational institutions and that effectively managed advisory committees can contribute immensely to the process.

Course content focus

The role of the advisory committee in course advisement is just that: to provide advice and suggest improvements regarding the content of instruction. It is not the purpose of the committee to address or critique the "hows" of learning, teaching, counseling, or administrating as they are related to the content. Experience has shown that the expertise of the committee can be productively utilized if curriculum concerns related to *content* rather than process are addressed. Educational process questions are within the purview of the professional educator and should remain there.

It is difficult, however, to separate content advice from advice regarding the process or the practice of education. The creation of a new vocational program can, for instance, require the addition of staff members with some unique credentials. In order to hire or certify such individuals, changes may be needed in hiring practices or state certification requirements. The advisory committee may choose to acknowledge that changes are needed, but it should not attempt to specifically map out how the changes shall be instituted.

Utilizing state and/or national curriculum materials

Different types of educational advisory committees at local, state, and national levels have been involved in curriculum development or revision. What has emerged from most state and national committee work has been a set of curriculum guidelines, a curriculum guide, a composite listing of objectives, a series of instructional materials, or some other form of curriculum specification. While these documents are helpful as guides for local educators, local committees still must serve a highly functional role in adapting curriculum to local or specialized needs and programs. To illustrate, a consortium of states (referred to as V—TECS) has recently been formed to develop catalogs of vocational education performance objectives to be shared among member states. The consortium suggests that local advisory committees play an active role in screening and refining the objectives and performance criteria for use in specific programs.

CURRICULUM CONTENT ADVISEMENT ACTIVITIES

There are a number of basic activities that an advisory committee can engage in as part of the curriculum advisement function. Appropriate selection of activities will depend upon the nature of the assignment given to the committee by the school board, dean of instruction, or whoever authorized the establishment of the committee; the availability of written curriculum materials and descriptions; and the purpose of the course advisement activities as perceived by individual committee members. Seven areas, however, typify the major curriculum advisement activities that may be initiated.

Employment and program needs assessment

A major criterion used by advisory committees for determining whether or not to establish, continue, or expand a career or occupational education program is whether the program is meeting local and regional employment needs and whether it is doing it effectively. The decisions inherent in this task must evolve from the objectives of the total program evaluation effort. Once the objectives of the program and of the evaluation effort are integrated, the information needed to determine how well the program objectives are being achieved can be collected. Several techniques and procedures may be necessary to collect the data.

The viability of the entire program is dependent on the care with which this information is collected. Assurances must be made concerning the validity of the data and the effectiveness of the data collection procedures. Without such exactness, the recommendations of the committee and the program itself can become suspect. Furthermore, the planning continuum itself comes under question, because without effective assessment based on sound data and interpretations, it is no more than a paper process.

The advisory committee can play an integral role in the development of instruments and data interpretation procedures. Depending on the nature of the information needed, the staff and committee must consider the following questions in designing the various data collection techniques: What is the relevant labor market? How well are the program objectives being met? What are the short-term and long-range employment and educational needs of the community? What are the placement records of the graduates? What are the opinions of parents toward proposed courses? What community resources are available to support new course offerings?

Vocational education advisory committees must play an active role in assessing and interpreting community desires for new vocational programs. Occupational projections may indicate a need for persons trained in custodial services, but parent expectations may strongly prohibit students from enrolling in these programs. Other factors unique to the community need to be reviewed by advisory committees when program changes are being considered.

Although the committee can assume major responsibility for the assessment process, the role of the committee is primarily one of assisting with the design of the study and interpreting the data. The committee should first identify the major questions to be asked. The answers to these questions should provide the necessary information for deciding whether to update, expand, or discontinue the program. The advisory committee should also keep in mind that the group that makes the final decision about the recommendations looks for detailed and comprehensive survey information. If advisory committees are involved in the planning and review of the questionnaires and studies, these surveys will provide a more accurate picture of the need for new programs or for certain changes in existing programs.

Review of program goals and objectives

Initially, an advisory committee may be interested in examining the goals and objectives relative to a specific program or set of programs. Such questions as the following might be examined by the committee: To what extent should the curriculum focus on exploration of career options or preparation for specific careers? To what extent should career decision making or employability skills be emphasized?

Obviously, schoolwide, general, and departmental level advisory committees will spend a great proportion of their time reviewing program goals and objectives. At any one of these levels the total curriculum in an area vocational school might be examined for the purpose of providing recommendations regarding the amount of work experience provided to students. Through a process of this type, the general goals of the occupational or career education program could be clarified in light of the ever-changing employment and program needs of the community.

When examining program goals and objectives, a program advisory committee might:

• Review and compare program goals and objectives with those of a similar program in a nearby community.

- Examine the goals and objectives of a secondary school level program in relationship to a local community college program offering advanced training in the same occupational field.

- Discuss the level of mastery that should be attained by students on individual objectives.

- Identify the industrial or specific working conditions under which students should demonstrate their abilities to perform the objectives.

- Analyze the list of goals to be certain it is complete. Are appropriate goals or objectives listed describing specific job skills, related math and reading skills, decision-making skills, employment-seeking skills?

Review of instructional goals and objectives

Competency-based instruction became popular in many vocational and career education programs during the early 1970s. As an approach to developing instructional objectives, it emphasized the identification of observable behaviors, skills, or competencies that students should be capable of demonstrating following instruction. The major outcome of the competency-based movement has been to require educators to place more emphasis on curriculum and instructional planning. The fundamental purpose of most of the efforts has been to identify and validate competencies and basic curriculum content, which enable the learner to obtain satisfying, meaningful, and productive work. Vocational and practical arts educators are in a unique position to analyze what skills, concepts, and information should be learned for a specific occupation or cluster of occupations.

The specificity of competencies and instructional objectives identified by curriculum specialists, teachers and researchers varies considerably. General objectives, such as "all learners will be capable of locating current occupational information," can be focused on by administrative, general, or departmental advisory committees. The identification of specific occupational competencies and objectives, such as "learners will be able to weld in the overhead position," may be emphasized more extensively by individual program or craft advisory committees. Advisory committees may choose to initiate the following activities related to competency identification and instructional objectives:

- Listing specific occupational competencies and related instructional objectives.

- Listing key related competencies (e.g., math, reading, safety, measuring, career awareness, personal-social skills, human relations skills).

- Reviewing and evaluating lists of competencies and instructional objectives prepared by teachers, researchers, curriculum developers, or state department of education staff.

- Suggesting sequences for presenting instructional objectives and activities.

- Identifying competencies that are performed in more than one occupation in a cluster of occupations.
- Verifying the criticality of each competency or objective success in the occupation(s).
- Identifying specialty competencies that may be uniquely appropriate for handicapped or disadvantaged students.

Figure 3-1 presents one format to identify critical and desirable competencies in a given occupational cluster. The instructor identified a list of proposed competencies for the occupations included in the program. The committee members individually rated each competency for the various occupations. Following the individual ratings, the committee discussed each competency and developed a "consensus rating." The information provided to the instructors through this process was helpful for refining the curriculum and suggesting instructional sequences.

Review of instructional activities and materials

Program and craft advisory committees can play a useful role in reviewing and evaluating the instructional materials and activities utilized in a program. On occasion, general or schoolwide advisory committees will examine instructional materials to be used in or developed for selected objectives. For instance, in recent years, general advisory committees have been increasingly interested in examining instructional materials for the purpose of eliminating or minimizing sex-role stereotyping in several occupational fields. More commonly, however, program or craft advisory committees have reviewed instructional materials and activities for the following:

- Accuracy of technical information and procedures
- Recency of technical information and procedures
- Reference to appropriate occupational standards (e.g., use of standard specification charts)
- Depth of information presented in tests, reference material, and instructional activities
- Realism associated with the assigned student projects
- Accuracy of occupational information (e.g., current wages and salaries)

Student organization involvement

Student organizations are an important aspect of the total program in many occupational and career education programs. While organizations and clubs are frequently viewed as extracurricular in nature, they are, in essence, a critical component in the career development of youth. Typically, the goals and purposes of student organizations such as the

FIGURE 3-1. Cluster analysis matrix

Auto Body Maintenance Occupational Cluster

Directions: Listed below are a series of tasks performed in one or more of the selected entry occupations identified for this cluster. For each task that is "essential or critical" for successful entry performance in the identified occupation, place an "x" in the appropriate box. For each task that is a "desirable" competency in a worker entering the identified occupation, place an "o" in the appropriate box. Add any tasks that are essential (x) or desirable (o) to successful occupational performance which are not listed.

Name of Respondent _____ Al Hersh
Place of Employment _____ Al's Body Shop
Occupation _____ Estimation – Supervision
No. of Years in Occupation _____ 16

CLUSTER OCCUPATIONS

ID Code	Task Inventory	Shop Estimator	Automobile Body Repairman	Painter, Automobile	Automobile Body Repairman Helper
ABM 01	Remove, overhaul, and replace trim and hardware		X	o	x
ABM 02	Perform bumping operations	X	X	o	o
ABM 03	Remove and replace body components		X	x	x
ABM 04	Prepare surface for painting		o	x	x
ABM 05	Apply masking tape and paper			x	x
ABM 06	Operate spray paint equipment			x	o
ABM 07	Perform lacquer refinishing			x	o
ABM 08	Perform enamel refinishing			x	o
ABM 09	Remove and install glass		X	o	x
ABM 10	Prepare vehicle for delivery	o	o	o	x
ABM 11	Estimate damage repairs	X	X	o	
ABM 12	Select and use appropriate materials and supplies	X	X	x	x

Adapted from M. L. Reynolds, R. J. Lutz, C. B. Johnson, and L. A. Phelps, *Cluster Guide* (Series). Mt. Pleasant: Central Michigan University, 1973. Copyright © 1973 by Central Michigan University. Used with permission.

Vocational Industrial Clubs of America (VICA) and the Future Farmers of America (FFA) focus on the following:

Developing leadership through educational, vocational, civic, recreational, and social activities.

Relating school experiences to a young person's personal search for meaning, identity, and achievement.

Promoting high standards in work ethics, craftsmanship, scholarship, and safety.

Developing an understanding of the functions of labor and management organizations and recognition of their interdependence.

Providing opportunities for community service to youth. [129:4]

An advisory committee serves an important communications link between the community and the student organization. A committee plays an instrumental role in helping the club to build strong, responsible citizens; and the committee can also bring about a better understanding of the club program by local industry, business, the home, and the school. More specifically, advisory committees can assist student organizations by

Evaluating the club's program of activities and its relationship to the curriculum

Informing the public of the purposes of the club

Sponsoring open houses and speakers from industry and business

Suggesting fund-raising activities for the club

Reviewing candidates for club achievement programs

Attending recognition banquets and other club functions [129:17–18]

Curriculum articulation

The rise of career education and the demand for program accountability have required schools to examine closely the courses offered at all levels. Curriculum articulation between elementary, middle/junior high, and high schools has become particularly critical. Obviously, effective articulation is essential for insuring that students have sequential and developmental experiences, beginning with career awareness and culminating in preparation for meaningful work roles.

Concern has also arisen regarding the potential duplication of vocational programs and of expensive facilities. The need to identify and determine the entrance and exit competencies of learners proceeding through a series of occupational courses also has raised concern for the articulation of curriculum.

A program or craft advisory committee can examine (1) the relationship of sequential courses (e.g., Auto Mechanics I, Auto Mechanics II)

and (2) relationship of related occupational courses offered at junior high schools, high schools, area vocational centers, local community colleges, and/or postsecondary vocational-technical institutes.

Vocational curriculum articulation has also emerged as a concern of several community agencies such as CETA prime sponsors, vocational rehabilitation, and the employment service. Efforts have increased nationally to encourage vocational educators to work in providing vocational education and training to unemployed, underemployed, and disadvantaged persons. In fact, under the Vocational Education Amendments of 1976, state advisory councils for vocational education are charged with

> assessing the extent to which vocational education, employment training, vocational rehabilitation, and other programs assisted under this and related Acts represent a consistent, integrated, and coordinated approach to meeting such needs (i.e. the identified employment and training needs of the state) . . . . [53:53832]

In states with rural populations, such as Kentucky, regional advisory councils are used to coordinate and articulate vocational course offerings for several school districts and postsecondary programs [80]. In larger cities, citywide committees have been formed to articulate occupational course offerings. The administrative advisory committee as described in Chapter 2 is frequently concerned with curriculum articulation between area vocational schools and sending schools. For increasing in-school articulation, program advisory committees can include representatives of sending programs (such as junior high or elementary school teachers or sending school counselors or teachers), as well as representatives of high school or postsecondary programs whose programs are being reviewed. Also, joint committees representing members of vocational education advisory committees may be established to increase communication and articulation of vocational education.

IMPLEMENTATION STRATEGIES

To implement effectively these curriculum advisement activities, the advisory committee might review information on employment and community needs, conduct a curriculum advisement meeting, engage in an in-depth curriculum study, or conduct a curriculum evaluation meeting. Working guidelines for these strategies are presented in the following sections.

Reviewing information on employment and community needs

By assessing employment needs, advisory committees provide information for programmatic decision making, thereby affecting the seven advisory committee functions. While information concerning the employment needs of the community may come from formal and informal sources, the more structured approach to collecting data is commonly the most critical to the recommendations formed by the committee. There are three types of occupationally related surveys that school personnel and committee members are concerned with, whether conducted by school personnel alone or in conjunction with community groups or segments, state employment service personnel, or specially employed consultants. First, the study of a single craft or occupation may be undertaken in an area such as carpentry, radio repair, food preparation, or offset presswork. Second, a survey may be undertaken of an entire business or industry such as construction, data processing, or office services. Third, a study of the community may encompass all or some of the principal careers or occupations in which individuals are employed.

The nature, scope, and assignment of the committee usually determine which type of study is undertaken. These surveys are designed to obtain the following kinds of information:

1. The number of people in a geographic area currently employed in a given occupation, and the additional members needed currently and through the next (usually) five years.

2. The occupation(s) in greatest demand.

3. The jobs within an occupation in which training is needed.

4. The number of graduates from school occupational education programs who might be accepted for employment in a community.

5. The interest of young people and adults in training for selected occupations.

6. The need for supplemental training for people already employed.

7. New areas in which school preparators or updating education and training are needed.

8. Which school programs should be expanded, discontinued, or established.

9. The education and training requirements of the occupation, job, or industry which can be met by the school program. [29:82]

Since the purpose of the occupational education program is to produce occupationally prepared individuals, an accurate determination of labor needs in the community is an essential part of program planning. Therefore the survey must provide data that will form the basis for making recommendations about the curriculum in order to place in priority those programs that best fulfill the community's labor needs. The most common areas of study in this context can be illustrated by the tasks identified for the Career Education Planning Districts (CEPD) in Michigan* [160:II. 6-10].

*Touche Ross and Company. *Vocational Education Local Manpower Planning Handbook.* Lansing, Mich.: Michigan Department of Education, 1972. Used with permission.

I. MAJOR ISSUES REQUIRING POLICY DECISIONS
  A. The Scope of the Relevant Labor Market
    1. Extent to which the CEPD should train for migration from the area.
    2. Extent to which the CEPD should emphasize state-wide versus local labor demand objectives.
  B. The Geographical Source of the CEPD Labor Supply
    1. Influx of skilled labor to the CEPD.
    2. Source and type of vocational training in CEPD.
  C. The Desired Rate of Annual Vocational Education Program Expansion during Five-Year Period.
  D. The Areas of Probable Program Expansion for the CEPD
    1. Apparent employment opportunities through occupational *Expansion* demand.
    2. Apparent employment opportunities through occupational *Replacement* demand.
  E. Other Issues Specific to Individual CEPDs

II. IDENTIFY AND ANALYZE RELEVANT DATA
  A. Define the Relevant Labor Market
    1. Extent to which CEPD should train for migration from the area based on:
      a. Labor force size of CEPD
      b. Rate of unemployment in CEPD
      c. Growth of CEPD population or labor force
      d. Proximity of CEPD to a Job Center
      e. Commuting patterns of CEPD residents
      f. Geographical placement of vocational education graduates, if data available
    2. Extent to which the CEPD should emphasize state-wide versus local labor demand objectives based on:
      a. State labor force composition (urban, rural farm, rural nonfarm) as compared to CEPD or regional composition
      b. State labor force composition (private industry, self-employed, unpaid family or government worker) as compared to CEPD or regional composition
      c. Occupation or industry employment as a percent of state labor force as compared to CEPD and/or regional labor force.
      d. State ranking of a particular occupation or industry as compared to CEPD and/or regional ranking
      e. State-wide growth of a particular occupation or industry as compared to CEPD or regional growth
  B. Define the Geographical Source of the CEPD Labor Supply
    1. Influx of skilled labor to the CEPD
      a. Growth of CEPD population
      b. Growth of CEPD labor force
      c. Rate of CEPD unemployment
      d. Commuting patterns in CEPD and adjacent CEPDs
    2. Source and type of occupational training in CEPD
      a. Private training schools in area (telephone directory, directory of private training schools)
      b. Local MESC [Michigan Employment Security Commission] office
      c. Major private industry
      d. Inventory of public vocational programs

C. Define the Desired Rate of Annual Expansion for Vocational Education Programming over Five-Year Period
  1. Develop annual growth objectives based on:
      a. Projected CEPD enrollment
      b. Goals for percent of total enrollment to be enrolled in vocational training (State plan for Reference)

D. Identify Areas of Probable Program Expansion Opportunity for CEPD Based on Labor Demand Criteria
  1. Apparent employment opportunities through occupational *Expansion* demand based on:
      a. Growth of a particular occupation or industry in the region or CEPD
      b. Total employment of a particular occupation or industry in the region or CEPD
      c. State of Michigan/Detroit Metropolitan area projections
  2. Apparent employment opportunities through occupational *Replacement* demand based on:
      a. Total employment of a particular occupation or industry in the region or CEPD
      b. Percent of total labor force accounted for by a particular occupation or industry in the region or CEPD
      c. Absence of negative growth of a particular occupation or industry in the region, CEPD or state
      d. State of Michigan/Detroit Metropolitan Area projections
      e. Other issues specific to individual CEPDs

III. DEVELOPING AND VERIFYING HYPOTHESES

A. Define specifically Program Expansion Opportunities
B. Evaluate Each Apparent Program Opportunity against Basic Data Limitations
C. Verify the Demand Potential of Selected Occupations
  1. Determine number of establishments relevant to occupations to be analyzed and their approximate employment size
  2. Select information required for each establishment or group of establishments
  3. Select survey technique
  4. Determine the optimum sample source
      a. If few establishments exist employing desired number of people, identify establishment name from:
          Empirical observation
          MESC
          Trade associations or unions
          Public utilities
          Chamber of Commerce
      b. If numerous establishments exist employing the desired number of people:
          Review Dun & Bradstreet DMI Printout for specific establishments relevant to occupation and identify:
            Four-digit Standard Industrial Classification
            Size of establishments
            Geographical location of establishments
          Contact VECDS [Vocational Education Curriculum Development Service] for assistance in obtaining required data

      5. Implement interviewing tasks
  D. Analyze Results against Previous Hypotheses
      1. Assign priorities to occupations based on the number of job openings identified
      2. Identify optimum type of program funding
        a. Extended day
        b. Extended year
        c. Shared time
        d. Funding sources other than VECDS
        e. Regular school year
      3. Determine priority programs to be funded by VECDS based on statewide labor demand criteria
      4. Estimate number of students enrolling in each nonfunded program identified
      5. Allocate available discretionary vocational education funds to each program in order of demand priority
      6. Adjust program mix to funds available

IV. DEFINE AND DOCUMENT THE DESIRED ACTION PROGRAM

When the committee members meet to review and discuss the data from the survey, they should discuss the following questions: What kind of general trends can be identified from the data or information? Does the data collected answer the questions in a manner consistent with the design of the assessment instrument? Does the data provide an accurate and adequate information base for making the necessary recommendations? How can the data be presented so that it is readily understood and interpreted. Discussing, interpreting, and summarizing the results of this effort are important committee activities essential to completing the planning cycle.

The survey must focus on those questions addressed to the general community (including students, parents, business and industrial personnel). Information from this survey will complement needs data accumulated through the employment assessment and provide comprehensive information from all parties served by the educational program. The committee should identify the major questions to be answered by the survey; the personnel actually involved in conducting the survey should formulate the specific questions and questionnaires. The following are some of the topics generally considered part of such an assessment:

1. Opinions and attitudes of parents toward proposed program offerings

2. Interests of students in new programs

3. Parental expectations for their children and their education

4. Willingness of the community to support new and additional school programs

5. Identification of community resources for new programming

6. Type and accessibility of community resources for new programming

7. Follow-up data of past graduates

8. Population trends

9. Student abilities [37:A-13]

The appearance of the study will differ depending on the data available and the specific purpose and scope of the study.

Most school personnel recognize and appreciate the importance of comprehensive survey information as a base for making decisions regarding program changes. Like the employment needs assessment, the form of the program needs assessment may vary. Very often the technique used is the mail survey. It is an effective procedure for obtaining facts and opinions; however, care must be taken that there is incentive to respond, that too many questions are not included, that questions are not ambiguous, that questions are presented in the proper format, and that requests for the same information are not made in other forms. Telephone interviews are another quick way of obtaining certain data.

Curriculum advisement meeting

It is generally recommended that at least one-fourth to one-third of the advisory committee meetings held each year be devoted to some aspect of curriculum advisement. The number and substance of these meetings will vary, of course, depending on the type of advisory committee involved. The topics planned for such a meeting could encompass selected or all of the basic activities (analysis of general curriculum emphasis or needs, identification of competencies, review of program goals and objectives, or review of instructional activities and materials).

Figure 3-2 provides a sample agenda for a curriculum content advisement meeting. In this particular meeting, the committee is both reviewing and evaluating the program performance goals. When curriculum advisement meetings are planned, attention must be given to the type and extent of advice needed relative to curriculum content, to the selection of appropriate committee activities, and to the development of an agenda that attacks key questions regarding curriculum content.

In-depth curriculum study

Advisory committees may be asked to conduct an in-depth curriculum study. Frequently these are schoolwide or general advisory committees that have been formed to examine a series of courses or major vocational education programs. An in-depth curriculum study requires considerable planning and management to be effective and usually requires a series of committee meetings as well as open discussion meetings with the parents and the general public. When organizing and managing an in-depth curriculum study, the committee must

- Define specific objectives for the study.

- Prepare appropriately detailed background information.

- Involve those advisory committee members who have positive and substantial interests in curriculum revision.
- Develop an overall plan for the study, which includes realistic dates for completion of specific steps or activities.
- Insure that the results of the study are available and used appropriately by key audiences.

FIGURE 3-2. Sample agenda for a curriculum content advisement meeting

---

AGENDA FOR THE AUTOMOTIVE TECHNOLOGY ADVISORY COMMITTEE MEETING

Local Community College

7:00 P.M.	Meeting Call to Order	Chairperson
	Approve Minutes from Last Meeting	Secretary
	Presentation of Course Content and Performance Goals of Automotive Technology Program	Instructor(s)

Discussion Questions   Chairperson

What general areas do these goals cover?

- Specific job skills
- Occupational information
- Human relations skills
- Employability skills
- Basic skills
- Mathematical/Computational Skills
- Career decision-making skills
- Continuing education

Completion of the checklist evaluation of course content and performance goals by committee   Chairperson

Evaluation Discussion Questions

Is the course content in the above areas current?

- What specifically needs to be added and/or deleted from the course content?
- Are there more recent instructional materials or references that might be used?
- What new field trips or co-op work experiences should be added to the course?
- Should the criteria for evaluation of student performances by instructors or participating employers be changed?
- How can the course content be more effectively coordinated with the community college and area vocational school locally?

9:30 P.M.	Adjournment

Adapted from Leslie H. Cochran, L. Allen Phelps, and Joseph F. Skupin. *A Guide for Effective Utilization of Advisory Committees.* Lansing: Michigan Department of Education, 1974. Used with permission.

FIGURE 3-3. Curriculum evaluation form

INSTRUCTION:

1. *Characteristic of Quality:*
   The program performance objectives represent the entry level job skills and knowledge required for employment.

   Reference Materials:
   A binder containing *"State Minimum Performance Objectives for Vocational Education"* for this code may be obtained from the school district administrator in charge of the vocational-technical education program. Some programs have locally developed performance objectives.

Reviewer's Score	COMMENTS:

   N/A — Not applicable
   ? — Insufficient data to answer
   1 — Poor (major improvements needed)
   2 — Fair (improvement needed)
   3 — Adequate (meets minimum standards)
   4 — Good (exceeds minimum standards)
   5 — Excellent (outstanding)

2. *Characteristic of Quality:*
   Each student is issued a copy of the program performance objectives and the vocational-technical education teacher maintains records of each student's achievement of performance objectives.

   Reference Materials:
   Michigan Department of Education, Vocational-Technical Education Service competency based education inservice training modules.

Reviewer's Score	COMMENTS:

3. *Characteristic of Quality:*
   Students who complete the program possess the job skills and knowledge reflected in the performance objectives required for successful initial employment.

   Reference Materials:
   Locally adopted performance objectives.

Reviewer's Score	COMMENTS:

76

4. Characteristic of Quality:
The program is designed to provide students the opportunity to practice job skills through the cooperative technique, student organizations and/or clinical laboratory experiences.

Reference Materials:
"Administrative Guide for Vocational-Technical Education" — Secondary Vocational-Technical Education, Section F.

Reviewer's Score	COMMENTS:

5. Characteristic of Quality:
The advisory committee and the instructor periodically review and modify the program performance objectives to maintain relevancy with job requirements and opportunities.

Reference Materials:
Program Standards of Quality, Section C, *"Administrative Guide for Vocational-Technical Education."*

Reviewer's Score	COMMENTS:

To be used for additional characteristics of quality if needed:

Reviewer's Score	COMMENTS:

Curriculum evaluation

A third strategy that could be used is curriculum evaluation. In this strategy the committee may be asked to directly evaluate the curriculum content, instructional sequence, or instructional materials. Several state departments of education require local vocational advisory committees to submit detailed program evaluations on an annual basis [99]. The overall evaluation function of advisory committees is presented in Chapter 7, but it is described briefly here with reference to the evaluation of curriculum content. Since the concept of an ongoing evaluation permeates the entire planning continuum, this activity is critical to recommendations related to establishing, continuing, modifying, and expanding curricular offerings—the assessment of the program is at the core of the same set of recommendations. Such factors as students' interests, parental expectations, student abilities, community resources, population trends, and other concerns must also be given consideration.

A curriculum evaluation checklist developed by the Michigan Department of Education to be used by local advisory committees is presented in Figure 3–3. An advisory committee should follow these steps when performing curriculum evaluation work:

1. Formulate specific evaluation questions

2. Obtain committee consensus on the content of evaluation questions (In some situations this may involve reviewing questions prepared by state departments, state advisory councils, or other external agencies.)

3. Prepare evaluation instrument

4. Test and revise instrument

5. Administer the evaluation

6. Compile and analyze the data and information

7. Develop an evaluation report that provides substantive recommendation for curriculum improvement

8. Insure that evaluation results are utilized appropriately

As noted in the procedure, curriculum evaluation instruments may already be available through state departments and other agencies. Such instruments usually provide space for additional curriculum evaluation items or questions to be added by the local advisory committee.

THE CURRICULUM CONTENT ADVISEMENT FUNCTION
IN ACTION

The following case study describes a special advisory committee that was formed to develop and review a curriculum for teaching occupational survival skills.* The strategies used by this committee reflect the concepts presented in this chapter, as well as some innovative approaches to curriculum advisement.

In May 1976, the Board of School Commissioners of Baltimore mandated a two-semester course in Survival Skills as a requirement for high school graduation. The department of home economics was given the responsibility of developing curriculum for Survival Skills and implementing it. This course consisted of a nine-week unit (forty-five lessons) in Consumer Education and a nine-week unit (forty-five lessons) in Preparation for Work.

In developing the curriculum content for Preparation for Work, representatives of business and industry as well as members of the educational and lay community had to be consulted. An informal survey of students, parents, and community members was conducted to determine which concepts and topics should be included in the course. Following the survey, a questionnaire asking for lists of topics to be included was sent to regional superintendents, curriculum coordinators and specialists, school principals and administrators, guidance counselors, and home economics and office occupations teachers. Compiled from these lists was a master list of concepts to be included in the course.

An advisory committee of Baltimore business leaders was formed to react to the survey results and provide guidance for curriculum content. The committee included the president of the Baltimore Retail Merchants. Association, the chairperson of the Voluntary Council, and representatives of large industries and businesses in Baltimore.

All committee members participated fully, not only in the formal meetings but also by individually studying the master list of concepts and materials presented to them and by stating their reactions and beliefs in writing. Several committee members arranged for vocational staff members working on the project to spend time at various plants and offices, where they conferred with key personnel and observed plant operations. Generous quantities of applications, evaluation sheets, and orientation materials were supplied by the businesses for use in the course.

The advisory committee was instrumental in determining the final course content and also made recommendations concerning the amount of time to be allocated for each segment of the course. Two members of the advisory committee served as keynote speakers for the workshop that was held to prepare teachers to use the curriculum materials. Because of the interest and input of this advisory committee, a realistic and relevant course that will help students prepare more effectively for the world of work was created.

*This case study was abstracted from the January, 1977 issue of the *American Vocational Journal* and is used here with the permission of the American Vocational Association.

COMMUNICATIONS EXERCISE

THE CURRICULUM CONTENT ADVISEMENT FUNCTION

The following communications exercise, by allowing you to apply your knowledge to a specific setting, can increase your understanding of the curriculum content advisement function. This exercise was designed and field tested as a self-instructional or small-group activity that stresses the application of concepts and ideas presented in this chapter.

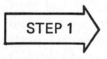 **THE FOLLOWING SECTION PROVIDES A BRIEF OVERVIEW OF A SPECIFIC SITUATION RELATED TO AN ADVISORY COMMITTEE. READ THIS SECTION COMPLETELY BEFORE PROCEEDING TO STEP 2.**

You are a member of an occupational advisory committee for a community college's two-year technical program in Automotive Service. The purpose of the program is to prepare service people, whose job it is to inspect, service, and overhaul hydraulic, mechanical, and electrical components and accessories of automobiles, buses, trucks, tractors, and other powered vehicles. Graduates of this program are awarded the Associate of Applied Science degree.

The next advisory committee meeting is to be devoted entirely to a content review of the Automotive Service courses in the curriculum. As the committee chairperson, it is your responsibility to prepare the agenda for the meeting. You have decided that the agenda will be in the form of a series of questions you feel should be considered.

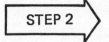

STEP 2

USING THE WORKSHEET BELOW, CHECK THE BOX(ES)
REPRESENTING THE ITEM(S) THAT MOST APPROPRIATELY
REFLECT(S) THE SITUATION DESCRIBED IN STEP 1.

Are the appropriate employability skills reflected in the performance goals? _____ 1	How is the student's level of skill development evaluated? _____ 2	What support counseling services are available to the handicapped and disadvantaged students in the program? _____ 3	What are the major performance goals of the Automotive Service program? _____ 4
Are the appropriate Automotive Service skill areas reflected in each course? _____ 5	What cooperative work experiences are provided for in the course sequence? _____ 6	Is occupational information regarding Automotive Service careers reflected in the performance goals? _____ 7	What placement services are available? _____ 8
Is information regarding continuing education included in the performance goals? _____ 9	Is the relationship and sequence of the Automotive Service courses appropriate and consistent with the performance goals? _____ 10	What new Automotive Service innovations should be added to the program? _____ 11	What instructional materials, information, experiences, or ideas can the advisory committee contribute to update the course content? _____ 12
What new 3-speed transmissions are on the market? _____ 13	Are the appropriate Automotive Service skills reflected in the specific course objectives? _____ 14	Is career counseling provided for the Automotive Service courses? _____ 15	What extra-curricular role does the student organization play in relationship to the Automotive Service program? _____ 16

STEP 3 EVALUATE THE RESPONSES ON THE WORKSHEET BY COMPARING THE INDIVIDUAL RESPONSES WITH THOSE RECOMMENDED BELOW. READ THE APPROPRIATE COMMENTS AND CONTINUE ON TO STEP 4.

If you checked _____ 2, 4, 5, 11, 14 _____ , read Comment A.

If you checked _____ 1, 3, 6, 7, 8, 9, 10, 15, 16 _____ , read Comment B.

If you checked _____ 12 _____ , read Comment C.

If you checked _____ 13 _____ , read Comment D.

Comment A   These responses should definitely be included. They reflect direct concern for what is being taught and for the appropriateness of the course content. Since this is a community college course, the committee is concerned with the series of Automotive Service courses and the related curriculum for the two-year program.

The major course content advisement concerns, as included in this set of responses are (in this preferred sequence):

- What are the student's major performance goals? (4)
- Are the appropriate skills to support the performance goals included? (5)
- Are the appropriate specific skills also reflected in the specific automotive service course objectives? (14)
- Are these skills evaluated in a realistic manner? (2)
- What innovations from the industry should be added? (11)

This series of five questions, if completely answered, should provide the committee with an excellent basis for providing course content advisement. As these questions are framed and discussed by the committee, the function of course content advisement is indeed *happening*.

Comment B   This set of responses represents a secondary level of concern for course advisement and could be included in the meeting's agenda.

These responses represent the components of a comprehensive occupational program, and as such they deserve consideration. As suggested in this chapter, course content should go beyond the specifics of skill development and focus upon the total educational development of the individual.

As the committee begins to discuss goals of the program which relate to concerns other than specific skill development, these questions will undoubtedly arise. Most advisory committees spend as much time discussing these general concerns as they do discussing the needed job skills.

Comment C   This question should appear as the last item on the committee meeting agenda. Once the committee has thoroughly discussed the status of the course content, the question of "Where do we go from here?" has to be addressed. If presented in the appropriate manner, this question will generate a series of positive ideas and information as to how the course content can be improved, updated, or expanded.

Comment D   This question is out of place here. If the question can be rephrased so that the committee could consider a new three-speed transmission in terms of new performance objectives that should be written, the question would be relevant. If it cannot be rewritten, it should be omitted from the agenda.

STEP 4   BASED ON THE DISCUSSION COMMENTS ABOVE, REEVALUATE THE RESPONSES MADE IN STEP 2. IF THE CONCEPTS ARE CLEAR, PROCEED TO STEP 5.

STEP 5   TO IMPLEMENT SOME OF THE KEY CONCEPTS IN THE CHAPTER AS THEY RELATE TO YOUR SPECIFIC SETTING, COMPLETE AT LEAST ONE OF THE FOLLOWING OPTIONS.

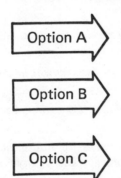

Option A   Review the chapter, select one concept, and develop a procedure for applying it to an advisory committee.

Option B   Select one of the situations outlined in the Suggested Activities section and make an application to an advisory committee.

Option C   Choose one of the sources in the Selected References section and integrate additional insights gleaned from that source into a plan for advisory committee action.

SUGGESTED ACTIVITIES

1. Order and review the following filmstrip-cassette tape presentations (free loan basis) from the Rurban Educational Development Laboratory, 357 Education Building, University of Illinois, Urbana, Ill. 61801: "Proper Functions of Citizens' Advisory Councils," "Citizens' Advisory Councils of Career Education."

2. Read and review Chapter 6, "Developing Curricula," in *Industry and Vocational-Technical Education* by Samuel Burt.

3. Interview a director of a nearby area vocational school to determine ways in which advisory committees are used for curriculum advisement.

4. Review and analyze the curriculum study questions presented in *Advisory Committee Member*, Bulletin No. 29–672 of the Department of Adult, Vocational and Technical Education, Illinois Office of Education, Springfield, Ill. 62777.

5. Contact the director of your state's Advisory Council for Vocational Education for information and guidelines related to the curriculum advisement function of local advisory committees.

6. Meet with a director of a nearby vocational education program and ask to review the employment and labor market data that he or she collects on a regular basis. Design an agenda and a procedure for reviewing this information with an advisory committee.

7. Organize and conduct a curriculum articulation meeting with your advisory committee. The purpose would be to identify and evaluate the courses and programs from which students enter your program. The typical educational programs that students enter when they complete your program could also be reviewed. General recommendations for articulating the curriculum content of these programs should be forwarded to the appropriate instructors.

8. Develop a modified version of the curriculum evaluation form presented in Figure 3–3 to fit the goals of your occupational or career education program. Review the form with an advisory committee. Incorporate any suggested refinements in the evaluation form prior to having the committee use it for evaluation of the curriculum content.

SELECTED REFERENCES

Alexander, William M. "Citizen Advisory Committees on Curriculum." *Curriculum Trends,* Craft-NEI Publications (subscription series), (April 1975): 1–4.

American Vocational Association. *The Advisory Committee and Vocational Education.* Washington, D.C.: American Vocational Association, 1969.

Burt, Samuel M. *Industry and Vocational-Technical Education.* New York: McGraw-Hill Book Co., 1967.

Burt, Samuel M. *Industry and Community Teachers in Education.* Kalamazoo, Mich.: Upjohn Institute for Employment Research, 1969.

Burt, Samuel M., and Lessinger, Leon M. *Volunteer Industry Involvement in Public Education.* New York: Irvington Publishers, 1970.

Evans, Rupert N., and Herr, Edwin. *Foundations of Vocational Education,* Second Edition. Columbus, Ohio: Charles E. Merrill, 1978.

Hofstrand, Richard K., and Phipps, Lloyd J. *Advisory Councils for Education: A Handbook.* Urbana: Rurban Educational Development Laboratory, University of Illinois, 1971.

Michigan Vocational-Technical Education Service. *Administrative Guide for Vocational Education.* Lansing: Michigan Department of Education, 1974.

Pennsylvania Bureau of Vocational Education. *Pennsylvania VICA Advisor's Handbook.* Harrisburg: Pennsylvania Department of Education, 1977.

Phipps, Lloyd, J.; Hofstrand, Richard K.; and Shipley, W. E. *Course of Study: Citizens' Advisory Councils in Education.* Urbana: Rurban Educational Development Laboratory, University of Illinois, 1972.

Phipps, Lloyd J.; Jackson, Franklin D.; and Shores, Lee F. *Activities of Citizens' Advisory Councils and Committees.* Urbana: Rurban Educational Development Laboratory, University of Illinois, 1973.

4 The equipment, facilities, and instructional resources review function

The quality and variety of equipment, supplies, and instructional resources are vital elements of occupational and career education programs. Almost since their inception, advisory committees have frequently assisted in evaluating and obtaining up-to-date equipment, learning materials, and instructional resources. Advisory committees have also been extremely helpful in establishing new vocational and educational facilities, as well as in completing major renovations.

Identifying and using up-to-date equipment, industrial materials and supplies is essential for maintaining relevancy in instructional activities for all learners. School laboratories, shops, and classrooms must mirror as closely as possible the contemporary environments of the world of work if students are to gain occupationally relevant competencies. The use of outdated equipment, processes, and materials in a given occupational field seriously inhibits the learner's opportunity for obtaining competitive employment in that field.

The growth of career education has raised even greater concerns for the use of current facilities and equipment for learning. In the face of rising building costs, general inflation, and increased fiscal efficiency, career education has stimulated the cost-effective strategy of using "the community as a classroom." Through work-observation field trips, students in elementary and junior high schools have gained exposure to the contemporary materials, tools, equipment, and facilities used in different careers at various work sites. Such experiences tend to reinforce the need for contemporary educational facilities and equipment from both the educator's and businessperson's perspective. This chapter will outline and discuss advisory committee activities in the realm of reviewing equipment, facilities, and instructional resources.

SCOPE OF THE EQUIPMENT, FACILITIES, AND INSTRUCTIONAL RESOURCES REVIEW

This function can be initiated in career-oriented educational programs at the elementary through postsecondary school levels. Included in the function are such activities as reviewing present equipment, facilities, and instructional resources, surveying equipment in business and industry, assuring that facilities and equipment allow for the effective participation of handicapped students, suggesting replacement equipment, aiding in the calculation of equipment depreciation allowances, suggesting equipment and facility bidding procedures, and seeking gifts, donations, and discounts for equipment, materials, and supplies.

The advisory committee can also be of assistance in interpreting and making recommendations for insuring compliance with Occupational Safety and Health Act (OSHA) standards. As advisory committee members or as consultants, safety and health personnel from local industries can assist in interpreting federal and state standards for occupational facilities. Training personnel from business and industry should also be involved in this function, because they can aid in identifying new instructional materials or media (such as self-instructional audio-visual programs) that are available for teaching concepts or skills for specific occupational areas. They can also assist in identifying new teaching materials and media.

Frequently a building advisory committee fulfills this function. Typically, this general advisory committee is charged with providing substantial input for the planning of a new facility or the renovation of an old facility. For example, the Illinois Office of Education [73:10] requires that a general advisory committee be established during the development of area vocational centers to lend assistance and direction in the overall planning.

> Such a committee composed of adequate representation of business, industry, management, organized labor, civic organizations, junior college representatives and lay persons can provide valuable direction to the educators in providing for the needs of all interested groups in the area.

Generally, building advisory committees serve for extended periods of time and are concerned with everything from the building floor plan to the layout of an individual laboratory to the selection of specific equipment, floor coverings, and so on. Depending on the nature of the building activity, there may be one or several advisory committees involved. Obviously, if multiple building advisory committees are used, close coordination of their efforts must be insured by the appropriate administrative personnel.

ESSENTIAL COMMITTEE ACTIVITIES

The primary activities of this function are inspection and evaluation, and providing assistance in obtaining equipment, facilities, and instructional resources.

Inspection and evaluation

Evaluation of equipment and facilities is a major responsibility of advisory committees. Several state departments of education have included items on advisory committee evaluation checklists that focus on the representativeness, adequacy, and condition of equipment and vocational facilities.

Wentling [175:8–6] has identified four distinct types of facility evaluation studies that may be undertaken:

1. *Utilization survey.* An analysis of facilities in light of their intended use. This can include both a survey of which laboratories or classrooms are being used during specified time periods as well as an analysis of student load for each lab or classroom.

2. *Safety survey.* A survey of the facility by a team of individuals who use a checklist to guide their observation. The outcome is the identification of unsafe or potentially unsafe facilities.

3. *Adequacy study.* A study of existing facilities that focuses on the state of repair, access to, and appropriateness of the facilities for conducting planned programs.

4. *Planning study.* A study of program need, enrollment forecasts, and facility requirements for several alternative programs and alternative building layouts.

Advisory committees can guide and develop strategies for one or more of these types of evaluations. Depending on the scope of the committee's responsibility, there may be a need to conduct several studies related to facilities. For example, if an adequacy study or utilization survey reveals the need for an addition to the area vocational center facility, a planning study may follow.

Inspections that are focused on adequacy and safety will, of necessity, involve the committee in examining the Occupational Safety and Health Act (OSHA) standards and the Architectural Barriers Act standards. Businesspersons who have participated in inspections will be familiar with the OSHA standards. If advisory committee members work or own facilities that provide federally supported services or assistance, they will be familiar with the Architectural Barriers Act standards. Recent federal legislation has required all public schools to eliminate architectural and transportational barriers faced by the handicapped. It should also be noted that most states have adopted OSHA and Architectural Barriers Act standards to be applied in concert with other federal standards.

Advisory committees can also help to evaluate facilities and equipment prior to on-site inspections by federal or state agencies. Inspection and evaluation activities can be initiated in three critical areas. General and program advisory committees should be concerned with the facility in which the program(s) operates; they should examine the appropriateness of equipment and materials used in the program to insure that they are similar to those used in business and industry; and, finally, they should examine the instructional resources (teaching-learning materials, technical and reference manuals, instructional media) to see if they are up-to-date.

Advise and assist

Advisory committees can give advice and assistance in purchasing equipment or they can obtain donated materials and equipment. Prior to obtaining materials, school personnel must be aware of the equipment, processes, and materials that are currently used in the relevant occupational field(s). Generally, the advisory committee can keep the instructional staff informed of current industrial or business practices. However, in large communities it may be necessary for the committee to conduct a survey to examine the specific types of equipment, processes, and materials used by various types of workers. For example, an advisory committee for an exploratory (middle school) program in communications media might survey the local printing businesses to identify the major reproduction, binding, and packaging processes used. The survey information could then be used for planning work-observations and field trips. The advisory committee could plan other industrial surveys to meet the specific needs of occupational education programs.

Advisory committees have also been helpful in the direct purchase of equipment and materials and by establishing, for example, procedures for the solicitation of bids for the purchase of major pieces of equipment. Some local companies may be willing to sell materials and supplies to schools at an educational discount. Knowledgeable advisory committee members can assist instructors and administrators with the preparation of purchase specifications for facilities or equipment. Advisory committees have also been instrumental in encouraging equipment manufacturers to donate or lend equipment to schools.

Case studies indicate that a great deal of equipment is donated or loaned to schools by industrial groups and employers [29]. Employers and committee members have been extremely generous in assisting occupational education programs by donating expendable supplies, materials, and special tools, by loaning equipment, and by allowing the use of company facilities for special activities. By frequently visiting local businesses, teachers and coordinators can obtain donations of equipment that is being phased out or replaced. Advisory committees, teachers, or supervisors should consider the following when soliciting donations of equipment and materials for educational use:

- The need for and intended instructional use of current materials and equipment should be clearly expressed to business and industry personnel.

- Teachers should accurately assess their need for equipment, supplies, or materials before approaching local businesses or industries.

- It is important to know which local businesses are highly interested in school programs. Cooperative education coordinators can aid in compiling this information since they have more extensive contact with local employers than do most teachers.

- Those employers who are contacted and appear interested in the program should be considered for future advisory committee involvement.

- Occasionally it will be necessary diplomatically to refuse equipment that businesspersons wish to donate but that is of little value to the occupational or career education program.

- The donation of *any* quantity of materials or supplies or any piece of equipment should be appropriately acknowledged. In some instances a warm, positive letter from the instructor, chairperson of the advisory committee, program director, or chief school official is sufficient. For larger donations, certificates of appreciation can be presented. Engraved plaques identifying the donor, can also be attached to equipment. When large donations or equipment loans are accepted, arrangements should be made for coverage by the local news media.

IMPLEMENTATION STRATEGIES

Each advisory committee will approach the review of facilities, equipment, and instructional resources differently, depending on the type of committee and its programmatic focus. Schoolwide advisory committees, for example, may be concerned with questions relating to the general adequacy of the building, the safety and accessibility of facilities, and the extent to which program advisory committees are monitoring the adequacy of instructional materials, equipment, and resources. Craft advisory committees may be concerned with specific questions relating to the adequacy, quality, safety, accessibility, size, and functionality of the facilities, equipment, and materials in a given occupational program. Because of different programmatic goals, career education advisory committees may be concerned with similar questions, but they may examine them in a somewhat different context.

> The goals and characteristics of career education have implications for the physical setting in which career education is to take place. An active learning process geared to the real world implies providing opportunities for students in diverse settings, both inside and outside the school. It implies providing physical activity as well as sitting and listening; this can mean, for example, providing tools and space in which to use them. The facility might consist of an "invisible" network of placement locations in community businesses, service agencies, government facilities, and industries. [60:7]

There are two basic strategies for implementing the equipment, facilities, and resources review function. The first focuses on techniques for evaluating the facility, equipment, and available instructional resources. The second strategy suggests procedures for surveying local businesses and industries to identify new processes, equipment, materials, procedures, or technical information that need to be incorporated in the occupational or career education program. Both of these strategies emphasize the evaluation and planning role of the advisory committee with regard to this function.

Planning and conducting evaluations

In planning any type of evaluation it is important to first outline the purposes of the evaluation. The advisory committee and school staff should develop an overall statement of scope that will guide the evaluation. For example:

- Determining the need for new facilities
- Determining the need for renovation of existing facilities
- Determining the adequacy of the instructional and learning materials used by students
- Identifying facilities or equipment that are not receiving optimum or efficient use
- Checking the compliance of the facilities and equipment with safety, health, and accessibility standards

Once the committee has stated the purpose of the evaluation, it can initiate several evaluation activities.

Facility evaluation. In evaluating a facility, an advisory committee can be instrumental in the construction of new buildings, in the major renovation of existing buildings, or in the updating and improvement of educational facilities on a smaller scale. Figure 4–1 lists sample questions that an advisory committee might consider. Comprehensive facility evaluation efforts should include questions related to facility utilization, adequacy, safety, and accessibility. The questions contained in Figure 4–1 are stated broadly and would require additional specificity when the committee develops checklists or other evaluation instruments. In planning a facility evaluation, a critical step is the identification of key questions. Once the committee identifies and agrees on these, it is easy to assemble a checklist. This process can be greatly facilitated if school personnel prepare the preliminary key questions and then ask for an advisory committee review.

Several facility evaluation checklists are available. Some state departments of education have developed facility evaluation checklists for use by vocational education advisory committees, and a number of the references at the end of the chapter contain additional checklists.

Figure 4–2 presents a sample checklist for facility evaluation, which could be filled out by individual committee members during a walking tour of the facility. When the individual checklists are complete, the committee could discuss each of the items on the checklist and formulate

FIGURE 4-1. Sample key questions for facility evaluation

Facility Utilization

1. To what extent is the facility fully utilized by students as well as adults from the community?

2. To what extent are classrooms and labs receiving optimum use?

3. To what extent is faculty, counselor, and administrative office space utilized?

4. To what extent is student recreational and leisure space appropriately furnished?

5. To what extent is the facility utilized by various community groups?

6. Are the instructional areas sufficiently flexible to accommodate different learning activities?

Facility Adequacy

1. Is the building adequate for the present and projected student enrollment?

2. Are the current library resources adequate for the facility?

3. Is adequate storage space provided throughout the building?

4. Are the acoustics and illumination adequate?

5. Are passageways large enough to accommodate student flow?

6. Are the space allocations appropriate for current program needs?

7. Are the service systems (electrical, plumbing) adequate?

8. Are the general acoustical design elements (floors, walls, ceilings) appropriate?

Safety and Accessibility

1. Does the building conform to state and federal standards for occupational safety and health (OSHA)?

2. To what extent does the building comply with the barrier-free architectural standards?

3. To what extent is the facility generally accessible to the community?

4. Do the ventilation and dust collection systems have sufficient capacity?

a consensus response. In this way the committee benefits from the independent observations of each member. The questionnaire presented in Figure 4–2 requires the respondent to provide a rating between one (excellent) and four (poor) for each item. Space is provided below each item for the rater to indicate specific strong points, weak points, and recommendations.

Lab and classroom evaluation. Program or craft advisory committees play an important role in the evaluation of laboratories, shops, classrooms, and support areas for individual occupational programs. Advisory committee members, because of their responsibilities in business and industry, are capable of critically evaluating the laboratory and classroom facility in terms of their potential for providing realistic occupational experiences.

As you will note in reviewing Figure 4–3, many of the key questions from the facility, or building, evaluation are also appropriate for the laboratories and classroom evaluation. Committees should be concerned with questions of utilization, adequacy, safety, and accessibility of the lab and classroom space for an occupational program and should consider the following factors:

- Lighting
- Ventilation
- Heating/cooling
- Environmental control systems
- Fire protection
- Plumbing and electrical services
- Acoustical design
- Color scheme
- Office facilities
- Classroom facilities/teaching areas
- Material handling and storage
- Cleanliness
- Walking/working surfaces
- Exit passageways
- Safety posters/procedures
- Ceiling, wall, and floor surfaces

Figure 4–4 is a sample checklist developed for use in evaluating a food service program. It is included here because (1) It illustrates the relationship of the key questions (identified by the advisory committee) to the specific questions. Each key question is divided into several specific questions. (2) The key questions are comprehensive in nature. (3) A simple rating system is used (i.e., 1 = excellent, 4 = poor). (4) Specificity in a checklist is essential for adequately evaluating a particular occupational facility. Because of the basic differences in most occupational education labs, different evaluation questions are necessary.

The recommended procedure for conducting a laboratory evaluation is similar to that for conducting a facility evaluation. The committee should review and refine the proposed evaluation checklist provided by the program instructor or director. Once individual member evaluations are completed, the committee should conduct a discussion to determine its consensus on each item on the checklist. Finally, the committee should draft a set of overall recommendations for improvement of the facility.

FIGURE 4-2. Sample questionnaire to assess teaching areas (general)

DIRECTIONS   Rate the following items on a scale of one to four; one representing excellent and four representing poor

1. A central communication system is used to send information from one area of the building to another.
   Comment _____

2. Acoustics and illumination are optimum for student learning.
   Comment _____

3. A central alarm system is provided and code signals are posted in appropriate places.
   Comment _____

4. Storage spaces are sufficient in size and conveniently located.
   Comment _____

5. An adequate number of electrical outlets are conveniently located in various areas.
   Comment _____

6. Space is provided for group and independent study.
   Comment _____

7. Size and arrangement of instructional areas are flexible for a variety of learning activities.
   Comment _____

8. Classroom size is sufficient to accommodate existing class enrollments.
   Comment _____

9. Entrance and exit passageways are free of obstacles and sufficiently wide to insure safe travel.
   Comment _____

10. Temperature and ventilation systems are sufficient for proper circulation and zoned for separate or partial use.
    Comment _____

11. Fire extinguishers are readily accessible to the teaching area and personnel are trained to use them.
    Comment _____

12. Ceilings and windows have appropriate reflection value.
    Comment _____

13. All writing surfaces are designed to minimize glare in the student's field of vision.
    Comment _____

14. Custodial services are performed daily and are adequate for effective learning.
    Comment _____

15. Furniture and equipment are adequate for operation of spaces for various activities and organizational patterns. (Check those available.)

    _____Display cases
    _____Work surfaces
    _____Writing areas
    _____Instructional media
    _____Television and other communication media
    _____Storage
    _____Shelving
    _____Seating
    _____Other (Pleast list.)

    Consider the information collected, and develop recommendations and suggestions for improvement.

1	2	3	4

Tim L. Wentling, *Locally Directed Evaluation Guide 8: Evaluation of Facilities.* Springfield, Ill.: Department of Adult, Vocational and Technical Education, Illinois Office of Education, 1976. Reprinted with permission.

FIGURE 4-3. Sample key questions for laboratory and classroom evaluation

Utilization

1. Is the laboratory and classroom space arranged efficiently?
2. To what extent is available equipment utilized?
3. Are adequate supplies and tools available?
4. Is the laboratory facility utilized fully throughout the day and evening?

Adequacy

1. Overall, does the facility provide the best educational environment possible for the occupational program?
2. To what extent is the facility equipped to provide students with experiences that are applicable to the occupational area?
3. Is the laboratory and classroom space flexible, functional, and capable of providing for the foreseeable program needs?
4. Does the area provide adequately for exchange of air, lighting, equipment arrangement, storage, and heating/cooling?

Safety and Accessibility

1. To what extent does the classroom and laboratory comply with OSHA safety standards?
2. To what extent does the classroom and laboratory comply with accessibility specifications for the physically handicapped?
3. Do the laboratory, classroom, and storage areas comply with the safety and health standards of the state departments of labor and health and safety?
4. Are the class enrollments and laboratory space provided consistent with formulas for computing optimum square footage per student?

FIGURE 4-4. *Sample questionnaire to assess food services facilities*

Directions: Rate the following items on a scale from one to four; one representing excellent and four representing poor. Check "NA" if the statement is not applicable.

Supplementary Information

1. Service is provided from a _____central kitchen, _____self-contained unit, satellite from another LEA _____.
2. Seating capacity of the lunchroom or dining room _____.
3. Number of student shifts necessary _____.

	NA	1	2	3	4

KEY QUESTION
How adequate is the dining area?
1. The dining area and furnishings are attractive, durable, and easily cleaned.
2. The dining area is designed so that it can be used for other purposes.
3. The dining area meets the needs of the LEA's program.
4. The dining area is available to students who bring their lunches.
5. The dining area is designed and furnished to promote a safe and efficient traffic pattern.

KEY QUESTION
How satisfactory are the lighting, ventilating, and aesthetic aspects of the food service facility?
6. The illumination in the dining area meets lighting standards.
7. The dining area is well ventilated.
8. A separate dining area is provided for staff.
9. Acoustical provisions reduce noise to a minimum.
10. Illumination in the kitchen meets lighting standards.
11. Aesthetic aspects of the dining area are pleasing.

KEY QUESTION
How adequate and efficient is the equipment for service?
12. Sanitary drinking water facilities are provided in the dining area.
13. Sufficient and appropriate receptacles and service are provided for disposal of refuse.
14. Refrigeration facilities are appropriate and easily accessible.

KEY QUESTION
How well designed and equipped is the kitchen area?
15. Facilities permit thorough cleaning of dining and kitchen areas on a regular basis.
16. All pieces of mechanical equipment are provided with safety devices.
17. Electrical outlets are located in accessible areas.
18. The floor surface is in good condition, free from obstructions, and easily cleaned.

KEY QUESTION
How satisfactorily are sanitary conditions maintained?
19. Facilities, materials, and maintenance are available to keep dining and serving areas clean and neat.
20. Lavatory facilities are readily accessible to students entering or leaving the dining area.
21. The kitchen is ventilated.
22. The kitchen and service areas are furnished with equipment that meets local and state sanitation standards.
23. Mechanical dishwashing facilities are provided.
24. Proper disposal methods are used for garbage and refuse.
25. Dressing, toilet, and lavatory facilities are provided for food service personnel.

KEY QUESTION
How adequate are the dry storage facilities?
26. Storage facilities are located adjacent to the kitchen area.
27. Storage facilities are of sufficient size to handle the needs of the food service area.
28. Storage facilities are easily accessible.
29. Food storage is maintained in an orderly and sanitary condition.

Tim L. Wentling. *Locally Directed Evaluation Guide 8: Evaluation of Facilities.* Springfield: Department of Adult, Vocational and Technical Education, Illinois Office of Education, 1976. Reprinted with permission.

FIGURE 4–5. Sample key questions for instructional resources evaluation

1. To what extent do the instructional materials reflect technically accurate information and content relative to the occupational area?
2. Are the instructional materials reflective of any traditional sex-role or racial stereotypes in the occupational area?
3. Are there new instructional materials available from sources within the industry that should be incorporated in the program?
4. To what extent do the instructional materials reflect up-to-date practices?
5. To what extent is the occupationally related information (e.g., wages, fringe benefits) provided in the instructional materials accurate?

Instructional resources evaluation. To date, advisory committees have not been utilized as actively in the evaluation of instructional resources as they have been in evaluating facilities and equipment. However, advisory committees can be extremely helpful in reviewing the currency and accuracy of the content presented in texts, reference guides, films, laboratory manuals, charts, and other instructional resources used in the program. Advisory committees must focus such evaluation activities only on the *content* of the material. They are not qualified to evaluate such factors as the readability level of the material, the cost/benefit considerations in selecting materials, or the extent to which the material is consistent with the instructional objectives. These factors are clearly within the professional responsibility of school personnel and should not be discussed in an advisory committee meeting.

Figure 4–5 lists some general questions that advisory committees are concerned with when evaluating instructional materials. As you will note the focus is on the accuracy and currency of technical information; on the accuracy of occupational information provided for guidance, counseling, and career selection functions; and on the potential sex-role and racial stereotypes presented in instructional materials. The latter consideration has become a major focus in occupational education programs as a result of federal legislation that prohibits schools from using materials that reflect sex-role and racial bias.

The committee can also focus evaluation and discussion questions on recent instructional materials that are available from business and industry sources, such as new editions of specification manuals, technical references, safety posters, or other materials that could be used in the instructional program. Forms for evaluating instructional materials and resources can be found in most methods or curriculum development textbooks.

Checking safety and accessibility compliance. As a result of federal legislation, industrialist and educators have been asked to become increasingly responsive to the needs of individuals. The Occupational Safety and Health Act of 1970 (OSHA) was enacted to protect the occupational, health, welfare, and safety of "workplace America." The Architectural Barriers Act, which preceded OSHA in 1968, was focused on eliminating the architectural and transportation barriers faced by physically handicapped citizens. Both of these pieces of legislation speak directly to insuring the welfare and full involvement of individuals in safe occupational education environments and eventually the work places of the nation.

Advisory committees need to be concerned with two issues posed by these pieces of legislation. First, the curriculum provided in career and occupational education must emphasize the safety standards required under OSHA as well as be sufficiently flexible to accommodate the instructional needs of the physically handicapped and other persons with special needs. Second, the facilities in which these programs operate must comply with standards for occupational safety and health and accessibility.

To implement advisory committee action in this area of concern, local or regional personnel from state agencies responsible for occupational safety and vocational rehabilitation can be invited to serve on advisory committees or can be used as consultants to meet with advisory committee members when facility evaluations are being planned. Representatives from local chapters of organizations such as Disabled American Veterans or the United Cerebral Palsy Association could also be made advisory committee members or consultants, and as such they could readily provide resource information, facility checklists, and information on national and state standards for accessibility and occupational safety.

Local industry surveys

Advisory committees can also conduct informal surveys of local businesses and industries to help identify new equipment, operations or processes, materials, and training materials that need to be included in the program. Conducting informal surveys of industry is an activity that has occurred more frequently with career education advisory committees all of whose members may not be fully acquainted with the various occupational fields or clusters that students may be studying. In these instances the survey activity can also serve as an in-service activity for the committee members.

The surveys described in this section have a different purpose from those described in Chapter 3. Here the focus is not on determining occupational demand or community needs but on identifying new equipment, tools, and related technical information that should be incorporated in the career or occupational education program.

Local business and industry surveys can also provide data to support the purchase of new instructional equipment. For instance, if 80 percent of the tool and die shops in a large metropolitan area have recently added electrical discharge machining (EDM) equipment, the purchase of such equipment for addition to a machine shop course may be well justified.

In addition, informal surveys can identify prospective donors of equipment or materials, can identify new and revised editions of technical manuals, service manuals, and related materials for purchase as instructional materials for the program(s), and can serve to acquaint new employers with the existence of the program and its purposes. Employers may be interested in accepting students seeking part-time work experience, or they may be interested in serving on future advisory committees. The committee should take the following steps when conducting the survey:

1. Discuss the purposes of the survey with local trade associations and chambers of commerce.

2. Review technical and trade journals to identify new developments and processes in the occupational field. The advisory committee members can aid in identifying new equipment, processes, and techniques to be reviewed in the survey.

3. Develop and review a series of survey questions or topics. The following list suggests topics for a local industrial survey:

   • New equipment installed in the industry or business
   • Processes or operations recently introduced
   • Recently published training or technical materials
   • Current occupational and employment information (e.g., new job titles, current wages and salaries, fringe benefit packages)
   • Equipment and materials available for donation
   • Sources and contacts for additional equipment donations

4. Conduct the survey by mail or personal, on-site interviews. The latter approach is strongly recommended. Once the major questions for the survey are identified, a brief interview form can be developed.

5. Whenever possible, groups of employers and educators should be used to collect the survey information. This team approach demonstrates to new employers a positive working relationship between industrial and school personnel.

6. Following the survey, prepare a brief report or summary memo. The report should describe the survey effort and include specific conclusions and recommendations for school officials. The committee chairperson should send a copy of the memo or survey to each of the employers contacted and thank each for his or her contribution.

THE EQUIPMENT, FACILITIES, AND INSTRUCTIONAL
RESOURCES REVIEW FUNCTION IN ACTION

The following case study* describes the efforts of an advisory committee in Baltimore, Maryland, to develop an occupational program for preparing packaging machine mechanics [118].

Studying employment projections to determine the need for new vocational programs is unscientific at best. The difficulties encountered in obtaining reliable data have been well documented. Therefore, in the fall of 1974, when representatives from a group of interested businesses contacted the Baltimore City Public Schools about the need for packaging machine mechanics, the advisory committee enthusiastically welcomed the opportunity to discuss the feasibility of initiating a program to meet their needs. Representatives from Amstar Corporation, Coca-Cola Bottling Company, J. H. Filbert, Inc., Lever Brothers, Inc., McCormick and Company, Noxell Corporation, and Package Machine Manufacturers Institute attended the first meeting.

To help clarify their thinking on how the program would operate, eight members of the committee traveled to Elizabeth, New Jersey, to see a packaging machine mechanics program in operation at the Edison Vocational-Technical Center. Armed with this experience, the committee was ready to plan a program for Baltimore. Subcommittees were established to work on proposal development, course content, equipment requirements, location of facilities, and selection of teachers. Business and industry members served on each of these subcommittees and proved to be a valuable resource to educational personnel. The short-range goal of the committee was to have the program operational within one year. In September 1975, the evening program in packaging machine mechanics was opened to interested adults.

The start of the day school program was delayed until a machine shop teacher, who had many requisite skills, was retrained for the new course. The retraining was accomplished by having the teacher attend the night school program, which was taught by an expert mechanic. The teacher also was provided with on-the-job experience at the plants where members of the advisory committee were employed. In February 1976, the program became fully operational. This committee made the following significant contributions:

• Getting donations of packaging machines and other equipment required for the program (The cost of this equipment was in excess of $100,000 when it was originally purchased.)

• Providing training sites for the teacher

• Securing a grant of $2,500 to purchase miscellaneous parts, materials, and supplies

---

*This case study is abstracted from the January, 1977 issue of the *American Vocational Journal* and is used here with the permission of the American Vocational Association.

Articles about this program, which appeared in trade magazines, have stimulated widespread interest. The Ciba-Geigy Corporation in New Jersey, the Doboy Package Machine Company in Wisconsin, and the Nordson Corporation in Ohio have supplied additional equipment for use in the program. At the invitation of dedicated committee members, the mayor of Baltimore, William Donald Schaeffer, attended a ribbon-cutting ceremony for the program during American Education Week in November 1976. The advisory committee's work to date has been largely developmental in nature, converting a concept into a reality. The committee has decided to concentrate next on developing work-study sites and evaluating the program.

COMMUNICATIONS EXERCISE

THE EQUIPMENT, FACILITIES, AND INSTRUCTIONAL RESOURCES REVIEW FUNCTION

The following communications exercise, by allowing you to apply your knowledge to a specific setting, can increase your understanding of the equipment, facilities, and instructional resources review function. This exercise was designed and field tested as a self-instructional or small-group activity that stresses the application of concepts and ideas presented in this chapter.

 THE FOLLOWING SECTION PROVIDES A BRIEF OVERVIEW OF A SPECIFIC SITUATION RELATED TO AN ADVISORY COMMITTEE. READ THIS SECTION COMPLETELY BEFORE PROCEEDING TO STEP 2.

You are a member of a new occupational advisory committee for the machine technology program. The program is being launched on the basis of a recent community survey that revealed a great need for machine tool operators and machinists. This expanded labor need is the result of the recent local opening of a small parts plant by one of the large automotive manufacturers. The committee is composed of several machinists, a local union official, the instructor, a prospective student, and two machine shop supervisors. What procedures for equipping the machine shop program would you recommend in the committee meeting?

STEP 2 ⟹ USING THE WORKSHEET BELOW CHECK THE BOX(ES)
REPRESENTING THE ITEM(S) THAT MOST APPROPRIATELY
RESPOND(S) TO THE SITUATION DESCRIBED IN STEP 1.

Survey the committee to see if any donations of equipment can be solicited. ____ 1	Pursue avenues to determine possible funding sources. ____ 2	Have a sales representative for large educational equipment manufacturer write equipment specifications. ____ 3	Review assessment study. ____ 4
Let the instructor for the program order all the equipment. ____ 5	Develop an equipment priority listing. ____ 6	Analyze accessibility of facility for handicapped students. ____ 7	Conduct a survey of industrial/business equipment. ____ 8
Recommend a faculty committee be organized to establish criteria for planning equipment purchases. ____ 9	Review curriculum materials as proposed by instructor. ____ 10	Survey other comparable programs for equipment and facility utilization. ____ 11	Determine types of equipment necessary to meet performance objectives. ____ 12
Recommend possible equipment specifications. ____ 13	Determine budgetary requirements for facility and equipment. ____ 14	Review OSHA standards for equipment and facilities. ____ 15	Survey community to identify adequate existing facility. ____ 16

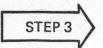

STEP 3

EVALUATE THE RESPONSES ON THE WORKSHEET BY
COMPARING THE INDIVIDUAL RESPONSES WITH THOSE
RECOMMENDED BELOW. READ THE APPROPRIATE COMMENTS
AND CONTINUE ON TO STEP 4.

If you checked	2, 14	, read Comment A.
If you checked	3, 5	, read Comment B.
If you checked	4, 6, 7, 8, 9, 10, 11, 12, 13, 15, 16	, read Comment C.
If you checked	1	, read Comment D.

Comment A   While these tasks are important they frequently are the sole responsibility of the administrative staff of the program. The director must take the initiative in locating sources of funds (2) to equip initially, maintain, and update the facility. Budgetary requirements (14) related to the facility and equipment are also managed by the director in most cases.

Comment B   Responses 3 and 5 are not sound recommendations. While sales representatives for equipment manufacturers can be helpful to the teacher, director, and advisory committee, they should not be asked to write the equipment specifications (3). One of the primary functions of the advisory committee is to assist the instructor with program planning. It is not recommended, therefore, that he or she be permitted to order all equipment without a review of the planned purchases by the committee (5).

Comment C   These eleven responses are excellent, reasonable suggestions for the situation. The community and labor market needs assessment survey should be reviewed in depth to analyze equipment and facility needs (4). It may be necessary to conduct a local survey of machine shop equipment being used (8), and use the results to develop an equipment priority list (6). A review of the course objectives (12), the proposed curriculum materials (10), and other vocational machine shop programs in the area (11) can be helpful in the process of recommending specific pieces of equipment to be purchased. Finally, it is important that facilities and equipment be reviewed for OSHA compliance (15) and for accessibility by handicapped learners (7).

Comment D   The major role or purpose of the advisory committee is not the solicitation of equipment donations. As noted in the chapter, the up-to-dateness of donated equipment and materials should be a major concern of the instructor and committee. It is quite possible that donations of out-dated equipment will be offered. However, the possible donation of some integral and current equipment is quite feasible, and the option should be left open to advisory committees and their local associates.

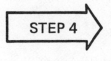

BASED ON THE DISCUSSION COMMENTS ABOVE, REEVALUATE THE RESPONSES MADE IN STEP 2. IF THE CONCEPTS ARE CLEAR, PROCEED TO STEP 5.

TO IMPLEMENT SOME OF THE KEY CONCEPTS IN THE CHAPTER AS THEY RELATE TO YOUR SPECIFIC SETTING, COMPLETE AT LEAST ONE OF THE FOLLOWING OPTIONS.

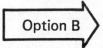

Review the chapter, select one concept, and develop a procedure for applying it to an advisory committee.

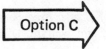

Select one of the situations outlined in the Suggested Activities section and make an application to an advisory committee.

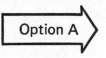

Choose one of the sources in the Selected References section and integrate the additional insights gleaned from that source into a plan for advisory committee action.

SUGGESTED ACTIVITIES

1. Obtain and review a copy of the *American National Standard Specifications for Making Buildings and Facilities Accessible to, and Useable by, the Physically Handicapped,* American National Standards Institute, Inc., 1430 Broadway, New York, N.Y. 10018. Develop a plan for discussing the standards with an advisory committee.

2. Contact your state department of labor and request a copy of the OSHA (federal) and state standards for occupational safety and health. Develop a plan for discussing the standards with an advisory committee.

3. Identify a local or nearby school district that is in the early stages of planning a new building or major renovation. Ask the director or superintendent if you can attend a meeting of the building advisory committee. Following the meeting, develop a list of the planning steps.

4. Contact your state director of vocational education and request guidelines or information describing the role of a local advisory committee in reviewing facilities, equipment, and instructional resources. Review the information for future use.

5. Review several of the documents listed in the references at the end of the chapter and identify facility and equipment evaluation checklists that could be used by your advisory committee.

6. Develop an equipment or facility evaluation checklist for your program(s). Invite your advisory committee to review and use the checklist in evaluating your program(s).

7. Identify the officers of various trade associations in your community. Initiate communications with these individuals to determine their willingness to endorse a local industrial survey aimed at identifying new equipment and processes being used in local businesses.

8. Review pages 22–23 in *Managing the Occupational Education Laboratory* [155] to identify strategies for soliciting gifts and donations of equipment. Identify five local businesses that are strong prospective donors for your program.

SELECTED REFERENCES

Gill, William B., and Luke, Ann W. *Facilities Handbook for Career Education.* Washington, D.C.: National Institute of Education, 1976.

Haffner, Alden N. *Vocational Education: A Manual of Program Accessibility for the Physically Disabled Two-Year College Applicant.* New York: State University of New York, Coordinating Area #4, undated.

Illinois Division of Vocational & Technical Education. *Area Secondary Vocational Center Planning Guide.* Springfield: Illinois Office of Education, 1971.

Nerden, Joseph T. *Vocational-Technical Facilities for Secondary Schools: A Planning Guide.* Columbus, Ohio: Council of Educational Facility Planners, undated.

Ramey, Walter S. *A Guide for the Organization and Operation of Local Advisory Committees for Vocational Education.* Richmond: Virginia State Department of Education, Division of Vocational Education, 1975.

Storm, George. *Managing the Occupational Education Laboratory.* Belmont, Calif.: Wadsworth Publishing Co., 1976.

Technical Handbook for Facilities—Section 4.12: Design of Barrier-Free Facilities. Washington, D.C.: Department of Health, Education, and Welfare, Office of Facilities Engineering, November, 1977.

Wahl, Ray. *A Safety and Health Guide for Vocational Educators.* Volume 15, Number 1. Harrisburg: Bureau of Vocational Education, Pennsylvania Department of Education, 1977.

Wentling, Tim L. *Locally Directed Evaluation Guide 8: Evaluation of Facilities.* Springfield: Department of Adult, Vocational and Technical Education, Illinois Office of Education, 1976.

5 The community resource coordination function

Since their inception, advisory committees have been used to identify and coordinate the use of community resources in local educational programs. In fact, the advisory committee itself is considered a major resource for educators. In a practical sense, the role that an advisory committee plays in each of the other functions (for example, curriculum advisement, program evaluation, student placement, and so on) could be considered a resource role. In this chapter, however, the term community resource is given a more specific definition. Generally, community resources are the persons, places, organizations, activities, or things in the community that have educational value [16]. They can include anyone or anything that directly facilitates or improves the teaching/learning process. Examples of resources include potential training stations for placement of cooperative education students; knowledgeable individuals who are capable of making speeches at career day meetings or of providing career counseling for individual students; agencies that provide support services for handicapped learners; parents who can provide an overview of their occupations; organizations that offer specialized literature related to various occupations, such as local trade associations and the chamber of commerce.

Within this broad spectrum of community resources, it becomes apparent that the advisory committee takes on several roles relative to obtaining community resources. Chapter 5 deals with community resources that do not exist in the advisory committee itself. The community resources discussed here are those that play an integral part in the learning experiences provided for students, instead of those resources that provide funding, teacher in-service activities, program evaluation, or management expertise.

The emergence of career education has emphasized the importance of closer relationships between the school and the workplace. While career education is consistent with many goals of general education, it does suggest an increased need for curricula that examine in depth the various life roles that students will assume (for example, producer of goods or provider of services, family member, social and political participant). In describing the role of community resources in career education, the school district of the city of Royal Oak, Michigan, noted that:

> Career education provides meaning to the learning of basic subject matter skills and understandings by relating them to the world outside the classroom. Through field trips, resource persons, advisory groups, work observation, work-study and work experience for students, teachers, and counselors; school will take on new meaning for all youth. It is inconceivable to believe that teachers and guidance counselors can provide the vast amount of career information needed by youth without using the community and its resources. [149:3]

The National Association for Industry-Education Cooperation has also strongly endorsed the increased use of community resources to expand the relevancy of present-day schooling:*

> Today's youth need more than can be gotten from books. The modern school seeks increasingly to enable pupils to learn through real life experience. The whole community may be used as a laboratory for this undertaking. Just as today's physics, chemistry, and auto mechanics can never be mastered, . . . through mere reading of books, so today's educator knows that our social and economic skills can only be appreciated, comprehended, and learned through real experience of their use.
>   When the school and community combine their efforts to this end, so that the child receives a nurture and training adequate for our time, the life of the entire community is ultimately enriched in meaning and enhanced in value. [16:1]

The recent economics of public education have also stimulated the increased use of community resources. With generally fewer tax dollars available to support education and with rapidly rising costs, administrators stress the need to solicit assistance from appropriate areas within the community. Community-based cooperative education and work-observation programs continue to be low-cost programs when compared to the per pupil costs for in-school training. Teachers are frequently asked to request donations or gifts of materials, equipment, and/or supplies.

Personnel involved in occupational education programs have long recognized the importance of strong community-based, employer/employee relationships in the process of preparing students for active participation in the work force [137]. To substantiate this statement, 119 school superintendents, community college presidents, school board members, and trustees were surveyed in Michigan regarding the extent to which

*From A. L. Ayars and C. Bovee. *How to Plan a Community Resources Workshop.* Buffalo, N.Y.: National Association for Industry–Education Cooperation, 1975. Used with permission.

vocational education advisory committees were involved in different functions. The survey, which was completed in 1974, revealed that over 75 percent of their advisory committees had been "moderately or greatly involved" in obtaining community resources. However, they also noted that over one-third of the members on the same committees demonstrated less than satisfactory performance in effectively obtaining community resources [38].

The effective use of community resources involves consideration of the needs of the teacher and of the resource person. The National Association of Industry-Education Cooperation [16] suggests that teachers generally focus their attention on becoming familiar with and planning to utilize the local instructional resources. A reverse of this process may also occur. The schools, the students, and the teachers may explore processes of becoming resources to the community. Community resource workshops that have been sponsored in numerous communities have placed students and teachers in service roles in neighboring schools, hospitals, attorney's offices, city government offices, and even political parties. In the school/community partnership, either partner can give or receive.

SCOPE OF COMMUNITY RESOURCES COORDINATION

The effective use of community resources is a continuing concern for elementary and middle school programs, as well as for high school and postsecondary occupational programs. Advisory committees should be actively involved in the identification and evaluation of community resources at all levels.

At the elementary school level, for example, program advisory committees can assist in identifying resources to be used in facilitating career awareness. Involving parents with unique occupations and identifying field trip sites for various career clusters are two key resource coordination activities that can be undertaken by an advisory committee. To illustrate, in the LET (Learning Experiences in Technology) program for grades kindergarten through sixth in Royal Oak (Michigan), parent resource committees are used "for the purpose of developing community resources to be used by the teachers and project staff."

> The Parent Resource Committee is of great assistance in seeking and securing community resources . . . it is impractical to expect either the teachers or the project coordinator to perform this task without this important resource. [149:134]

The parent resource committee focuses on identifying resources that

> Expose students to a variety of careers through contact with someone in the field and to provide students firsthand career development experiences by taking field trips to places of employment and/or exposure to occupational role models.

1. To develop lists of community resources (speakers and field trips)
2. To serve as an advisory group for the development and organization of the project
3. To serve as a liaison between project staff and the local P.T.A. executive board. [149:134]

At the junior high or middle school level, the coordination of resources for career orientation, exploration, and decision making activities becomes the central focus. To assist learners in these activities, advisory committees can aid teachers and coordinators in identifying such resources as work-observation sites, guest speakers, sources of occupational information, field trip sites, or consultants for teachers. Providing background information for obtaining these resources is an important first step. The advisory committee can also help in making the first contact with parents, employers, and other persons who represent the resources.

At the high school and postsecondary level, advisory committees have assisted occupational education teachers for many years especially in developing cooperative education (co-op) programs, which enable students to spend part of their school day working in the community. Depending on the types of students being served and the specific in-school program, students are placed on entry level, semiskilled, skilled, or technical jobs. Often in postsecondary programs students will be employed full time for one or two semesters through an internship to gain their on-the-job experience. In these programs the employers provide an extremely valuable resource for the occupational education program.

Curriculum relevance

At whatever level the advisory committee is functioning, the identification of resources to be used in instruction must relate directly to the curriculum, program, or course objectives. Prior to engaging in surveys to identify resources, each committee member should be informed of the major instructional goals. Teachers can help by listing the instructional units for which field trips, guest speakers, or other resources are needed. Obviously the instructional staff is responsible for the final selection of the resources to be used, but time and effort can be saved if the identification of community resources is focused on specific instructional goals or units. New instructional units could, however, be discovered in the process. Occasionally, new technical information that suggests the addition or revision of certain instructional objectives or units may be uncovered in a community survey. Teachers and advisory committee members can use the information provided through resources to critically evaluate their curriculum.

Comprehensive resources

The range of community resources that can be used in career and occupational education programs is extensive in most communities. Wentling

(176:5) suggests that a community resource file for an occupational program should include information on

> Resource personnel (for instructors)
> Field trips
> Advisory committee members
> Local, state, and federal agencies
> Professional and service organizations
> Youth organizations
> Media and publications
> Cooperative work stations

Parents could also be added to the list of prospective resources. When seeking business and industry resources, it is important to identify resources that represent organized labor as well as those that are provided by employers and management personnel.

COMMUNITY RESOURCE COORDINATION ACTIVITIES

The community resource coordination function can entail several basic activities. Many of the specific activities could easily be considered a part of the student placement (Chapter 6) or community public relations (Chapter 8) functions. To fulfill its community resource coordination function, the committee engages in three activities: identifying potential resources to be used, contacting and developing these resources as an integral part of the instructional program, and evaluating the effectiveness of community resources. Although cooperative work experience training stations are a community resource, strategies for identifying and using this resource through the advisory committee are discussed in Chapter 6.

Identification of resources

The advisory committee serves as an initial link in the identification of community resources. Through meetings devoted to the community resource topic, program or craft advisory committees can discuss the following questions:

- What types of resources are critical to student attainment of the course objectives?

- Which community resources are currently being used?

- What additional resources are available from the businesses or agencies that the members represent?

- Which local associations (e.g., chamber of commerce, trade associations) could be helpful in identifying additional resources?

- Have previous attempts been made to tabulate or identify community resources for a certain industry or occupational field?
- Which additional businesses or agencies might have resources of importance to the program?
- Which regional, state, or national associations might be contacted to identify locally available resources?

From a discussion focused on these questions, the specific needs relative to community resources can be readily identified.

This information is especially helpful to program-level advisory committees. Schoolwide or districtwide advisory committees would be concerned with the same questions but on a broader scale. Elementary career education advisory committees, for instance, would be concerned with identifying resources to support a broad set of student goals related to self-awareness, career awareness, decision making, orientation, and other factors related to the early stages of career development. Most occupational education committees, on the other hand, are concerned with resources that will aid students in obtaining job-related competencies.

A first step in identifying community resources is to check for existing local resource directories. Volunteer and service organizations frequently compile directories of available services or sources of information. For instance, most communities have directories that describe the services obtainable from local human service agencies such as mental health, family planning services, or service clubs. Such directories are helpful for coordinating support services for special needs (handicapped or disadvantaged) students. Similar local directories categorizing educational resources may have been prepared by unions or trade or professional associations.

Resource development

There are several ways in which advisory committees may assist with the development of community resources. Once the committee has identified the potential resources, it can obtain specific data describing these resources. Frequently the committee does this through mail or interview surveys. The advisory committee may become involved in planning the survey questionnaire, wording the items appropriately, or conducting interviews. The chairperson of the program advisory committee often writes the survey cover letter.

Once the critical community resources for a program have been identified, they can be further developed through a community resources workshop. The National Association for Industry-Education Cooperation describes the community resources workshop as "a combined venture of education and business, industry, labor, agriculture, government, cultural, professional, and other groups to acquaint teachers with our industrial and commerical world at work and other aspects of community life." [16:16]

Through such workshops teachers have developed various types of materials, including resource files and teaching units. In communities where workshops have been held, research indicates an increase or upgrading in

Community understanding of school objectives and methods

Teacher understanding of industry, business, government, and other phases of the community's economic and social life

Cooperative relationships between the schools and community groups

Participation of teachers in community activities

Attitudes on the part of teachers toward vocational opportunities open to youth locally, the achievements of the free enterprise system, the importance of the community, and the motives of industry and business people

The use of effective, modern teaching methods and tools

Teacher's confidence in their ability to produce curriculum materials

Teacher involvement in career education. [16:20]

The implementation strategies section contains additional ideas for planning and conducting community resource workshops under the sponsorship of local advisory committees.

Evaluation of resources

Advisory committees can be of assistance in evaluating the extent and effectiveness of the use of community resources in the program. Such evaluative questions as the following are appropriate for committee discussion:

- Which instructional units (courses) presently use field trips, guest speakers, occupational consultants, and so on?
- Are these resources underutilized or overutilized?
- Do the students consider these resources valuable to their learning experiences?
- To what extent are these resources appropriate for the specific course (program) objectives?

Continuous evaluation of the efficiency and effectiveness of community resources is vital to any program. The advisory committee can help determine evaluation criteria for "good" guest speakers and field trips. As resources are used, whether for the first time or on a continuing basis, teachers, students, and, in some cases, the resource personnel should compile evaluation data. At least annually the committee should summarize and discuss the evaluation data. The committee can then make recommendations for adjusting and improving techniques for using the resources, for discontinuing the use of certain resources, or for locating new resources.

IMPLEMENTATION STRATEGIES

To fulfill its community resources coordination function, the committee can decide on one or more of the following: planning community resource surveys, organizing community resource workshops, or evaluating the use of community resources. Procedures and techniques for each of these are discussed in detail in the following sections.

Community resource surveys

Organized surveys have proven to be the most efficient means of identifying the available resources in a community or locale. Initially, the committee can help with the survey by defining the overall purpose and anticipated uses of the survey results and by determining the appropriate geographical area to cover (e.g., school district, city, township, county, or region). The committee may also discuss the selection of the specific types of resources (e.g., parents, business and industry, organized labor, human service agencies, individual citizens). Most frequently, several different types of resources are identified in one survey. Once these initial directions are established, the committee may be of great assistance in identifying and selecting the specific companies, agencies, and persons to be contacted. The committee may also review the questionnaires to clarify individual items and evaluate the appropriateness of items.

Wentling [176] recommends that the chairperson of the advisory committee prepare a cover letter for surveys that are mailed. This helps to insure a better return and a generally favorable response from the community. If the survey is conducted by interview, it is also helpful to have a letter of endorsement from the chairperson as well as having committee members do the interviewing. Additional recommendations for administering, tabulating, and following-up community resource surveys may be found in Wentling's *Locally Directed Evaluation Guide 16: Analysis of Community Resources.* These procedures are not discussed here because school personnel have primary responsibility for such tasks.

The Tri-County Industry-Education-Labor Council of East Peoria, Illinois developed the community resource survey questionnaire presented in Figure 5-1[176]. The questions are brief and concise, yet considerable information is elicited for identifying field trip locations (career visits), classroom consultants, career counselors, and teacher in-service opportunities. The survey is designed to identify resources for both elementary and secondary career education programs.

FIGURE 5–1. *A community resources questionnaire*

Name of Business _____

Address _____

Person(s) to Contact _____ Phone _____

Circle One

Yes   No   Do you have resource people available to visit the classroom, inform students, and answer students' questions? (A teacher will furnish the area of interest.)

Yes   No   Do you have resource people available for individual student career information interviews? (Example: A student is interested in a pharmaceutical career. The council will arrange for the student to talk with a registered pharmacist.)

Yes   No   Are you willing to accept requests for classroom visits or career visits?

How much advance notification is required for classroom visits?_____

Check the age groups with which the resource person(s) would be willing to meet in a classroom setting:

   6-7___   8-9___   10-11___   12-13___   14-15___   16-18___

Number of classroom setting visits you will accept per school year:_____

Person(s) to contact regarding the details of classroom setting visits:

   Name _____ Phone _____

Maximum number of students per group for career visit (tour): _____

Best month(s) of the year: _____

Best day(s) of the week: _____

Best time of the day: _____

How much advance notification is required for career visits? _____

Check the age groups you would be willing to accept for career visits:

   6-7___   8-9___   10-11___   12-13___   14-15___   16-18___

Approximate amount of time needed for a career visit:_____

Are parking facilities available to students and teachers? _____
_____

Description of possible areas or departments which can be visited on career visits:
_____

Person(s) to contact regarding the details of a career visit:

   Name _____ Phone _____

Specific safety precautions to be observed by students: _____
_____

Suggested follow-up activities you may desire after career visits:_____
_____

Short descriptive statement about your business or products? _____
_____
_____

Tim L. Wentling. *Locally Directed Evaluation Guide 16: Analysis of Community Resources.* Springfield: Illinois Office of Education, 1976. Reprinted with permission.

FIGURE 5-1.   (continued)

In what other ways can Business, Industry, Agriculture, Professions and Labor contribute to the education of our children?

_____

_____

_____

_____

Circle One

Yes   No   Are you willing to accept one or more groups per school year of five to twenty teachers for a career visit (tour or facilities), briefing of your operations, products or services, and interviews with employees to learn more about an individual career or occupation from the individual performing the work? Teachers would be with you for approximately two hours.

The number of teachers you would be willing to accept for a career visit: _____

Yes   No   Would you consider employing high school juniors and seniors so that they could learn more about the realities of the world of work through the school's cooperative program?

As career education programs have expanded at the elementary level, many school districts have found parents to be a valuable resource. To facilitate the involvement of parents, Project ABLE at Northern Illinois University [181] developed several strategies for using parents in pilot career education programs. Figure 5–2 presents an informational memo and response form that is to be used by advisory committees or teachers to identify the occupational expertise of parents and other individuals interested in contributing their time.

Once the resource information is compiled, it can be organized in card files, with the essential information from each resource contained on a file card as shown in Figure 5–3 [132]. Different arrangements for organizing, reproducing, and centrally locating the resource card files can be developed based on the type of program being served.

Resource rosters or directories are another way of organizing the information. This format is generally appropriate for communitywide distribution. In situations where employers, other nearby schools, agencies, or the general citizenry also have a use for the resource information, the publication of a resource directory by the school district or advisory committee can be of other than educational service to the community. The case study presented in the next section describes an effort to develop a community resource roster.

Community resources workshops

Advisory committees can sponsor community resources workshops to facilitate the identification and development of community resources for

FIGURE 5-2.   Parent resource survey

```
SCHOOL _____ GRADE_____ TEACHER_____

Dear Parents,

    As a part of our regular instructional program, we would like parents
to come to our class and tell the students about their occupations.  Our
children will benefit by contact with an adult who is contributing to him-
self and his society.  We are sure they will have many important questions
to ask.

    Please fill out and return this form.  You will be contacted to arrange
a definite time and date.  The general objectives of the program and sug-
gestions for the things we would like to know about will be available.  We
are interested in all occupations.

_____



Please return to the teacher.

Name_____ Phone_____

Address_____

Occupation_____

Company or Firm_____

It would be most convenient for me to be at your school on (days and times).

_____

_____

_____

                          _____
                               Signature
```

School District of the City of Royal Oak. *Career Awareness—Grades K-6: Guide for Implementation,* Second Edition. Royal Oak, Mich. School District of the City of Royal Oak, 1974.

use in all types of educational programs. Such workshops can build a
closer relationship between the schools and community, as well as enabling teachers to develop useful materials and learning experiences. The
committee should encourage community members and school personnel
to participate actively in workshops. The National Association for

FIGURE 5-3. *Community resource data cards*

Instructional Resources

```
CAREER-RELATED INSTRUCTION RESOURCE

Career cluster or occupation  Janitor
Name of resource person  Harold Graves
Title  Janitorial Supervisor    Address  411 Long Lake Blvd.
Phone  467-3322                  Creston, Illinois
Appropriate for (students, grade level, etc.)  Special needs students,
grades 9-12


Type of resource (check all that are appropriate)

___ Field trip                    ___ Speaker
_✓_ Classroom consultant          ___ Individual student tutor
___ Instructional materials       ___ Sponsor of short-term
_✓_ Instructional content resource     work experiences

Detailed description of resource  Likes to work with students;
has a full range of custodial services; excellent
attitude toward the world of work
```

Service Resources

```
SUPPORTIVE SERVICE RESOURCE

Type of service                   Source of service (name of agency or
_✓_ Student assistance                organization)
___ Parent/family assistance      Neighborhood Youth Corps
___ School/teacher assistance
___ Other (describe)_____


Name of contact person  Ron Barrett
Address  1400 W. Jasper                 Phone  467-3228
         Creston, Illinois              Office hours  9-5

Record previous contacts or referrals below

Date        Student          Action
11/7/78     Harvey Devin     3 counseling sessions
                             scheduled
```

L. Allen Phelps and Ronald J. Lutz. *Career Exploration and Preparation for the Special Needs Learner.* Boston: Allyn and Bacon, 1977. Used with permission.

Industry-Education Cooperation has developed a comprehensive set of guidelines for conducting such workshops [16]. Although these workshops are designed to achieve general objectives (e.g., to develop a better working relationship between education and other organizations and individuals of the community), the guidelines can be readily modified to suit a specific purpose or program. Obviously, the advisory committee sponsoring the workshop must define the specific purposes of a community resources workshop. Figure 5-4 outlines several guidelines for organizing and conducting a community resources workshop.

FIGURE 5–4.   Guidelines for conducting a summer community resources workshop

1. A full-time director, consultants, and secretary should be designated, based on the number of participants. The staff should be highly skilled in workshop organization and management.

2. Since most of the work is done in small groups, the number of participants is usually flexible.

3. The purposes and scope of the workshop should be defined during the initial sessions. Specific problems and concerns of the participants can be identified for group project work.

4. Participants choose the problems they desire to tackle. Advisers and consultants act as resource and facilitating personnel, but do not prescribe a program for the participants to follow.

5. Most workshop groups form committees to work on phases of problems in which they are most interested. Sometimes the entire workshop group attacks a common problem, and occasionally participants work alone. Committees sharing common interests may select such activities as:
   - Planning a teaching unit
   - Producing a resource unit
   - Identifying community problems
   - Establishing community service programs
   - Surveying the community for career education possibilities
   - Developing resource files of materials, people, or places

6. Administrative committees for managing the workshop are also helpful. These committees focus on categories such as obtaining curriculum materials, scheduling field trips, providing public relations for the workshop, scheduling open house and social hours, and developing the resource catalog.

7. General sessions are needed to provide opportunities to get acquainted, hear visiting speakers, plan field trips, exchange progress reports, identify relationships among various committee activities, and analyze and adjust the direction and scope of the workshop as needed.

8. If possible, involve individuals from a nearby university or college in the planning and operation of the workshop. It may also be possible to reach an agreement for offering credit to the participants.

9. Adequate facilities for the workshop are essential. Space for general sessions, committee meeting rooms, library facilities, audiovisual equipment, and typing and reproduction facilities are all crucial factors in successful workshops.

10. Continuous evaluation is also important. Ongoing activities should be critiqued daily to insure that the outcomes and products are on target with the workshop objectives.

11. After the workshop, appropriate reports should be issued and needed follow-up activities planned.

Abstracted from A. L. Ayars and C. Bovee. *How to Plan a Community Resources Workshop.* Buffalo, N.Y.: National Association for Industry-Education Cooperation, 1975. Used with permission.

Evaluation of community resources

Advisory committees can help to evaluate the extent and effectiveness of community resources utilization. Phipps and his coauthors [137] note that evaluation of community resources is critical to determine who has used various resources, how many resources have been used, and to what extent the resources have been appropriately used. The committee can address these and other evaluation questions both during and at the conclusion of a school year. The purpose of evaluation is to improve the selection, use, and effectiveness of all community resources employed in the program.

Figures 5–5 and 5–6 provide sample instruments for evaluating two common resources: guest speakers and field trips. Teachers and older students can use such forms to assess the educational value of a field trip or of a guest speaker's remarks. The appropriate evaluation form can be shared with the field trip guide or the guest speaker ahead of time to aid the guide or speaker in planning the upcoming learning experience. The advisory committee can review the summarized evaluation data and offer recommendations for the future use of selected resources (for example, instead of using only the assistant plant manager, the committee could request different tour guides for different departments in a plant). The advisory committee might also develop a general evaluation form for local resource persons to use for themselves when they are working with career or occupational education programs. Chambers of commerce or local trade or professional associations could distribute these evaluation forms.

THE COMMUNITY RESOURCES COORDINATION
FUNCTION IN ACTION

In small rural districts the need for effective utilization of community resources frequently takes on additional importance. The Clare-Gladwin Intermediate School District is located in the middle of Michigan's lower peninsula and serves five rural kindergarten-through-twelfth-grade school districts. When the Michigan Career Education Act was passed in 1974, the Clare-Gladwin Intermediate School District was designated as the Career Education Planning District (CEPD) for the five school districts of Beaverton, Gladwin, Harrison, Farwell, and Clare. The kindergarten-through-twelfth-grade enrollment in each school district is less than eight hundred students.

To facilitate career education program development, the CEPD Council accepted a proposal to develop a human resource roster. The roster was established to assist educators, students, and other citizens interested in human resources. A mail survey was conducted to identify persons living in the district who had a special expertise that could contribute to the career development of human resources. Advertisements

The community resource coordination function

FIGURE 5–5. *Guest speaker evaluation*

SPEAKER _____DATE _____

CLASS _____

STUDENT _____ (optional)

Please respond to the following questions by circling the appropriate answer (NA = Not Applicable, Ex = Excellent, P = Poor, and Av = Average). Please make comments that you feel are relevant.

ITEM	RESPONSE			COMMENTS
1. Was the purpose (objectives) of the speaker's visit made clear?	Yes	No	NA	
2. Was the presentation well organized?	Yes	No	NA	
3. Were the important ideas of the speaker clearly presented?	Yes	No	NA	
4. Did the speaker encourage the audience to ask questions?	Yes	No	NA	
5. Was the speaker stimulating? Did he or she increase your desire to learn more about the topic?	Yes	No	NA	
6. In comparison to other speakers you have heard, how would you rate this speaker?	Ex	Av	P	
7. Did the topic relate to your class discussion?	Yes	No	NA	
8. Was the preparation done prior to the speaker's presentation complete?	Yes	No	NA	
9. Was the follow-up activity assignment clear and related to the speaker's presentation?	Yes	No	NA	
10. Other comments				

Ideas and items taken from Tim L. Wentling's *Locally Directed Evaluation Guide Series,* and from *Manual for Community Resource Utilization,* University of Illinois, Urbana, and the Division of Vocational and Technical Education, Springfield, Illinois.

describing the roster and soliciting the involvement of interested persons were placed in local newspapers. Over four hundred persons willing to tutor or provide their expertise at no cost were identified in the initial survey.

The roster of human resources contains two major sections. The student or teacher using the roster first looks up the area in which assistance is needed. Figure 5–7 is an excerpt from the first section that lists the 321 areas in which resources are available. The right-hand column

FIGURE 5-6. Field trip evaluation form

PLACE VISITED _____ DATE_____

REASON FOR VISIT _____ INSTRUCTOR _____

On the scale that follows each item, please place an (X) at the point that represents your evaluation of that item. If the statement is not applicable, please circle the letters NA to the right of the rating scale.

	Definitely No				Definitely Yes		
1. The purpose of the field trip was made clear and definite.	0	1	2	3	4	5	NA
2. The students shared in determining the purposes of the trip.	0	1	2	3	4	5	NA
3. The trip was a learning experience that related to the classroom instruction.	0	1	2	3	4	5	NA
4. An orientation regarding the purpose of the trip was conducted.	0	1	2	3	4	5	NA
5. Appropriate questions to be asked by the class were developed prior to the trip.	0	1	2	3	4	5	NA
6. Specific directions were developed for all phases of the field trip.	0	1	2	3	4	5	NA
7. Responsibilities to be assumed by participants were discussed and clearly assigned.	0	1	2	3	4	5	NA
8. A high degree of interest was shown throughout the trip.	0	1	2	3	4	5	NA
9. Appropriate notations and observations were made by the group.	0	1	2	3	4	5	NA
10. The time schedule was appropriate to the observation made.	0	1	2	3	4	5	NA
11. The students participated in evaluating the trip.	0	1	2	3	4	5	NA
12. Appropriate conclusions were drawn by the class following the trip.	0	1	2	3	4	5	NA
13. New interests resulting from the trip were evidenced through informal comments, extended reading, contributions in class.	0	1	2	3	4	5	NA

Ideas and items taken from Tim L. Wentling's *Locally Directed Evaluation Guide* series and from *Manual for Community Resource Utilization,* University of Illinois, Urbana, and the Division of Vocational and Technical Education, Springfield, Illinois.

FIGURE 5-7. *Human resource roster for career education planning district no. 15 (Section I)*

Area	Resource Reference Number
Agriculture	
Animal Husbandry	1
Animal Training	227
Elevator Management	164
Farming	30, 164, 165, 299
Forestry	31, 117, 164
Horticulture	164, 165, 275, 288
Natural Resources	164
Shorthorn Cattle	32
Art	
Cartooning	34

Abstracted from *A Human Resource Roster for CEPD 15,* Clare-Gladwin (Michigan) Intermediate School District, 1973. Reprinted with permission.

FIGURE 5-8. *Human resource roster (Section II)*

Resource Reference Number	Name	Phone	Tutor	Free	Time Available
1	Marilyn Grant	435-7088			1-2 hours weekly
2	Martie Ehinger	465-2181			
3	Arnold Nutt	435-9813	x	x	Evenings
4	Judy Nichols	435-7771	x	x	Weekends & evenings
5	Beverly Rise	435-9350	x	x	Anytime except Monday & Tuesday nights
6	Mary Huber	426-5680			

Abstracted from *A Human Resource Roster for CEPD 15,* Clare-Gladwin (Michigan) Intermediate School District, 1973. Reprinted with permission.

provides the code number(s) for the resource personnel who can provide the needed expertise.

Once the appropriate resource code numbers are located, the second section of the directory is consulted to identify the name and phone number of the person who can provide the needed resource assistance. Figure 5–8 illustrates the second section of the directory. Information stating when the person is available is also included.

Teachers in elementary, junior high, and high schools throughout the CEPD as well as students have used the roster to plan and carry out career education-related experiences. Efforts are now underway to expand the roster to include *all* human service agencies and organizations in the two-county area. The expanded agency and human resources roster will include resources available from veterans organizations, fraternal groups, civic and service clubs, governmental agencies, occupational and professional groups, and church and religious organizations. The local CETA prime sponsor is providing funds to support the development of the roster.

COMMUNICATIONS EXERCISE

THE COMMUNITY RESOURCE COORDINATION FUNCTION

The following communications exercise, by allowing you to apply your knowledge to a specific setting, can increase your understanding of the community resource coordination function. This exercise was designed and field tested as a self-instructional or small-group activity that stresses the application of concepts and ideas presented in this chapter.

 THE FOLLOWING SECTION PROVIDES A BRIEF OVERVIEW OF A SPECIFIC SITUATION RELATED TO AN ADVISORY COMMITTEE. READ THIS SECTION COMPLETELY BEFORE PROCEEDING TO STEP 2.

You have been appointed to an ad hoc career education council for the local junior high school. This council has been asked to devise a survey that will identify the community resources to support the junior high school (grades 7, 8, and 9) career exploration program. The major goal of the career exploration program is to provide each student with exploratory experiences in three or five of the fifteen career clusters identified by the U.S. Office of Education. Select from the following work-sheet a list of general items or information to be included in a community resource survey. The survey will identify and describe the existing community resources for the junior high school career exploration program.

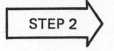 **STEP 2** USING THE WORKSHEET BELOW, CHECK THE BOX(ES) REPRESENTING THE ITEM(S) THAT MOST APPROPRIATELY RESPOND(S) TO THE SITUATION DESCRIBED IN STEP 1.

Name, address, phone number, and employer of the person responding to survey ____1	Statement of purpose of the survey ____2	Question focusing on the respondent's preference for working with individuals or group from the school ____3	Possible resources the survey respondent might provide to school administrators ____4
Possible field trips for students ____5	Career/occupations of the survey respondent ____6	Question identifying consultants for classroom instruction (personnel from industry/business/management-labor) ____7	Short-term work-experience stations for students ____8
Possible field trips for educators ____9	Contact representatives from such agencies as Council for Exceptional Children and Neighborhood Youth Corp. ____10	Possible work-observation stations for students ____11	Questions identifying consultants for career counseling (personnel from industry/business/management-labor) ____12
Work-experience positions for educators ____13	Goals of the career exploration program ____14	Previous services offered by the survey respondent ____15	Description of the survey respondent's "area of expertise" ____16

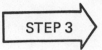

EVALUATE THE RESPONSES ON THE WORKSHEET BY
COMPARING THE INDIVIDUAL RESPONSES WITH THOSE
RECOMMENDED BELOW. READ THE APPROPRIATE COMMENTS
AND CONTINUE ON TO STEP 4.

If you checked _____1, 2, 6, 14_____ , read Comment A.
If you checked __5, 7, 8, 10, 11, 12__ , read Comment B.
If you checked _____9, 13_____ , read Comment C.
If you checked _____3, 4, 15, 16_____ , read Comment D.

Comment A   This set of responses should be included in the survey for the purpose of collecting basic information from the respondents (1) and describing the purpose of the
survey (2). A description of the goals of the exploration program will enable the
respondents to understand clearly the purpose of the survey and thus enable them
to be specific in their responses (14).

      The occupation of the survey respondent will enable the educator to determine
under which of the fifteen clusters the potential resource should be placed (6).

Comment B   The identification of community resources for classroom and field experiences
is a major purpose of the survey; therefore, these items will definitely be included.

      This survey should address the areas of possible field trips, potential work-
experience stations for students, and consultants for instruction and counseling in
terms of the potential resources for the career exploration program at the local junior
high school.

Comment C   Identification of community resources for educators is another major purpose of
the survey; consequently, these items should definitely be included in the survey. Not
only do students benefit from the utilization of community resources but experiences
and educational programs for educators can also be facilitated. On occasion, businesspersons have sponsored special training programs for educators. In still other instances,
teachers at all levels (including junior high school) have had opportunities to visit with
employers, tour facilities, attend seminars (9), and gain significant experiences through
specialized work experiences (13).

Comment D   This set of responses represents items that *could* be included depending on the
specific intent of the survey. A description of the respondents' "area of expertise"
will further describe those services, resources, or information the individual can contribute to the program (16). An accurate description of the resources identified will
enable the committee to develop a comprehensive roster of community resources.
Item 16 should be included as an open-ended response if that can be done without
making the questionnaire too long.

      In certain instances, the resources uncovered by surveys have reflected potential
management services for school administrators (4). This item may be included in the

survey if the committee feels it is important. Responses 3 and 15 may be included if the committee is concerned about the respondent's preferences for contributing his or her resources to the school's program.

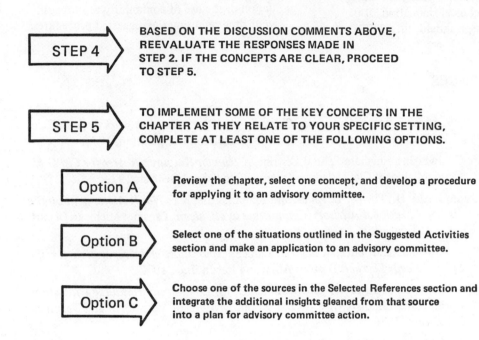

STEP 4 — BASED ON THE DISCUSSION COMMENTS ABOVE, REEVALUATE THE RESPONSES MADE IN STEP 2. IF THE CONCEPTS ARE CLEAR, PROCEED TO STEP 5.

STEP 5 — TO IMPLEMENT SOME OF THE KEY CONCEPTS IN THE CHAPTER AS THEY RELATE TO YOUR SPECIFIC SETTING, COMPLETE AT LEAST ONE OF THE FOLLOWING OPTIONS.

Option A — Review the chapter, select one concept, and develop a procedure for applying it to an advisory committee.

Option B — Select one of the situations outlined in the Suggested Activities section and make an application to an advisory committee.

Option C — Choose one of the sources in the Selected References section and integrate the additional insights gleaned from that source into a plan for advisory committee action.

SUGGESTED ACTIVITIES

1. Contact the local or state chamber of commerce to determine (1) what educational resource information is available and (2) whether resource directories (listings) have been prepared in the past or are currently available.

2. Write to the National Association for Industry-Education Cooperation (NAIEC, 235 Hendricks Boulevard, Buffalo, N.Y. 14226) and request information regarding community resources workshops. Prepare a plan for conducting a community resources workshop in your school.

3. Develop a list of the community resources currently used in your program or another local program.

4. Analyze the differences between the types of community resources frequently used in career education programs and those used in occupational education programs.

5. Prepare a list of the potential resources available from the businesses and agencies represented by the members of the advisory committee.

6. Contact the state vocational education office to determine if information or materials are available to assist teachers in identifying and using community resources.

7. Develop a list of the types (e.g., field trip sites, in-class speakers) of community resources needed in your program.

8. Read pages 36–45 in Phipps et al., *CRU System: A Manual for Community Resource Utilization* [137], where techniques for evaluating community resources are discussed, and evaluate the use of community resources

in an instructional program for which you are responsible.

9. Obtain a copy of Tim Wentling's *Locally Directed Evaluation Guide 16: Analysis of Community Resources* from the Illinois Office of Education, Department of Adult, Vocational, and Technical Education, 100 North First Street, Springfield, Ill. 62777.

This document contains detailed procedures and sample instruments for conducting a team evaluation of community resources. A filmstrip/cassette tape presentation is also available to orient an evaluation team to the activity. Organize and conduct an evaluation of the use of community resources in your program using the suggested procedures.

SELECTED REFERENCES

Ayars, A. L., and Bovee, C. *How to Plan a Community Resources Workshop.* Buffalo, N.Y.: National Association for Industry-Education Cooperation, 1975.

Clare-Gladwin Intermediate School District, *A Human Resource Roster for CEPD 15.* Clare, Michigan: Clare-Gladwin Intermediate School District, 1973.

Cochran, Leslie H.; Phelps, L. Allen; and Skupin, Joseph F. *Needs Assessment on the Use of Vocational Advisory Committees in Michigan.* Lansing: Michigan Department of Education, 1974.

Phelps, L. Allen, and Lutz, Ronald J. *Career Exploration and Preparation for the Special Needs Learner.* Boston: Allyn and Bacon, Inc., 1977.

Phipps, Lloyd. J., et al. *CRU System: A Manual for Community Resource Utilization.* Springfield: Illinois Office of Education, Division of Vocational and Technical Education, 1976.

School District of the City of Royal Oak. *Career Awareness—Grades K-6: Guide for Implementation,* Second Edition. Royal Oak, Michigan: same, 1974.

Wentling, Tim L. *Locally Directed Evaluation Guide 16: Analysis of Community Resources.* Springfield: Illinois Office of Education, Department of Adult, Vocational, and Technical Education, 1976.

World of Work: Resource Units for Elementary School Teachers. Dekalb: ABLE Model Program, Northern Illinois University, undated.

6 The career guidance and placement services function

Career education is, largely, a product of the perceived failure of education to assist students leaving the formal educational system to understand the changing relationships between education and work [70]. The rate of societal and occupational changes has been far more rapid than the changes within schools. Obviously, advisory committees play a critical role in narrowing this gap in the future.

The central theme of career education has been to focus educational efforts on the total career development of youth and adults. Hoyt [6] refers to career development as a process through which persons develop the capacity for and engage in work as part of their total life-style. It includes the developmental stages of career awareness, career exploration, career decision making, career planning and preparation, career establishment, career maintenance, and career decline. In this process, guidance and placement services are vital in providing students with educational and occupational experiences that are productive, satisfying, and meaningful.

Information from recent student follow-up studies also suggests that schools must provide more in the way of guidance and placement services. A follow-up study of 1973 vocational program graduates and dropouts in Illinois revealed that

- Over 54 percent of the respondents recommended that more career guidance be provided in high school occupational programming.

- Over 24 percent felt they needed more assistance in obtaining a job following graduation.

- More than 77 percent of the vocational program graduates went on to enroll in some type of postsecondary education. [54]

As schools refocus their emphasis on providing more experiences related to preparation for the world of work, the support services provided to students become increasingly critical. Counselors and teachers must have current occupational information to share with students. Opportunities to sample various occupations in the real-life setting must be available in order for students to make informed decisions about the occupational education programs or occupations they wish to enter.

The role of advisory committees in stimulating the development of career guidance and placement services can best be described as "emerging." In many school districts, special advisory committees have recently been formed to assist with the development of school-based placement services for occupational education programs. Program or craft advisory committees have provided increased assistance in locating part-time co-op training stations for students. With the development of area vocational centers, advisory committees have been asked to give guidance to counselors and administrators for the recruitment and selection of students to attend these centers.

Results from a statewide assessment of vocational advisory committees in Michigan suggest that a more extensive role in student placement efforts is needed. Nearly 60 percent of the local administrators and board members surveyed felt their advisory committees were either ineffective or only slightly effective in facilitating the placement of students. A number of placement-related activities were cited as needing greater attention by advisory committees, including recommending potential co-op work stations, reviewing follow-up studies, organizing employer/student conferences, and facilitating consultation with the state employment service [38].

This chapter focuses on strategies that advisory committees can undertake relative to career guidance and placement services. The role of the committee concerning the review and development of occupational information, and the recruitment, selection, and placement of students is highlighted.

SCOPE OF CAREER GUIDANCE AND PLACEMENT SERVICES

To describe adequately the career guidance and placement function, it is important to first define the function in a programmatic context. Career guidance can be viewed as a set of services provided to students to aid them in their career development [70]. It includes such services as increasing the individual's awareness of available educational and occupational opportunities, assisting students with career decision-making processes, and aiding students in implementing career decisions. Placement can best be described as the active, implementation phase of the career development process. Barrow and her coauthors describe placement as the "implementation of a step in the career plan of a student involving employment, transition to another educational or training setting, or other career alternative consistent with individual aptitude, interest values, and ability." [17:3]

In this definition, placement takes on an individual-based perspective. It becomes more global than simply placing a student in some form of part-time or full-time employment. Placement is essentially the effective transition from a particular program the student is completing to the next appropriate experience in his or her career development plan. From this perspective, advisory committees must play an important role in the placement of students as they enter, progress through, and exit from a program(s).

Several authors have pointed out the need to consider career guidance and placement assistance as a comprehensive array of services. Depending on the availability of services from other agencies, the essential components include needs assessment and program planning, orientation, career planning assistance, testing, referrals to placement, public relations, contacts with business and industry, job development, referral and interview services, and follow-up services. Obviously, advisory committees can play a larger role in some of these components than in others. The most frequent roles involve activities associated with student recruitment, selection, and placement. Appropriate committee activities might include:

- Meeting with counselors from junior and senior high schools to assist in describing occupational and career education programs and related employment possibilities.
- Meeting with parents, students, and community groups to inform them of the school's educational and employment opportunities.
- Suggesting functional criteria for the selection of students for admission to occupational programs.
- Assisting school personnel with the placement of students in part-time and/or full-time jobs.

Many of these activities are also appropriate for elementary and middle school career education programs. Advisory committees for these programs will likely focus their efforts on fulfilling the career guidance function through the use of community resources.

The advisory committees involved in the career guidance and placement function include the placement advisory committee, cooperative education advisory committee, and program or craft advisory committee. The organizational structure and administrative policies of the occupational education program will determine which of these committees is appropriate.

Placement advisory committee

This special advisory committee is generally formed where high schools, community colleges, or area vocational centers have organized services and staff members with assigned responsibilities for the placement of students following program completion. The use of such committees is usually related to the state's endorsement of funding of school-based placement programs. In Michigan, for instance, school districts are funded to provide areawide placement services jointly. Placement advisory committees composed of teachers, students, community representatives, labor groups, employers, and parents must be formed to assist with the program. The advisory committee exists to identify placement needs, opportunities, and problems. It also provides guidance in the development of vocational programs with emphasis on placement [95].

Cooperative education advisory committee

Another special advisory committee concerned with placement is the cooperative education advisory committee, which is similar to the placement advisory committee in composition. This committee is generally found in an occupational program that has cooperative education programs operating in several areas (i.e., agricultural occupations, distribution occupations, industrial occupations). The cooperative education advisory committee usually advises the coordinators on sources of training stations for placement, types of instructional materials, organization of the employer appreciation banquet, and other organizational and instructional matters [94].

Program or craft advisory committees

Program or craft advisory committees will be more actively involved in the guidance and placement function if neither cooperative education nor the placement advisory committees are in existence. If full-time counseling, placement, or cooperative education personnel are not employed, the responsibilities generally fall on the occupational teacher or teacher-coordinator. The program or craft advisory committee that serves the occupational teacher's program must be prepared to give advice on guidance and placement.

In many larger school districts, however, placement and cooperative education advisory committees exist alongside program advisory committees. To insure that career guidance and placement services are fully integrated with occupational instruction, close coordination between these advisory committees is essential. School personnel from either the cooperative education or placement committees may also serve on the program or craft advisory committees to facilitate communication. Newsletters are another means of effectively coordinating advisory committee efforts for large school programs. Due to the interrelatedness of the programs being served by the committee, no attempt has been made to distinguish between which inputs can best be handled by placement, which by cooperative education, or which by program or craft advisory committees.

CAREER GUIDANCE AND PLACEMENT ACTIVITIES

Advisory committees can play an integral role in the four major components of a comprehensive career guidance and placement system:

FIGURE 6-1. Comprehensive career guidance and placement system

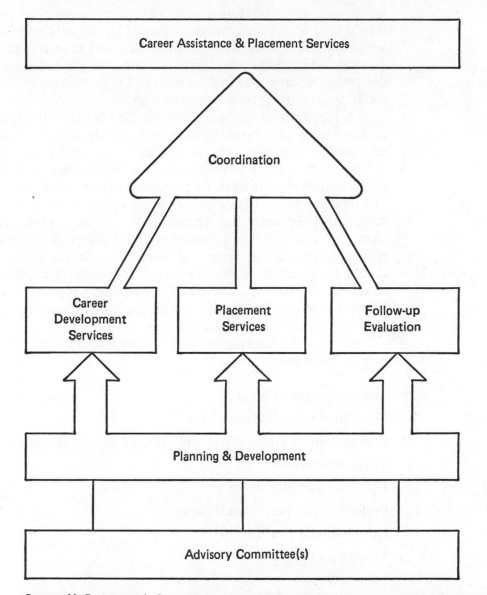

Connye M. Barrow et al. *Career Assistance and Placement Services Resource Manual, Report—Contract Number RDC-A5-225.* Springfield, Illinois: Department of Adult, Vocational and Technical Education. July 1976. Used with permission.

coordination, career development services, placement services, and follow-up and evaluation services [17]. Special, general, or program advisory committees can assist in the planning, development, and evaluation of the components. Figure 6–1 illustrates the operating relationship of the components of the career guidance and placement function.

Coordination of activities

To avoid duplication of effort and insure maximum effectiveness, two levels of coordination of the guidance and placement effort are especially important. First, guidance and placement services should be fully integrated in the on-going occupational education program. Faculty, counselors, and administrators should view these services as essential, they should have a thorough understanding of all the guidance and placement services available, and they should understand their role in assisting students in using the services. Both students and graduates should consider the available services as instrumental in the development of their careers and in the transition from school to work.

A second level of coordination is that between the in-school career guidance and placement services and similar services available in the community. Strategies for the use and coordination of community resources such as these were discussed in the previous chapter. However, the effective coordination of placement services is frequently difficult. The limited number of available jobs and slots in training programs creates competition between the agencies who are attempting to place their clients or students. To minimize negative effects of such competition, representatives of all or several placement services in the community should be involved in the advisory committee. The committee should direct its efforts toward establishing positive, cooperative working relationships among the agencies for the sharing of the guidance, counseling, placement, and related support services.

Among the community agencies that provide guidance and placement services are

State employment service

Vocational rehabilitation service

Comprehensive Employment and Training Agency (Department of Labor)

Trade associations

Industrial associations

Professional and civic associations

Neighborhood youth corps

Veteran's Administration

Labor unions

The advisory committee may wish to stimulate cooperation between these groups and the school district by suggesting such strategies as

- Developing local interagency coordination plans or agreements to be endorsed by governing boards of each party.
- Using representatives of these agencies or organizations as resource speakers for youth organization meetings, career days, PTA, and teacher in-service activities.
- Designating persons from the school district as liaison representatives for each agency.
- Arranging for vocational aptitude testing of students by the local employment service.

- Inviting representatives of all appropriate agencies to serve on both special and program advisory committees of the school district.
- Arranging field trips to local agency offices.
- Developing a roster of key community resource personnel and distributing it to all staff members involved in the guidance and placement function.

Career development services

Although the major responsibility for the career development services lies with the counseling and guidance staff, teachers, co-op coordinators, placement personnel, parents, and others are becoming increasingly involved in helping students define, clarify, and implement their career plans. In the career development process, students require experiences in assessing themselves, obtaining career information, making decisions, and developing specific employment skills (e.g., interviewing, preparing a résumé). The guidance, counseling, and support services that are instrumental in providing these experiences include individual appraisal, career planning, occupational information, educational information, career counseling, and placement services.

The advisory committee can assist career development services by

- Reviewing the currently used literature on career information, occupational opportunities, and educational and retraining opportunities.
- Recommending essential employability competencies to be provided to students (e.g., appropriate dress for an interview, information to include in a résumé).
- Recommending and providing current literature on career and educational opportunities and career requirements.
- Providing suggestions for aptitude and occupational interest testing programs.
- Identifying in-service experiences for counselors and teachers (e.g., industrial seminars and workshops).
- Serving as career mentors for individual students and counseling them in their career selection.
- Providing students with opportunities to spend an exploratory "day on the job."
- Arranging for resource speakers from personnel departments of local businesses and industries.
- Arranging for field trips to personnel departments of local business and industries.

Placement services

The effective placement of students in full- or part-time employment or in appropriate educational programs is the cornerstone of the placement process. While often a program is evaluated on the basis of *where* students obtain employment or advanced training, the essence of the placement process is placing students in the most appropriate setting for continued career growth and development. Barrow and her coauthors [17] identify four steps in the placement process: (1) reaching and interacting with students in order to serve them, (2) interacting with employers in order to identify career opportunities, (3) referring students to career opportunities, and (4) following through to improve placement effectiveness. While these steps represent the basic procedure, step number three must be expanded to read "career *and educational* opportunities." An important but less emphasized purpose of occupational and career education is to assist students in locating continuing education opportunities that are critical to their career growth and development. The advisory committee can provide assistance in recommending advanced and specialty training programs for students.

Follow-up and evaluation services

In addition to providing assistance with on-the-job follow-up studies, the committee must also direct its efforts to conducting follow-up studies that will help in evaluating the total occupational or career education program. Follow-up studies can provide information on the current status of persons who have completed the program, on their satisfaction with their current status, and on their satisfaction with their school experience. This information is essential for improving career guidance and placement services as well as other elements of the occupational or career education program.

The advisory committee can provide assistance in organizing follow-up surveys of employers to determine their assessment of students they have employed. However, in planning student follow-up surveys, the advisory committee should have an opportunity to review and react to the questions to be included in the survey. The advisory committee can review the compiled data, offer possible explanations for apparent problem areas and trends, and provide the staff with suggestions and recommendations to be included in summary reports. Chapter 7 provides additional information on the role of the advisory committee in planning and reviewing follow-up studies.

The advisory committee can assist in other activities designed to evaluate the guidance and placement service function. Some state departments request that advisory committees annually evaluate counseling services, placement assistance, occupational information, and other support services. Advisory committees can help to develop and analyze parent, student, and staff surveys that are designed to evaluate the career guidance and placement function.

IMPLEMENTATION STRATEGIES

Guidance and placement services are a concern of nearly all advisory committees involved with occupational and career education programs.

Thus it is difficult to identify implementation strategies that focus solely on guidance and placement. Frequently advisory committee efforts in this area are integrated with other functions. Many of the advisory committee activities described in other chapters (for example, curriculum advisement, community resource coordination, program evaluation, or professional development) can also be used to strengthen the guidance and placement elements of a program. The following strategies are discussed in this section: monitoring cooperative work-experience programs, recruiting students, selecting and in-school placing of students, sponsoring conferences and seminars, assisting in direct placement, and evaluating.

Monitoring cooperative work-experience programs

In this section, a broad view of cooperative education programs is taken. It includes cooperative vocational education, exploratory work-experience and work-observation programs, and work-training programs. The advisory committee can initiate a number of activities to review and strengthen the guidance and placement aspects of these various cooperative work-experience programs.

As noted earlier, many of the implementation activities are closely allied to other functions. For example, an advisory committee reviewing a cooperative education program might review the curriculum for a related course that is designed to assist students with career planning and employability skills. In such a case the curriculum advisement function and the guidance and placement service function overlap.

The special cooperative education advisory committee and the occupational program advisory committee are involved with the guidance and placement service from differing perspectives. Figure 6–2 lists some activities common to the two committees.

Most of these activities are self-explanatory. The experiences that students receive while observing or participating in community-based employment are of critical importance in the process of career exploration, decision making, career choice, skill development, and transition from school to work. The cooperative education opportunities provided to learners are probably the most important component in the guidance and placement services provided by a school. Advisory committees at all levels must be involved continuously in reviewing, evaluating, and improving cooperative work-experience programs.

Recruiting students

Participating in school programs and recruiting students are services that advisory committees can perform well [29]. The committee might consider two types of recruitment: student recruitment for occupational program enrollment and recruitment for employment. Advisory groups have traditionally been more active in recruitment of students for occupational education programs. Advisory committee members, as a result of their occupational and educational experiences, are well qualified to assist

FIGURE 6–2. *Common and unique placement activities of cooperative education and occupational advisory committees*

Common Activities

Identify potential work-training sites

Plan and sponsor employer appreciation banquets/breakfasts

Make presentations to related classes

Review training plans

Recommend operation policies for co-op programs

Recommend policies for recruiting or placing special needs students into co-op programs

Recommend strategies for limiting sex-role stereotyping in the placement of students

Plan and sponsor employer-student seminars

Unique Activities for a Cooperative Education Committee	Unique Activities for an Occupational Program Committee
Review recommendations from occupational committees regarding placement	Review student records prior to placement
Evaluate the need for new co-op programs	Recommend special or advanced training courses for selected students
Suggest co-op modifications and guidelines for disadvantaged and handicapped students	Provide current industry-specific occupational information (e.g., wages, working conditions)
Sponsor seminars for administrators, counselors, placement staff, coordinators, and students, on techniques for gaining employability skills	Sponsor seminars for teachers and students on new processes and technologies
	Recommend specialized co-op positions for disadvantaged or handicapped students

students with decisions and questions regarding programs that will meet their career goals and personal needs.

To recruit students advisory committees can:

- Develop resource material (brochures, pamphlets, portable exhibits) that can be used in speeches to civic organizations, student groups, parent groups.

- Make presentations to students in elementary or junior high school programs to acquaint them with the occupational program(s).

- Meet with counseling staffs of elementary and junior high school counselors to discuss the goals, learning experiences, and placement of students after the program is over.

- Contact local employers regarding upcoming day or evening courses that may be of interest to them. Specific occupational offerings may be helpful for retraining or upgrading of various employers.

- Provide program information for personnel offices of local industries or businesses. When personnel staff interview prospective employees, they may want to recommend occupational or educational programs offered locally to assist persons in acquiring specific marketable skills. This information should be provided locally to all potential referral agencies, including vocational rehabilitation service, state employment service, and the Comprehensive Employment and Training Agency (CETA) offices.

- Prepare presentations for use with parents. The focus of these presentations should be on the value of having marketable job skills and on the various options that would be open to their son/daughter once he/she has completed the program. Recently, a number of area vocational centers have sponsored two-day parent awareness programs that provide intensive hands-on experiences for parents in several occupational laboratories.

In planning and conducting student recruitment efforts, the committee must remember to approach each group that has a potential impact on the student's career decision or choice—including parents, guidance counselors, teachers in the lower grades, referral agency personnel, and personnel staffs of local businesses or industries. The second key point the committee must remember is concerned with recent federal legislation to minimize discrimination in education and employment. Title IX of the Education Amendments of 1972 requires that policies and materials for recruitment be free of statements that would discourage or limit persons of either sex from enrolling in any educational program. Similar requirements exist for minorities and handicapped persons. The advisory committee should be actively involved in developing recruitment materials and in other recruitment efforts that encourage persons from both sexes, those with different functional abilities, and those of different cultures and races to enroll in the program(s).

Selecting and in-school placing of students

Following recruitment efforts, the advisory committee might want to concern itself with the screening, selecting, and placing of students. This is primarily the responsibility of guidance personnel, administrators, and teachers. However, the extent of advisory committee involvement will depend on the nature and level of the program. In advanced, occupational or technical training programs, where previous experience is necessary, the advisory committee can assist in recommending procedures and exams for evaluating previous experiences, suggesting minimum entrance criteria (for example, vocational aptitude scores), and recommending alternative placements and referrals for students who do not meet the entrance criteria. In programs that have only limited criteria for entry, the advisory committee will be only minimally involved in this area.

With the recent emphasis on serving special-needs students and eliminating sex-role stereotyping, the in-school placement of students has become a major concern. The advisory committee can play an important role in recommending appropriate placements and experiences for females/males or for handicapped students. For instance, an advisory committee for a welding program might recommend that special instructional materials be used to describe the unique career opportunities for women in the welding field. The same advisory committee might suggest specialized training (for example as a cutter) for a mentally handicapped student. Also, the advisory committee may want to identify successful female or handicapped welders and involve them in providing career counseling for students and consultation for teachers.

Sponsoring conferences and seminars

Career days, career workshops, and employer/student conferences are advisory committee vehicles to facilitate career guidance and placement services. Such seminars and workshops can greatly increase awareness of local employment opportunities, postsecondary education and training opportunities, the type of work performed, and the skills and attitudes that are important to employers. They can also prove enlightening and informative for counselors, teachers, and parents. It might be helpful to invite parents to attend with their children.

Figure 6–3 presents an agenda for a career workshop for high school students. The workshop theme was "Career Opportunities in the 1980s." Participants representing business and industry and various school services (such as career counselors, area vocational schools, and cooperative work-experience coordinators) were involved in the workshop.

At the postsecondary level, the employer/student conferences are usually oriented toward employment recruitment. Community colleges. and four-year schools frequently conduct two- to three-day employer fairs that enable recruitment personnel for business and industry to set up displays and interview students who are being trained in fields in which business and industry are seeking personnel.

FIGURE 6–3.   Career workshop agenda

HAMMERTON TOWNSHIP HIGH SCHOOL

presents

CAREER OPPORTUNITIES FOR THE 1980s:
A Career-Planning Workshop

October 3, 1979
Auditorium 7:00 P.M.

Panel Moderator   Dr. Ed Jenkins, Career Counselor

Business/Industry/Governmental Agency Participants

Careers in the early 1980s   Mr. Peter Hansen, Employment Forecaster
                                                             County Employment and Training
                                                             Agency

Manufacturing Careers   Dr. John Johnson, Personnel Director,
                                                             Motor Division

Marketing Careers   Ms. Cheryl Lodkins, Owner, Fashions

Service Careers   Mr. Homer Horton, Director of
                                                             Personnel, Servo, Inc.

Military Careers   Maj. Carol Conlon, Director of
                                                             Recruitment, U.S. Army

Postsecondary Occupational   Dr. Art Herman, Coordinator of Student
   Education   Services, Vocational-Technical Institute

8:00–8:45 Small discussion/interaction groups
9:00–9:45 Small discussion/interaction groups

In planning and sponsoring these conferences, workshops, and seminars, advisory committees provide important input. To maximize the effectiveness of this input, the committee should take the following steps:

1. Analyze the specific needs for employer/student interaction regarding career guidance and placement.

2. Establish a set of goals and objectives for the conference; these goals might focus on providing students with specific career information, increasing awareness of career alternatives and career ladders, or providing students with employer contact to aid in locating full- or part-time work.

3. Identify employers and employer representatives and school personnel who could benefit from conference participation.

4. Plan an agenda that addresses the identified needs for career guidance and placement information.

5. Prepare conference announcement and registration information.

6. Distribute the information to all prospective participants, including students, employers, counselors, teachers, parents, school administrators, and union officials.

7. Conduct and evaluate the conference.

Many trade, civic, and professional associations have prepared material that can be used for special topical conferences. Burt [29: 227–28] describes two approaches that have been developed for nation-wide use by the United States Chamber of Commerce and by B'nai B'rith.*

The Business-Education Day program developed by the U.S. Chamber of Commerce and conducted by local chambers in many cities throughout the nation, arrange for tours of industrial and business organizations by teachers and counselors. Schools usually close for the day, and all teachers in the school or school systems are scheduled to visit one or more plants participating in the program. While this effort is expensive and time consuming on the part of all concerned, it is considered an extremely worthwhile activity by teachers and an important phase of business public relations in "getting their story across" to teachers, and hopefully, to students. A manual and case report on how to conduct B-E Days is available from the U.S. Chamber of Commerce, Washington, D.C.

The Career Day Conference is an extremely popular technique of school guidance counselors. The programs are arranged so that students indicate some particular industry or career area in which they are interested and for which the counselor has pre-arranged an industry speaker or group of speakers. Usually one–two days during the school year are set aside for this purpose. For interested school and industry people, a useful manual is available from B'nai B'rith Vocational Service, Washington, D.C., titled, "A Career Conference for Your Community."

Assisting in direct placement

In addition to placement assistance for part-time or full-time employment, the committee could provide assistance for placement in training programs (trade schools, apprenticeships, on-the-job training), military service, volunteer service, or higher education (community colleges, junior colleges, colleges). The advisory committee assists placement by identifying job openings. Generally, school personnel receive announcements of job openings at various businesses in the community from advisory committee members. Once they receive these announcements, they post them or place them on a list of job openings, which they then circulate regularly throughout the occupational program, for student and teacher review.

The advisory committee can facilitate the providing of announcement information by developing a procedure for locating and announcing job openings, encouraging all employers to list their openings, and keeping

*Reprinted with permission from: Burt, Samuel M. *Industry and Vocational-Technical Education.* New York: McGraw-Hill Book Company, 1967.

the listing as up-to-date as possible. During the process of developing a job openings list, the advisory committee should plan strategies for disseminating the list of openings as well as sharing the list with other nearby education and employment agencies. This would make the listing considerably more useful.

Businesses also frequently provide direct placement assistance in the form of financial assistance. In some occupational fields, such as nursing and engineering, scholarships are also available for advanced training. Advisory committee members frequently have or can obtain information about such industry-supported scholarship, loan, and grant programs. Also, some committees have been the recipients of grants or endowments to be used to assist needy students. Burt [29] notes that some committees administer these funds directly, while others turn the money over to school officials to use at their discretion. Direct assistance can also be provided to business and industry personnel. School personnel and advisory committee members can provide on-site assistance to supervisors and managers who are working with co-op students or other students being trained in the program. Such assistance is particularly critical for supervisors working with handicapped and disadvantaged students who may experience problems in social adjustment.

Evaluating the services

Effective and frequent evaluation of guidance and placement services is the key for the improvement of such services. The Vocational Education Amendments of 1976 emphasized the importance of evaluating local occupational education programs on a regular basis. The final federal rules and regulations reflect this concern as it pertains to guidance and placement services:

> evaluate in quantitative terms the effectiveness of each formally organized program. These evaluations shall be in terms of: (a) Planning and operational processes, such as:
>
> (2) Guidance, counseling, and placement and follow-up services; . . .
>
> (4) Employer participation in cooperative programs of vocational education. [53:53842]

In many school districts and community colleges, advisory committees play a critical role in designing, conducting, and interpreting evaluation efforts.

Planning evaluation efforts. Evaluations should examine how well career development services, placement services, and follow-up services are coordinated within the school as well as with local employers, community agencies, and other education and training programs. School personnel plan evaluations; the advisory committee reviews the key

FIGURE 6-4. Sample key questions for evaluation of guidance and placement services

Occupational Information

1. Do the materials currently used for providing occupational information reflect current and accurate information about the occupation?

2. Does the occupational information program adequately orient students to clusters of occupations in the world of work?

3. To what extent has the career information program had a demonstrated and positive effect on student career and educational decisions?

4. Are the career information materials used by students free of sex bias and sex-role stereotypes?

5. Do the occupational instructors adequately and appropriately incorporate occupational information in their instruction and counseling?

6. Have parents been adequately involved in the career information program?

7. Are special career information activities and services available to students who are handicapped and disadvantaged?

8. Are the results of students' personal inventories and tests reviewed with students?

9. Is the program of career information closely articulated and coordinated with feeder programs?

10. Are the occupational interests of students surveyed as they enter and exit from the program?

Career Counseling

1. Does the guidance and counseling staff have extensive and current occupational information?

2. Are adequate counseling services available to adults and out-of-school youth?

3. Is the guidance and counseling staff involved with general and occupational advisory committees?

4. Is appropriate in-service training provided for the guidance and counseling staff?

5. Are counselors knowledgeable about and able to assist students with employment opportunities, work programs, scholarships and loans, student activities, continued education and training opportunities, and community services?

6. To what extent do occupational instructors and counselors coordinate their efforts to meet student needs?

7. Is the role of the guidance and counseling staff well defined and understood by teachers, parents, and students?

FIGURE 6-4. (continued)

Placement Services

1. To what extent do placement and follow-up activities involve advisory committees, public and private agencies, business and industry, and other groups?

2. Are students, parents, employers, and teachers aware of the available placement services?

3. Are students who seek part-time work adequately placed?

4. To what extent is the instructional staff actively involved in placement and follow-up activities?

5. Is effective, regular communication maintained with public and private sources of the labor market and employment information?

6. Do students who are referred for placement have a reasonable possibility of successfully filling the job?

7. Are the placement services provided to graduates and out-of-school youth effective?

8. Is on-the-job follow-up assistance available for students needing such services?

Key questions are adapted with permission from Tim L. Wentling. *Locally Directed Evaluation Guide 5: Assessment of Student Services.* Springfield: Illinois Office of Education, 1976.

questions to be addressed and suggests the types of persons who ought to provide evaluative information. To insure that the evaluation effort is comprehensive, questions should be developed that cover all aspects of the available counseling, career information, and placement services. Figure 6–4 lists some sample key questions. Once school personnel prepare an initial list of key questions, the advisory committee should be involved in adding, deleting, and refining the major questions.

Several different groups of people can provide meaningful evaluative information about guidance and placement services. Mail, telephone, and personal interview surveys can be developed and used with employers, current students, program graduates, parents, instructional staff, guidance and counseling staff, out-of-school youth, public and private employment agencies, and other local education and training institutions such as community colleges and technical institutes. Figure 6–5 is a sample survey form that was developed for use with employers.

Interpreting evaluation information. Once evaluation information is compiled, the advisory committee can help to interpret the results. It is recommended that school personnel write a preliminary set of findings or conclusions. The advisory committee can review the findings and verify or clarify the supporting data if necessary. The committee can also develop recommendations for modifying or expanding guidance and placement services. An advisory committee's review and endorsement of an evaluation report adds credibility to the findings and recommendations and tends to stimulate greater involvement, commitment and contributions by individual committee members.

CAREER GUIDANCE AND PLACEMENT SERVICES
FUNCTION IN ACTION

A new/used car dealership owner in a small southwestern Pennsylvania community was asked to serve as a member of the general advisory committee for a local area vocational-technical school. A preliminary placement and follow-up report of the 1977 graduates was presented to the committee for review, discussion, and suggestions for dissemination. During the meeting the car dealer noted that, because of federal and state minimum wage requirements, he didn't feel that he could afford to hire inexperienced mechanics directly out of high school. His rationale was that it would be too costly to train these individuals before a reasonable profit could be realized from their employment.

After reviewing several of the area vocational school's programs and listening to other employers on the committee, he gave his situation some second thoughts. He became reasonably assured that the graduates of the auto mechanics program generally had employability skills that were well above entry level. They were being trained on up-to-date equipment that was similar to equipment used in his business, plus they seemed to perform well with little supervision. Two years ago, as an experiment, he decided to hire one of the school's graduates. As of February 1978, the car dealership discussed here had employed one mechanic and two auto body repair specialists from the school on a full-time basis. In addition to also employing co-op students, the dealership owner had become a real booster of the school in local community affairs.

FIGURE 6-5. *Sample questionnaire for employers*

Directions: Your answers to the following questions will assist the general advisory committee in evaluating the placement services of the Smith Area Vocational Center. Please answer the questions below and return the form in the self-addressed envelope at your earliest convenience. Thank you!

1. Does the Smith Area Vocational Center have someone who is assigned to the responsibility of job placement?

   _____ yes _____ no _____ don't know

2. Can you get a list of students seeking part-time jobs?

   _____ yes _____ no _____ don't know

3. Can you get a list of students seeking full-time jobs?

   _____ yes _____ no _____ don't know

4. Have you completed a survey of possible job opportunities for students seeking full- or part-time jobs?

   _____ yes _____ no _____ don't know

5. How much job placement assistance is provided to you by the Smith Area Vocational Center staff?
   _____ a great deal of assistance
   _____ some assistance
   _____ no assistance

6. Would you like to receive more or a different type of job placement assistance from the Smith Area Vocational Center staff?
   _____ yes _____ no

   If yes, what type of assistance is needed:

7. Have you ever served on an advisory committee?
   _____ yes _____ no

8. Would you serve on an advisory committee if asked?

   _____ yes _____ no

Adapted with permission from Tim L. Wentling. *Locally Directed Evaluation Guide 5: Assessment of Student Services.* Springfield: Illinois Office of Education, 1976.

COMMUNICATIONS EXERCISE

THE CAREER GUIDANCE AND PLACEMENT SERVICES FUNCTION

The following communications exercise, by allowing you to apply your knowledge to a specific setting, can increase your understanding of the career guidance and placement services function. This exercise was designed and field tested as a self-instructional or small-group activity that stresses the application of concepts and ideas presented in this chapter.

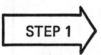 **THE FOLLOWING SECTION PROVIDES A BRIEF OVERVIEW OF A SPECIFIC SITUATION RELATED TO AN ADVISORY COMMITTEE. READ THIS SECTION COMPLETELY BEFORE PROCEEDING TO STEP 2.**

You are a member of the general advisory committee that has been asked to look into the placement of graduates and nongraduates (dropouts) of the high school program. Upon completion of a needs assessment of the current placement function, the committee has decided to recommend the establishment of a placement center within the comprehensive high school enrolling 1,200 students in grades ten through twelve. The center should include placement services for graduates, nongraduates (dropouts), co-op students, and students seeking part-time and summer employment.

From the following worksheet, select those considerations and recommendations that the committee should include in its proposal for the placement center.

STEP 2

USING THE WORKSHEET BELOW, CHECK THE BOX(ES)
REPRESENTING THE ITEM(S) THAT MOST APPROPRIATELY
RESPOND(S) TO THE SITUATION DESCRIBED IN STEP 1.

Recommend that placement center staff conduct annual surveys. ____1	Recommend that placement center staff and special education staff coordinate placement of handicapped students. ____2	Outline placement center staff needs and necessary qualifications. ____3	Sponsor employer/ student conferences. ____4
Recommend that placement center assist in conducting occupational demand surveys. ____5	Recommend that placement center staff serve on advisory committees. ____6	Collect in-depth follow-up of students enrolling in postsecondary programs. ____7	Recommend that placement center staff provide in-class seminars on how to apply for a job. ____8
Establish a comprehensive library of information on all available postsecondary education programs. ____9	Recommend that a central credentials file be set up and maintained for each student desiring one. ____10	Recommend that all students go through the placement center for an exit interview. ____11	Recommend that provisions be made for in-service training for placement center staff. ____12
Recommend the establishment of a comprehensive occupational/career information library. ____13	Collect individualized instructional materials focusing on employment skills (e.g., job interviewing). ____14	Follow-up school dropouts for potential enrollment in special-needs program. ____15	Coordinate information and services with other public agencies also providing placement services. ____16

STEP 3   EVALUATE THE RESPONSES ON THE WORKSHEET BY COMPARING THE INDIVIDUAL RESPONSES WITH THOSE RECOMMENDED BELOW. READ THE APPROPRIATE COMMENTS AND CONTINUE ON TO STEP 4.

If you checked _____ 1, 5, 7 _____ , read Comment A.
If you checked _____ 9, 10, 11, 13, 15 _____ , read Comment B.
If you checked _____ 4, 8, 14 _____ , read Comment C.
If you checked _____ 2, 3, 6, 12 _____ , read Comment D.
If you checked _____ 16 _____ , read Comment E.

Comment A   If you included these responses in your answer, you have gathered the appropriate impression that the placement center should be involved in providing support for or conducting surveys. The existence of a placement center facilitates contact with employers of all types; thus the center staff will have ready access to labor market demand information (5), as well as follow-up information on graduates (7).

In order to place students effectively as they exit from a program, the staff needs to collect and review graduate follow-up information (7). As this information is summarized, it can be passed along to the instructional staff and the school administration.

These follow-up surveys should be conducted on graduates and nongraduates as well. An extensive follow-up survey of those students entering postsecondary institutions will provide a comprehensive data base for review by the total faculty and staff of the high school as they attempt to upgrade all areas of the school curriculum (7).

Comment B   These responses should definitely be included in the proposal since they outline the specific student services to be offered by the center. Personnel of the center would be able to provide such direct services as interviewing exiting students (11), assisting students with preparation of their credentials, handling credentials for students (10), posting job openings on a central clearing board or in a regularly circulated publication, and maintaining a comprehensive library of in-depth occupational/career information (13) and postsecondary education opportunities (9). Students should also be afforded the opportunity of an exit placement interview.

Another dimension of the placement center would focus on nongraduates. A specific effort should be made through the placement center to follow up dropouts and attempt to reinterest them in school. Perhaps special-needs funding could be sought for this "recovery" program (15).

Comment C   Another function of the center would be to provide instructional support services. Responses 4, 8, and 14 outline activities of an instructional nature, which could be sponsored by the center staff. The instructional program generally focuses on the content of the course with little regard for "how" students apply for a job, where they will apply their knowledge and skills, or "how" they apply for admission to advanced educational programs. The placement center staff can effectively present this information to students through seminars (8) or self-instructional systems (14). Employers (through employer/student conferences) can also provide this information to students in an effective manner (4).

Comment D   The proposal should also include a description of the proposed placement center staff and their responsibilities. The actual makeup of the staff would depend on the goals and purposes of the center. In some instances the staff might be composed of vocational counselors; in other instances it might include co-op coordinators or teachers; or it might be composed of any combination of individuals with these backgrounds (3).

The placement staff should definitely be involved with advisory committees because of the committee's interest in placement (6). Since co-op placement is usually considered part of placement, the staff may be directly involved in this activity; or they may at least have some responsibilities for coordinating the activity. Provisions should be made for regular in-service sessions to keep the staff abreast of current developments and needs in the placement function (12).

Comment E   This is an absolutely essential component of the proposal. With the numbers of agencies currently offering job placement services (both public and private), the proposal must outline an *acceptable* strategy for interagency cooperation so as to avoid a duplication-of-effort charge, which might endanger the entire proposal.

STEP 4 BASED ON THE DISCUSSION COMMENTS ABOVE, REEVALUATE THE RESPONSES MADE IN STEP 2. IF THE CONCEPTS ARE CLEAR, PROCEED TO STEP 5.

STEP 5 TO IMPLEMENT SOME OF THE KEY CONCEPTS IN THE CHAPTER AS THEY RELATE TO YOUR SPECIFIC SETTING, COMPLETE AT LEAST ONE OF THE FOLLOWING OPTIONS.

Option A Review the chapter, select one concept, and develop a procedure for applying it to an advisory committee.

Option B Select one of the situations outlined in the Suggested Activities section and make an application to an advisory committee.

Option C Choose one of the sources in the Selected References section and integrate the additional insights gleaned from that source into a plan for advisory committee action.

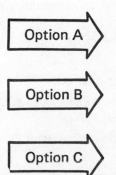

SUGGESTED ACTIVITIES

1. Write to some national professional organizations (American Personnel and Guidance Association, National Vocational Guidance Association, American Vocational Association) to obtain literature on career guidance. Review the material to identify various roles that advisory committees can undertake in the career guidance and placement process.

2. Attend a meeting of an occupational advisory committee and analyze the implications of the discussions for improving the career guidance function.

3. Contact the directors of several nearby school districts and area vocational centers to determine the extent to which discussions regarding career guidance services are effectively coordinated.

4. Interview several local vocational counselors and determine the type and extent of involvement they have had with local educational advisory committees. Share your findings with appropriate administrators or teachers.

5. Obtain and review a copy of the most recent annual report of your state's advisory council for vocational education. Identify the pertinent council recommendations regarding career guidance and placement services. Evaluate how these recommendations might affect your local program.

6. Review the suggested advisory committee activities for counseling and recruiting students in Samuel Burt's *Industry and Vocational-Technical Education* [29:225–28]. Determine which of these may be appropriate for use with your committee.

7. Obtain and review the results of a recent student follow-up survey. Analyze the data to identify the implications for career guidance and placement services. Develop an agenda for an advisory committee meeting that would provide suggestions and recommendations for strengthening the guidance and support services.

8. Review available community resources rosters and identify persons or agencies that are actively involved in providing job placement assistance. Determine which of these agencies are represented on occupational advisory committees and whether or not additional persons or agencies should become involved.

SELECTED REFERENCES

Barrow, Connye M., et al. *Career Assistance and Placement Services Resource Manual Report—Contract Number.* Springfield: Illinois Office of Education, 1976.

Burt, Samuel M. *Industry and Vocational-Technical Education.* New York: McGraw-Hill Book Co., 1967.

Cochran, Leslie H.; Phelps, L. Allen; and Skupin, Joseph F. *Needs Assessment on the Use of Vocational Advisory Committees in Michigan.* Lansing: Michigan Department of Education, 1974.

Federal Register. Vocational Education, State Programs and Commissioner's Discretionary Programs. 42 (October 3, 1977).

Felstenhausen, Joyce L. *If I Tell You, Will You Listen???* Charleston: Center for Educational Studies, Eastern Illinois University, 1974.

Hoyt, Kenneth B. *A Primer for Career Education.* Washington, D.C.: GPO, 1977.

McCurdy, John, and Johnson, Tommy. *Key Concepts in Vocational Education: Placement.* Lansing: Michigan Department of Education, 1976.

Mason, Ralph E., and Haines, Peter G. *Cooperative Occupational Education.* Danville, Ill. Interstate Publishers and Printers, 1972.

Wentling, Tim L. *Locally Directed Evaluation Guide 5: Assessment of Student Services.* Springfield: Illinois Office of Education, 1976.

7 The program evaluation function

The Education Amendments of 1976 placed an increased emphasis on the evaluation of vocational and technical education programs. To justify increased funding and provide the necessary data base for program improvements and refinements, state departments of education and other funding agencies now require that programs be evaluated for efficiency and effectiveness. To that end, numerous systems and models have been developed. The Education Amendments require state boards for vocational education to evaluate the effectiveness of local programs. Within a given five-year period, each local program needs to undergo a comprehensive evaluation, including an examination of planning and operational processes, student achievement, employment status of graduates, and the effects of support services provided for special populations [53]. A similar emphasis appears in the Career Education Incentive Act of 1977 [166].

This concern for detailed and comprehensive evaluation emerged in the early 1970s with the concomitant concern for accountability. The essential notion is that if occupational education is to be responsive to the occupational needs of a rapidly changing technological society, it must develop a capability for measuring and evaluating its performance relative to these changing needs.

This chapter discusses the role of advisory committees in planning, conducting, and interpreting such evaluation efforts as student and employer follow-up surveys. Nance [104] describes evaluation of the total program as one of the most important functions of the advisory committee. He notes that the evaluation function of the committee must be ongoing in nature and focused on the attainment of measurable goals and objectives. He further notes that the importance of evaluation can be viewed in programs that have failed to get public support because their program efforts could not be measured or because provisions for evaluation had not been made prior to program start-up. Wentling and Lawson [178:37] emphasized the special qualifications of advisory committee members in the evaluation role by stating that

> Since they [advisory committee members] are normally local business people who have already made a commitment to education, they can provide an excellent source for consultation regarding some programs. Advisory committee members can encourage other local personnel to cooperate with interviewers in an employer follow-up situation. Furthermore their expertise can be exploited when it comes to making recommendations for improvement after evaluative information has been gathered.

Evaluation can mean different things to different audiences, including the advisory committee. Persons being directly or indirectly evaluated, such as teachers, may view it as threatening or potentially disruptive. Those persons involved in conducting an evaluation, such as members of an advisory committee, may see it as a means for proving personal viewpoints. It is imperative that all parties concerned understand that the primary and overriding purpose of evaluation is to improve programs and services benefiting current and future learners. The Kentucky Advisory Council [105:2] states that

> The primary purpose of the Kentucky Advisory Council Evaluation System is to help *improve* Kentucky's vocational education programs, *not to prove* whether they are good or bad. . . . It is a method of helping advisory committees provide advice to vocational educators. The evaluation process will help determine which aspects of the program need the most improvement and which are most outstanding.

SCOPE OF THE PROGRAM EVALUATION FUNCTION

Evaluation by advisory committees can be both process oriented and outcome oriented. Part II presents process evaluation as a basic activity in the major advisory committee functions. Along with providing advice and assistance, evaluation is a critical activity of the committee as it engages in curriculum advisement (Chapter 3), review of equipment, facilities, and instructional resources (Chapter 4), coordination of community resources (Chapter 5), review of career guidance and placement services (Chapter 6), facilitation of community public relations (Chapter 8), and stimulation of professonal development (Chapter 9).

Several states have mandated the comprehensive process evaluation role for advisory committees. In Michigan, for instance, the regular use of advisory committees is essential in meeting the state-developed *Program Standards of Quality in Vocational-Technical Education* (see Appendix A.) To ensure that local occupational programs have actively involved advisory committees, the State Department of Education prepared an advisory committee review form. Local advisory committees use the form to evaluate and recommend improvements for each program's components or processes; namely, curriculum content, equipment and facilities, safety, job opportunities, placement, and guidance and counseling services. Once completed, the evaluation is forwarded to the state director of vocational education [99].

The advisory committee can also view evaluation as being outcome oriented. The recent competency-based and fiscal accountability movements have placed much greater emphasis on goal identification, goal attainment, and assessment of outcomes. Since the successful transition from school to work is a principal goal (outcome) of occupational education programs, assessing the extent to which this goal is attained is a major evaluation activity.

Advisory committees for programs at the elementary, secondary, and postsecondary levels have been active in evaluating the curriculum, reviewing facilities and instructional resources, and assessing the use of community resources. In addition, however, the advisory committee must examine the outcomes of the program—the students. Business executives are concerned with the performance of their product and continuously evaluate such factors as sales, profit margins, customer satisfaction, and the number of returns for warranty service. With this information on the market performance of their product, they are able to adjust production processes, quality control, and prices systematically to provide the customer with the best product at the lowest price. The follow-up evaluation of students leaving an occupational or career education program has a similar purpose. Information from former students and their employers can be extremely helpful in refining curriculum content to provide students with essential job skills or with skills needed in subsequent related courses. Follow-up information can also be used to strengthen guidance support and placement services, to update tools and equipment, and to increase the use and effectiveness of community resources.

Process and outcome evaluation

It is important to recognize and consider the interface between evaluation of processes (such as the career guidance function) and evaluation of outcomes. In most instances, the process and outcome questions asked of students, advisory committee members, employers, and parents are similar. Evaluation questions in general focus on the qualities, appropriateness, and effectiveness of instruction, materials and equipment, and support services. However, the important distinction is the time frame in which these questions are asked. Follow-up, or outcome, evaluation provides information and observations *after* students have completed a program. The reaction of students and employers to an educational experience is likely to be different following a period of time on the job or in an advanced course. Once students have had an opportunity to use the competencies they have gained, they have a realistic base for assessing the importance and quality of the educational experience they received.

Likewise, an employer's assessment of the need for career guidance or support services may change if he or she is placed in a position where employing out-of-school youth is necessary, and these individuals are found to lack essential basic skills.

A comprehensive evaluation system must interface process evaluation with outcome evaluation. Student observations must be obtained while students are in the program, as well as following their departure from the program. Through advisory committees and follow-up surveys, employers and the public must continuously assess both internal program components and processes and the performance of students once they have left the program.

Information sources

Outcome information can be obtained from a number of sources: Employers can provide information describing the performance of students and the adjustments they are making to the working environment. Students who have graduated or left a program for other reasons can provide evaluative information in light of their current occupational status and experiences. Teachers at the postsecondary level who are currently working with graduates of secondary occupational programs can also provide useful information indicating the performance level of students. Agencies (such as the employment service or vocational rehabilitation) that have served the student since his or her program enrollment have information that can be enlightening. Parents can also provide useful evaluative information.

Statewide evaluation systems

The role of advisory committees varies from place to place in the evaluation of occupational programs. In some states, like Kentucky, advisory committees have been given major responsibility for planning, conducting, and interpreting evaluations on a regional basis [80]. In Michigan, occupational program advisory committees are considered an essential standard for program operation. Within a three-year period, each advisory committee must provide the state's department of education with a comprehensive evaluation of the program including recommendations for improvements [99]. In Illinois, an external team evaluates each occupational program during a five-year period. The team usually interviews advisory committee members. Often members of local advisory committees participate as evaluation team members and visit other programs [74].

The strategies for program evaluation developed by the state department of education will influence the advisory committee's role in program evaluation. In some instances, advisory committees will be assigned the task of developing and administering evaluation surveys; while in others, advisory committee members will only be used as an information source. It is important to be familiar with the evaluation approaches used by the state department of education prior to developing or refining plans for evaluation efforts by advisory committees.

PROGRAM EVALUATION ACTIVITIES

Advisory committees can effectively direct and/or facilitate a number of basic activities in the program evaluation process. While the literature is somewhat limited on advisory committee–directed evaluation systems, they can engage in planning and orientation, collecting information, reviewing and analyzing information, and reporting and using outcomes.

A comprehensive evaluation system is composed of a series of systematic procedures. Before tackling these procedures, one must recognize the purpose of an advisory committee–based evaluation effort, which is to collect, compile, and interpret information about the program that is useful in making decisions regarding needed improvements in the program and related services. Wentling and Lawson [178] provide the following general procedures for systematically conducting evaluations:

1. Focus the evaluation by formulating key evaluative questions to be answered
2. Select appropriate evaluation activities (e.g., student follow-up survey, employer follow-up survey, etc.)
3. Identify specific data and information to be collected by each activity
4. Select personnel to be involved in conducting the evaluation
5. Assign personnel responsibilities for completion of activities
6. Develop a timetable for data collection
7. Develop data collection instruments
8. Compile, review, and analyze the collected data
9. Develop a format for reporting the evaluative information
10. Develop and distribute the evaluation findings
11. Assist others in interpreting and using the evaluative information

While advisory committees will not be engaged in all of these tasks, they can provide guidance and direction for several of them.

Planning and orientation

The most difficult and time-consuming activity is the initial step of planning and orientation. At the outset, advisory committees can identify the major purpose(s) of the follow-up survey effort and review key questions they feel need to be answered. General advisory committees will view the purpose of the follow-up broadly, while program, occupational, or craft advisory committees will seek information specific to their program (e.g., auto mechanics). When program and general advisory committees are involved with follow-up surveys, their efforts must be coordinated.

Advisory committees at the planning stage need to consider several important reasons for conducting follow-up evaluations. Follow-up surveys of students and employers can determine mobility of students, can assess the competency of graduates for entering advanced education or training programs, or can identify current occupational openings and entry requirements in the community. Through review and discussion, the advisory committee can also assist school personnel in identifying, refining, and deciding on the priorities or purposes in the follow-up effort. Advisory committees can be particularly helpful at this stage because they usually represent the major audiences that will receive the survey report, therefore they represent and can reflect the concerns of parents, the governing board, employers, teachers, counselors, students, and others.

Once the committee identifies the major purposes, it should draft key questions for each purpose. If one of the purposes of the follow-up is to determine the adequacy of the occupational education program in preparing for job entry, the following key questions might be appropriate: (1) How many students entered occupations for which they were trained? (2) To what extent was the instructional content consistent with job requirements? (3) What do former students feel were the major strengths and weaknesses of the program? Advisory committees should be involved in refining questions of this type and in reviewing the final instruments to be distributed to former students and employers, thereby insuring that major viewpoint differences are resolved and that the follow-up survey addresses the major concerns of the audiences that will eventually use the information.

Collecting information

Once the survey documents are prepared and the specific target audience of students or employers is identified, the next task is to conduct the survey. The advisory committee can expedite the collecting of survey information by having the chairperson of the committee prepare and sign the cover letter for a survey to be mailed to local employers, by having reviewed the plans for conducting the surveys with local chambers of commerce and trade associations ahead of time to solicit their input and support for the survey, and by telephoning employers to arrange for personal survey interviews.

If they have had proper training ahead of time, advisory committee members can conduct follow-up interviews with employers, supervisors, former students, or parents. Educational directors have noted that this experience gives committee members an excellent feel for the program.

Reviewing and analyzing information

Prior to the development of a follow-up report, advisory committees should have an opportunity to review the tabulated data and information.

Their insights relative to local employment trends and situations can explain and clarify the findings. Let's take a situation in which a group of former students who are employed by a large industrial firm all rated their initial introduction to labor organizations as "poor." An advisory committee member from that particular firm might offer the recent major changes in union membership requirements and increased union fees as an explanation for the former students' responses. Advisory committees can also offer suggestions for conclusions and recommendations to be included in the report. Once a preliminary report is drafted, the advisory committee can suggest refinements and appropriate language for specific sections.

Reporting and utilizing the outcomes

Once the final report is formulated, the advisory committee members should help to see that the appropriate boards and persons adopt the recommendations. Committee members, including school staff, should present the report to whichever group(s) the findings and recommendations are aimed. They could send a copy of the report to parents, local trade associations, and cooperating employers, or they could present the report orally to a school board or board of trustees. The nature and focus of the recommendations will determine who should receive the most attention from the committee. If the report suggests that major changes in curriculum are needed, then the committee should work closely with the instructional staff in making the necessary course revisions. If the report suggests new pieces of equipment are needed, then the committee's effort will be spent with local directors, governing boards, or employers to provide whatever additional information is needed to insure that the equipment is purchased or donated.

IMPLEMENTATION STRATEGIES

The following sections provide some ideas as to how the advisory committee might assist in the implementation of student and employer follow-up surveys. In most cases the examples are appropriate for program or craft advisory committees because most follow-up studies are organized to provide input for modifying and improving specific programs. Detailed strategies for using the data and recommendations from follow-up studies are also presented.

Student follow-up surveys

The essential purpose of the student follow-up survey is to ascertain from former students the strengths and weaknesses of the program. Students who have completed a program or who have dropped out or transferred to other programs can provide useful information regarding their feelings about the educational or training experience and about their transition to employment or further education. This information can be enormously helpful in redirecting, refining, and improving specific programs and services. Student follow-up surveys can be conducted by mail, telephone, or personal interview. The method selected will depend on the number of students to be contacted, the funds available for the survey, the amount of time allotted for completion of the survey. However, in most instances the mail survey is the most viable technique [172].

Student follow-up surveys have been used to collect a wide variety of information. Obviously, the type and extent of information collected will depend upon the purpose of the survey. In developing a statewide follow-up system for monitoring Illinois vocational program graduates, Felstehausen [54] suggests that the following information be included:

1. *Employment status* of respondents at the time of the survey. Knowing something of the status of former students will enable vocational educators to plan for better preparation of students for their early post-high school experiences. Supply data for occupational education program planning can be obtained from the percentage of respondents who were found:
   - in the labor force only
   - in the labor force and in school
   - unemployed
   - not available to the labor force

2. *Reason for part-time employment* was asked of respondents who had part-time jobs only. Implications for educational planning, placement, and guidance services can be drawn if students report they were unable to find other employment.

3. *Length of time required to find first job after leaving school* provides an indication of program strength.

4. *Reason for any job change(s) since leaving school* allows educators to profile the job retention rate. Non-personal reasons may indicate program weakness.

5. *Reasons for not obtaining a job since leaving school may* differentiate between factors within or beyond the control of local programming.

6. *Job title* is needed to determine whether or not employment was related to training.

7. *Satisfaction with present position* is asked so that both student career choice and program relatedness can be considered in assessing program effectiveness.

8. *Satisfaction with various job aspects.*

9. *Assessment of educational program* solicits feedback to educators. Items might ask:
   - Reason for choice of program
   - Helpful sources of career guidance
   - Suggestions for improving school
   - Assessment of program as preparation for current job

10. *Identification of job adjustment difficulties* could provide useful data for improving pre-employment preparation activities.

11. *Identification of continued education activities of former students* helps to evaluate academic programs and identify the types of goals for which students prepare. Items might be included to identify:

- type of school
- type of degree sought, if any
- major field of study
- assessment of program as preparation for present studies

The Kentucky Advisory Committee Evaluation System [105] uses a detailed interview guide for conducting interviews with vocational program graduates. Members of local craft committees conduct in-depth interviews with graduates for the purpose of collecting information and recommending program improvements. As shown in Figure 7–1, questions have been grouped under eight different headings.

In planning a survey, it is helpful to be familiar with the most recent follow-up efforts of the district, as well as with districtwide or statewide follow-up surveys that are conducted regularly. Another means of determining appropriate questions for a follow-up survey is to review other follow-up instruments. Surveys can be formulated to place emphasis on the student's perceptions of various program components. Figure 7–2 below presents a follow-up survey that was developed by the Career Placement Center staff of Triton College in River Grove, Illinois [17].

The actual conduct of a follow-up survey involves a number of specific planning considerations. For example, teachers and administrators must select the sample, locate current addresses, handle reproduction of the material and mailing, and schedule follow-up contacts to insure that a reasonable percentage of the surveys is returned. Consult the references at the end of the chapter for specific information regarding these and other management tasks.

Employer follow-up surveys

Employers who have hired former students can provide a considerable amount of evaluative information concerning these students and the training they received. Wentling [173] notes that employer surveys can be used to evaluate the performance capabilities of the students that have been hired, offer reactions to competency lists, identify instructional areas needing more attention, estimate local occupational supply and demand, provide comparisons of the capabilities of students from different local programs, and identify employer recruitment procedures. When employers or supervisors are contacted, they can provide a number of specific inputs that support program evaluation and improvement efforts. The following are useful, potential employer inputs:

1. Employer satisfaction with the employee's training and level of competency demonstrated.
2. Employer reaction to areas of competency that need to be strengthened.

FIGURE 7-1. Questions for interviewing vocational education program graduates

A. *Occupational Orientation and Exploration*

1. In what ways does your present job not meet the expectations you had when you were a student with respect to salary? working conditions? employment opportunities? day-to-day routine? opportunity for advancement? other expectations?

2. If you had it to do over, would you have entered this occupation?

3. What parts of your school work do you feel have best prepared you for your present job? (Ask the graduate to name particular courses, work experience opportunities, etc.)

4. What areas of your job do you wish your school work had covered in more detail? in less detail?

5. In what areas of your job did you feel you had out-of-date or inaccurate information when you started working?

6. Overall, how do you think your education could have better prepared you for your current job?

7. If you had it to do over, would you have enrolled in this vocational program and taken the courses you did?

E. *On-the-Job Performance*

8. What parts of your job do you feel the least comfortable doing?

9. What parts of your job do you feel you are the best at?

I. *Locating Employment*

10. How did you go about looking for a job?

11. What problems did you have looking for a job?

12. What could your school have done to better help you to find a job?

J. *Maintaining Employment*

13. Have you had the same job since you graduated? (If not, ask the student to describe why he left the job.)

14. Have any of the students in your graduating class quit their jobs voluntarily? Why do you think they quit their jobs?

15. Have any of the students in your graduating class been fired? Why do you think this happened?

K. *Interpersonal Relations with Supervisors, Co-workers, and Customers*

16. What problems have you experienced, if any, in getting along with other people you work with? For example: problems with your boss? problems with your co-workers? problems with customers?

L. *Work Habits and Attitudes*

17. Do you enjoy your job? What do you enjoy most about it? What do you enjoy least about it?

18. If you had to be absent from work for personal reasons, what would you tell your boss?

19. If your boss asks you to do something that you don't completely understand and then leaves, what would you do to learn more about the task?

20. If you make a mistake on the job that you know your boss will be very upset about, what would you do?

21. If you think of a better way to perform one of your job tasks than what your boss suggests, what would you do?

22. What would you do if one of your co-workers is taking goods from work without permission?

23. Do you think that your vocational program helped you to develop good work habits, such as responsibility? dependability? pride of craftsmanship? willingness to continue to learn new things? following safety rules? using time efficiently? How could your vocational program have helped you more in these areas?

N. *Reading, Communication, and Math*

24. Do any of your skills in reading, math, or communication need to be improved in order for you to perform your job? If yes, what skills?

O. *Continuing Career Development after Employment*

25. Have you participated in any further job training since you started working? If yes, what type?

26. Have you received any promotions or salary raises since you started working? What future opportunities for advancement do you have in this field?

27. In what related jobs do you feel qualified to seek employment if you could no longer work in this occupation?

National Center for Research in Vocational Education. *Kentucky Advisory Committee Evaluation System.* Columbus: The Ohio State University, 1976.

FIGURE 7-2. Former student career survey

NAME_____

ADDRESS_____

CITY_____ STATE_____ ZIP_____

```
┌─────────────────────────────────────┐
│                                     │
│                                     │
│        (attach mailing label)        │          *Make any corrections above.*
│                                     │
│                                     │
└─────────────────────────────────────┘
```

SINCE ATTENDING TRITON COLLEGE, WHAT IS YOUR CURRENT EMPLOYMENT STATUS?
(Check only one)

_____ Working full time in an occupation directly related to my college program. (*Directly related refers to the specific occupational category for which your program was designed to provide training*)

_____ Working full time in an occupation closely related to my college program. (*Check only if the skills you have used from this course are essential for satisfactory performance of the "closely related" job*)

_____ Working full time in an area different from my college training.

_____ Working part time (*Less than 30 hours/week*)

_____ Not employed but looking for a job.

_____ Not employed and uncertain about the type of job for which I should apply.

_____ Not available for employment.

_____ Other (*Please explain*) _____

IF YOU ARE NOT AVAILABLE FOR EMPLOYMENT PLEASE EXPLAIN WHY:

_____ Health _____ Personal reasons _____ Military service _____ Other

_____ Continuing education: School _____ Major _____

_____ Took the course for personal enrichment or recreational purpose

_____ Unwilling to move to a new locality to take available job

Details: (*Optional*)_____

DOES YOUR PRESENT STATUS REPRESENT WHAT YOU WANT TO BE DOING AT THIS TIME IN YOUR CAREER?

_____ Yes _____ No Comments_____

IF YOUR ARE EMPLOYED, PLEASE COMPLETE THE FOLLOWING:

Employer's Name _____

Address_____
　　　　　　　Street　　　　　　　　　　　　　　City　　　　　　　　　Zip

Job Title _____

Job duties or activities _____

Salary or wage before deduction (*Mark only one*)

$ Per Month: _____ Under $400 _____ $401–600 _____ $601–800 _____ over $800

$ Per Hour: _____ Under $2.50 _____ $2.51–$3.50 _____ $3.51–$4.50 _____ over $4.50

IF YOU WITHDREW OR LEFT THE COLLEGE BEFORE COMPLETING CERTIFICATE OR DEGREE REQUIREMENTS, PLEASE INDICATE THE REASONS: (*Check as many as apply*)

_____ Found employment
_____ Family problems
_____ Travel
_____ Financial
_____ Marriage

_____ Illness
_____ School schedule
_____ Completed enough courses to meet own objectives
_____ Program quality

_____ Instructor quality
_____ Entered military service
_____ Other (*Specify*) _____
_____

IF YOU ARE EMPLOYED, PLEASE INDICATE THE SOURCE WHICH AIDED YOU MOST IN GETTING YOUR JOB:

_____ Financial Aids & Placement Office
_____ Instructor
_____ Counselor
_____ Other college source

(*Specify*) _____

_____ State employment service
_____ Private employment agency
_____ Newspaper want ads
_____ Friends/relatives

_____ Other (*Specify*) _____

PLEASE INDICATE IF ANY OF THE FOLLOWING WOULD HAVE IMPROVED YOUR EDUCATION AT TRITON:

_____ More career & job information
_____ More personal or academic counseling
_____ More counseling about career plans
_____ More information about further education

_____ More help on how to get a job
_____ Better information on college placement services
_____ All programs satisfactory

Comments: _____

ARE YOU IN NEED OF CAREER COUNSELING OR JOB PLACEMENT ASSISTANCE NOW?

_____ Yes   _____ No

BEFORE OR DURING YOUR ATTENDANCE AT TRITON COLLEGE, WERE YOU EMPLOYED IN A FIELD THAT RELATED TO YOUR COLLEGE PROGRAM?   _____ Yes   _____ No

PLEASE EVALUATE THE FOLLOWING ASPECTS OF YOUR EDUCATION AT TRITON BY CHECKING THE APPROPRIATE BOX:

	Excellent	Good	Fair	Poor	Unable to observe
Quality of instruction					
Course content					
Counseling services					
Job placement services					

PLEASE COMMENT ON HOW YOU FEEL TRITON'S EDUCATIONAL PROGRAMS OR CAREER SERVICES COULD BE IMPROVED: _____

_____

_____

_____

THANK YOU FOR YOUR COOPERATION

Connye M. Barrow et al. *Career Assistance and Placement Services Resource Manual, Report— Contract Number RDC-A5-225.* Springfield, Illinois: Department of Adult, Vocational and Technical Education. July 1976. Used with permission.

3. Employer suggestions for training specializations that will be needed in light of technological advancements.
4. Employer observations regarding level of initial employment and advancement rate of program graduates as compared with other employees.
5. Employer suggestions for overall program improvements.

The employer survey serves the secondary purpose of improving community public relations. Most employers view the follow-up survey as an excellent opportunity to offer suggestions for improving educational programs and thereby providing a more adequately prepared prospective employee. Because the survey serves this critical function, employer surveys should be coordinated, well planned, concise, and require only a minimal amount of time to complete. The employer survey can be conducted by mail, telephone, or personal interview. In most instances, the mail questionnaire is the most cost efficient and feasible.

The Kentucky Advisory Committee Evaluation System uses interviews with employers to identify information in such areas as relevance of course offerings to job opportunities available; performance of job skills, co-op work experiences, work habits, and attitudes; and reading, communication, and math skills. In all, members of craft committees solicit follow-up information from employers in thirteen specific areas [105]. Figure 7-3 lists the questions that are commonly posed for employers.

Existing employer follow-up surveys can also provide potential questions and areas of concern. In most situations an existing employer follow-up survey can be revised to meet specific information needs. Figure 7-4 is an example of a survey form developed by the Illinois Follow-up System [55]. It asks the employer or supervisor to rate the former student on a number of factors, including preparedness for employment, suitability for the job held, and personal qualities.

One shortcoming of locally directed evaluation activities is that the results often are not appropriately disseminated and the necessary follow-up action is not taken. As the evaluation effort nears completion and some tentative recommendations are formulated, the advisory committee should begin to develop strategies for disseminating their recommendations. This last step in the process is often difficult to complete. However, to meet its full obligation in the evaluation function, advisory committees should engage in several activities that insure that the results of surveys and other types of evaluations are appropriately utilized.

An evaluation committee meeting. An important initial strategy involves devoting committee meetings, usually one near the end of the school year, to evaluation concerns. Borgen and Davis [22] suggest that such a meeting focus on reviewing and integrating all evaluation findings for the year, including evaluations of the program functions and of student and employer follow-up data. Figure 7-5 presents a sample agenda for an advisory committee meeting that includes a review of graduate and employer follow-up surveys, student evaluations, facility evaluations, ancillary

FIGURE 7-3. Questions for interviewing employers

B. *Relevance of Course Content to Current Job Practices*

   1. In what areas of their jobs do students tend to be poorly informed when they start working?

   2. Would you recommend any additional topics which should be taught to students preparing for this occupation?

   3. In what areas of their jobs do students tend to know the most about when they start working?

   4. Do you feel that students are taught any subjects in their vocational program that they don't need on the job?

C. *Up-to-date Equipment*

   5. From your experience, what equipment or technology used in this occupation are students typically unfamiliar with when they begin working?

D. *Relevance of Course Offering to Job Opportunities Available*

   6. For which jobs does your firm have the most difficulty in recruiting qualified employees?

   7. For which jobs does your firm have too many applicants?

   8. What training programs would you recommend limiting the enrollment in or dropping all together because employment opportunities are scarce?

   9. What are your recommendations for improving the coordination between your firm and vocational education for better developing employees to meet your manpower needs?

E. *Performance of Job Skills*

   10. In your candid estimation, what percent of the vocational students graduating from this program are in each of the following categories: (Read all the categories one time then ask the employer to estimate the percentage of students which fall into each.)

       a. Low proficiency in job entry skills
       b. Below average proficiency in job entry skills
       c. Average proficiency in job entry skills
       d. Above average proficiency in job entry skills
       e. High proficiency in job entry skills

F. *Laboratory and Cooperative Work Experience Opportunities*

   11. Do you think that vocational students receive enough practice of their job skills in real or laboratory work settings before they graduate?

   12. Have you employed work-study students? (students who work part time and attend school part time)

   13. What problems, if any, have you experienced in employing work-study students?

   14. How could the vocational school assist you in:

       a. Providing part-time jobs for more students?
       b. Providing a greater variety of part-time jobs for students?

   15. What recommendations do you have for improving the work-study program?

G. *Equal Education Opportunities*

   16. How could vocational education programs better help you fill affirmative action requirements?

   17. How could vocational education programs improve the chances of people with handicaps in finding and maintaining employment with your company? For example:

       a. Individuals with physical handicaps?
       b. Individuals with mental handicaps?
       c. Individuals with limited English-speaking ability?
       d. Males and females in non-traditional occupations?
       e. Others?

I. *Locating Employment*

   18. How do you usually obtain applicants to fill jobs? Would you like to see these sources changed or expanded in any way?

   19. What are your main reasons for rejecting an applicant after the initial interview?

   20. Once a choice of applicants has narrowed to a final few, what is the primary reason for hiring one applicant over another?

   21. What are the major areas of improvement needed by job applicants?

J. *Maintaining Employment*

22. What is (are) the primary reason(s) your firm terminates employees (excluding resignations and RIF's)?

K. *Interpersonal Relations with Supervisors, Co-workers, and Customers*

23. What are the major areas of improvement needed by your employees from vocational programs in interpersonal relationships with supervisors? co-workers? customers?

L. *Work Habits and Attitudes*

24. What are the major areas of improvement needed by your employees from vocational programs in their work habits—for example: dependability and follow-through? efficient time utilization? responsibility and initiative? safety precautions? neatness and pride of craftsmanship? use of instructions? What recommendations do you have for improving the school's role in developing students' work habits?

25. What improvements are needed in attitudes toward work held by your employees from vocational programs?

M. *Personal Habits*

26. What improvements are needed in the personal habits of your employees from vocational programs? For example: social behavior? dress? money management?

N. *Reading and Communication and Math*

27. Do your employees from vocational programs typically have adequate reading, communication and computation skills to do their jobs? If not, in what areas do skills need to be improved?

O. *Continuing Career Development after Employment*

28. Are your employees from vocational programs typically able and motivated to change and advance in their jobs? For example: are they willing to learn new job skills? Are they able to transfer skills from one job to a related job?

National Center for Research in Vocational Education. *Kentucky Advisory Committee Evaluation System.* Columbus: The Ohio State University, 1976, pp. 17–19.

FIGURE 7–4. Evaluation of employee's high school preparation for employment

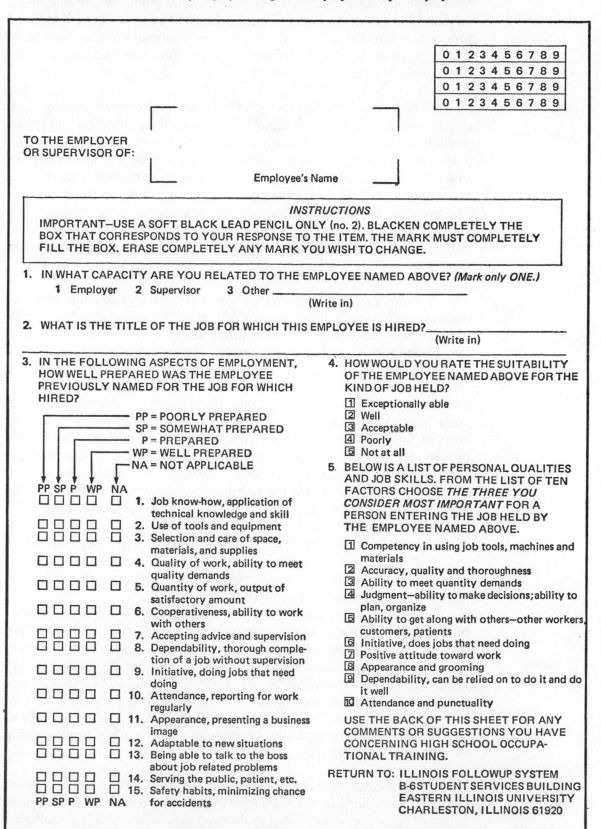

| 0 1 2 3 4 5 6 7 8 9 |
| 0 1 2 3 4 5 6 7 8 9 |
| 0 1 2 3 4 5 6 7 8 9 |
| 0 1 2 3 4 5 6 7 8 9 |

TO THE EMPLOYER
OR SUPERVISOR OF:

Employee's Name

INSTRUCTIONS

IMPORTANT—USE A SOFT BLACK LEAD PENCIL ONLY (no. 2). BLACKEN COMPLETELY THE
BOX THAT CORRESPONDS TO YOUR RESPONSE TO THE ITEM. THE MARK MUST COMPLETELY
FILL THE BOX. ERASE COMPLETELY ANY MARK YOU WISH TO CHANGE.

1. IN WHAT CAPACITY ARE YOU RELATED TO THE EMPLOYEE NAMED ABOVE? *(Mark only ONE.)*

1 Employer   2 Supervisor   3 Other _____

(Write in)

2. WHAT IS THE TITLE OF THE JOB FOR WHICH THIS EMPLOYEE IS HIRED? _____

(Write in)

3. IN THE FOLLOWING ASPECTS OF EMPLOYMENT, HOW WELL PREPARED WAS THE EMPLOYEE PREVIOUSLY NAMED FOR THE JOB FOR WHICH HIRED?

PP = POORLY PREPARED
SP = SOMEWHAT PREPARED
P = PREPARED
WP = WELL PREPARED
NA = NOT APPLICABLE

PP SP P WP NA

1. Job know-how, application of technical knowledge and skill
2. Use of tools and equipment
3. Selection and care of space, materials, and supplies
4. Quality of work, ability to meet quality demands
5. Quantity of work, output of satisfactory amount
6. Cooperativeness, ability to work with others
7. Accepting advice and supervision
8. Dependability, thorough completion of a job without supervision
9. Initiative, doing jobs that need doing
10. Attendance, reporting for work regularly
11. Appearance, presenting a business image
12. Adaptable to new situations
13. Being able to talk to the boss about job related problems
14. Serving the public, patient, etc.
15. Safety habits, minimizing chance for accidents

PP SP P WP NA

4. HOW WOULD YOU RATE THE SUITABILITY OF THE EMPLOYEE NAMED ABOVE FOR THE KIND OF JOB HELD?

1 Exceptionally able
2 Well
3 Acceptable
4 Poorly
5 Not at all

5. BELOW IS A LIST OF PERSONAL QUALITIES AND JOB SKILLS. FROM THE LIST OF TEN FACTORS CHOOSE *THE THREE YOU CONSIDER MOST IMPORTANT* FOR A PERSON ENTERING THE JOB HELD BY THE EMPLOYEE NAMED ABOVE.

1 Competency in using job tools, machines and materials
2 Accuracy, quality and thoroughness
3 Ability to meet quantity demands
4 Judgment—ability to make decisions; ability to plan, organize
5 Ability to get along with others—other workers, customers, patients
6 Initiative, does jobs that need doing
7 Positive attitude toward work
8 Appearance and grooming
9 Dependability, can be relied on to do it and do it well
10 Attendance and punctuality

USE THE BACK OF THIS SHEET FOR ANY
COMMENTS OR SUGGESTIONS YOU HAVE
CONCERNING HIGH SCHOOL OCCUPA-
TIONAL TRAINING.

RETURN TO: ILLINOIS FOLLOWUP SYSTEM
B-6 STUDENT SERVICES BUILDING
EASTERN ILLINOIS UNIVERSITY
CHARLESTON, ILLINOIS 61920

Joyce L. Felstchausen and Genie O. Lenihan. *Followup Report on Illinois "Class of '73" Occupational Program Alumni.* Charleston: Center for Educational Studies, Eastern Illinois University,
1974.

service evaluations, and cost/benefit evaluations. Evaluations of curriculum, community resource utilization, career guidance and placement services, and public relations efforts could also be included. An additional function might be to have the committee conduct a self-evaluation of their operations and efforts. Chapter 13 provides some useful ideas and forms for committee self-assessment.

Stating recommendations. The accurate and concise statement of conclusions and recommendations is critical to their adoption and implementation. The committee has to summarize the information from employer and student surveys and other sources, and then it must interpret this data. The committee must also take care, on important issues such as course revision, to validate the need for changes from different sources. For example, if a sizable number of former students, employers, and advisory committee members all suggest a need for a unit on tape-controlled milling in the machine tool program, the potential recommendation should deserve more attention than if it is mentioned by only one or two local employers.

A number of evaluation report forms are available to aid in structuring recommendations and suggested actions. Study each carefully prior to use. The Kentucky Advisory Committee Evaluation System [105] uses two basic forms to communicate results. Figure 7–6 is a program profile that evaluates local vocational programs across fifteen different areas. Once the committee has reviewed all of the data from students, teachers, and employers for a given area, it rates the area for the extent of improvement needed. When the committee gives similar ratings to the remaining areas of the program, a profile of the entire program emerges. The graphic profile clearly identifies the strengths and weaknesses of the program.

The Kentucky system also uses a program recommendations form. For each program reviewed, the Kentucky system provides recommendations for strengthening the various elements of the program. Figure 7–7 presents a sample form that provides specific, implementable recommendations for improving three program areas—occupational orientation and exploration, laboratory and cooperative work-experience opportunities, and learner skills for locating employment. The strengths of the program are described as "commendations."

A third reporting format is the one developed by the Illinois Office of Education for use in both a statewide and a locally directed evaluation system for vocational education. Figure 7–8 presents a sample format from the Resources Utilized section of the *Composite Evaluation Report for Occupational Education in the State of Illinois* [74]. This format is particularly useful because it illustrates the logical development of recommendations and suggested solutions from data-based conclusions, and it charges specific personnel or agencies with the job of implementing specific suggested solutions.

Facilitating adoption of recommendations. To bring about the improvements outlined in the evaluation report, the committee should make copies of the report available to key decision-making and policy-establishing

FIGURE 7-5. Sample advisory committee agenda

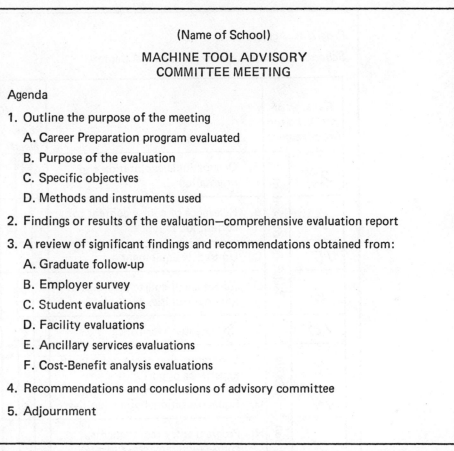

(Name of School)

MACHINE TOOL ADVISORY COMMITTEE MEETING

Agenda

1. Outline the purpose of the meeting
   A. Career Preparation program evaluated
   B. Purpose of the evaluation
   C. Specific objectives
   D. Methods and instruments used

2. Findings or results of the evaluation—comprehensive evaluation report

3. A review of significant findings and recommendations obtained from:
   A. Graduate follow-up
   B. Employer survey
   C. Student evaluations
   D. Facility evaluations
   E. Ancillary services evaluations
   F. Cost-Benefit analysis evaluations

4. Recommendations and conclusions of advisory committee

5. Adjournment

Joseph A. Borgen and Dwight E. Davis. *Planning, Implementing, and Evaluating Career Preparation Programs.* Bloomington, Ill.: McKnight Publishing Company, 1974, p. 463. Used with permission.

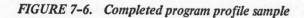

FIGURE 7-6. Completed program profile sample

Program: Agribusiness

School: Central Kentucky Vocational Center

Ranking of the Need for Improvement		*Evaluation Areas*	*Rating of the Need for Improvement*		
			Low Need	Medium Need	High Need
2	Relevance of Content	A. Occupational exploration and orientation			●
12		B. Relevance of course content to current job practices		●	
15		C. Up-to-date equipment	●		
6		D. Relevance of course offerings to job opportunities available		●	
13	Job Entry Skills	E. On-the-job performance		●	
10		F. Laboratory and cooperative work experience opportunities		●	
14		G. Equal educational opportunities	●		
7		H. Program entry requirements, course requirements, and student evaluation procedures		●	
1	Employability Skills	I. Locating employment			●
9		J. Maintaining employment		●	
11		K. Interpersonal and public relations with supervisors, co-workers, and customers		●	
3		L. Work habits and attitudes			●
8		M. Personal habits		●	
5		N. Reading, communication, and math skills		●	
4		O. Continuing career development after employment			●

FIGURE 7-7. *Completed program recommendations form sample*

Program: Practical Nursing

School: Blue Grass Vocational School

Recommendations

A. *Occupational Orientation and Exploration.* Many practical nursing students have an unrealistic view of their future career. They have limited knowledge about working conditions, typical daily routine, and opportunities for advancement. *Provide opportunities for every student in the program to spend time with a practical nurse while on the job.*

F. *Laboratory and Cooperative Work Experience Opportunities.* Teachers spend a large percentage of their time in lecture situations which leaves insufficient time for developing skills and techniques needed on the job. *Enable students to spend more time practicing job skills and less time listening to the teacher talk.*

I. *Locating Employment.* Employers indicated that a large number of students they had interviewed were not prepared for their initial job interview. Students do not know how to prepare a resume and were aware of only newspapers as a source to look for jobs. *Include topics on "how to apply for jobs" and "job interview techniques" for practical nursing students.*

Commendations

L. *Work Habits and Attitudes.* Graduates of the program showed highly positive attitudes toward their jobs and exceptional integrity in solving job related problems. The program should be commended for helping students develop highly positive work habits and attitudes.

O. *Continuing Career Development after Employment.* The program maintains contact with graduates through bi-monthly problem-solving seminars. These appear to be highly successful.

D. *Relevance of Course Offerings to Available Job Opportunities.* Over 95 percent of the graduates of the program have been placed in jobs related to their training. The program appears to be meeting job market demands very well.

National Center for Research in Vocational Education. *Kentucky Advisory Committee Evaluation System.* Columbus, The Ohio State University, 1976.

FIGURE 7–8. State of Illinois evaluation report format

RESOURCES UTILIZED

CONCLUSIONS	RECOMMENDATIONS	SUGGESTED SOLUTIONS
1. Ninety-one percent of the LEA's evaluated reported on the School and Community Data Form that they utilized citizens from their communities to serve on occupational advisory committees. (The Team Leader Questionnaire indicates that 67% of the LEA's involved community personnel to a limited degree or not at all in planning programs.)	1. LEA's should institute task oriented advisory committees for use in developing and maintaining occupational programs.	1. a. (DVTE) Reprint and send quantities of the publication *Advisory Council Member* to the directors of occupational programs in LEA's.
		b. (DVTE) Develop a short publication for LEA personnel who work with advisory committees on topic of "How to Orient Advisory Committees to the Identification and Accomplishment of Tasks."
		c. (DVTE) Publish samples of advisory committee meeting minutes which reflect a task-oriented approach to occupational education.
		d. (DVTE) Publish *Guidelines* on use of overall advisory committee vis-a-vis specific program advisory committees.
		e. (DVTE, U) Research effectiveness of overall advisory committee versus specific program advisory committee in LEA's of various sizes.
		f. (DVTE, U) Conduct a statewide survey to ascertain composition of advisory committees based on characteristics such as occupation, size of organization, etc.

2. A common shortcoming of LEA's as expressed in local evaluation reports was the limited use of external resources while conducting occupational courses. (The Team Leader Questionnaire indicates that over 78% of the LEA's utilized community resources to an average or low degree.

2. LEA's should greatly expand the utilization of community resources in the on-going occupational programs.

g. (LEA) Utilize DVTE Publication *Advisory Council Member* with local advisory committees.

h. (LEA) Integrate work of advisory committee with One and Five Year Plan objectives to insure task-oriented groups.

i. (LEA) Formulate and utilize Ad Hoc or subcommittees for advisory committees to work on specific tasks.

j. (LEA) Contact Rurban Education Development Lab—University of Illinois for resource materials.

k. (LEA) Utilize DVTE consultants.

2. a. (DVTE) Develop materials reflecting ways for LEA's to involve community resources in the occupational programs.

b. (DVTE) Through a research funded project, work with private and public agencies to identify sources to use in occupational courses. Make these sources available to LEA's

c. (DVTE) Sponsor comprehensive Regional Workshops for occupational educators on utilizing community resources (including Advisory Committees) in occupational classes.

d. (IOE, ICCB) Mobilize a public relations campaign aimed at private and public agencies encouraging them to offer their services in occupational classes.

Illinois Office of Education. *Composite Evaluation Report for Occupational Education in the State of Illinois, FY 1975.* Springfield: Illinois Office of Education, 1976.

personnel; namely, members of the school board or board of trustees; administrators; officers of local parent organizations; officers of local business, professional, and trade associations; officers of local unions; and other community and educational leaders. Obviously, to whom the report is disseminated will depend on the nature of the report and the volatility of the findings and recommendations. Once a dissemination plan is prepared, the committee should send copies of the report with a cover letter from the chairperson of the committee. The committee may conduct personal and public discussions of the report to urge the adoption of the major recommendations.

THE PROGRAM EVALUATION FUNCTION IN ACTION

The integral role an advisory committee plays in the planning and evaluation of programs can be exemplified by a recent evaluation of a summer program for economically disadvantaged youth in central Pennsylvania. For the past two summers the local prime sponsor conducted an eight-week summer program designed to provide disadvantaged youth with paid work experience, career exploration experiences, and career counseling and guidance services. Several advisory and supervisory committees from local agencies, including the local CETA planning council and the advisory committee of the area vocational school, suggested that the program be evaluated by an independent, third party. Individuals from a nearby community college, who had program evaluation experience, were contracted to conduct the evaluation.

The evaluators met with administrators and the advisory committees of the local prime sponsor, the vocational school, the intermediate school district, and two community agencies. In addition, several school superintendents and some parents were interviewed for input regarding the major evaluation questions to be addressed. Lists of evaluation questions for assessing the value and effectiveness of the program components (paid summer work experience, career exploration program, and career counseling services) were mailed back to each group for review and final reaction. Brief feedback forms were then developed for program supervisors, students, parents, program administrators. The forms contained some common questions relative to the objectives, effectiveness, and value of each of the program components.

The overall tone of the evaluation report was extremely positive. Data collected from students, parents, supervisors, and administrators consistently revealed a high degree of satisfaction with all aspects of the program. Several recommendations were offered for expanding the successful effort in order to serve more students and involve the private employment sector of the community. On the basis of the report, the program was expanded to serve an additional fifty students (an enrollment increase of 32 percent) during the following summer. Also, a number of additional supportive services were added to the program (e.g., purchase of an career exploration/assessment workbook series, expansion of counseling staff). Some of these services were supported by matching funds from the agencies who originally requested the evaluation.

COMMUNICATIONS EXERCISE

THE PROGRAM EVALUATION FUNCTION

The following communications exercise, by allowing you to apply your knowledge to a specific setting, can increase your understanding of the program evaluation function. This exercise was designed and field tested as a self-instructional or small-group activity that stresses the application of concepts and ideas presented in this chapter.

 THE FOLLOWING SECTION PROVIDES A BRIEF OVERVIEW OF A SPECIFIC SITUATION RELATED TO AN ADVISORY COMMITTEE. READ THIS SECTION COMPLETELY BEFORE PROCEEDING TO STEP 2.

Your advisory committee is a general advisory committee composed of the chairpersons of six occupational advisory committees. The program areas include agricultural mechanics, nurse's aides, food service staff, automotive mechanics, and office and distributive occupations personnel.

The six programs serve a total of 325 students in a comprehensive high school setting. The community population is 12,000, primarily composed of agricultural, agribusiness, and small industrial economic concerns.

It is the responsibility of your advisory committee to prepare a series of recommendations or suggestions for program improvement based on a program evaluation report recently completed by your committee. The first step is to determine a procedure for formulating the suggestions. From the following worksheet, select those statements that represent a logical and effective procedure for planning and implementing specific program recommendations.

STEP 2 — USING THE WORKSHEET BELOW, CHECK THE BOX(ES) REPRESENTING THE ITEM(S) THAT MOST APPROPRIATELY RESPOND(S) TO THE SITUATION DESCRIBED IN STEP 1.

Be sensitive to the political ramifications of recommendations. ___ 1	As chairperson, develop the report and submit it to the school board. ___ 2	Review several possible formats for presenting recommendations and commendations. ___ 3	Present recommendations or commendations for *all* programs and services evaluated. ___ 4
Appoint subcommittees to develop specific recommendation sections if necessary. ___ 5	As chairperson, be available to discuss the suggestions with decision-making groups. ___ 6	If necessary, hire consultants to supplement the initial program evaluation report information. ___ 7	Assess the validity of the program evaluation report data. ___ 8
Identify *who* will receive, review, and act on the recommendations. ___ 9	Collect additional evaluative data if necessary. ___ 10	Review the program goals. ___ 11	Present a preliminary draft of the report to key individuals for their review and reaction. ___ 12
Develop a goal-free program evaluation design. ___ 13	Include recommendations for support services (e.g., counseling) and occupational programs. ___ 14	Consider the final set of recommendations as school policy. ___ 15	Be sure that the final document is concise, accurate, and easy to interpret. ___ 16

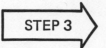

STEP 3   EVALUATE THE RESPONSES BY COMPARING
THE INDIVIDUAL RESPONSES WITH THOSE
RECOMMENDED BELOW. READ THE APPROPRIATE
COMMENTS AND CONTINUE ON TO STEP 4.

If you checked _____1, 8, 9, 11_____ , read Comment A.
If you checked __3, 4, 5, 7, 10, 14__ , read Comment B.
If you checked _____6, 12, 16_____ , read Comment C.
If you checked _____2, 13, 15_____ , read Comment D.

Comment A   These are excellent initial steps for planning the development of recommendations from a program evaluation report. Reports and evaluative recommendations, especially those that affect several occupational programs, can have extensive political ramifications (1). Recommendations should be focused on critical issues and offer reasonable alternatives for resolving the political dilemmas of administrators if they exist. The data on which recommendations are to be based must be recent and represent valid and accurate information (8). The specific audiences that will read and act on the recommendations should be identified early (9).

Comment B   Remember several logical and simple operational strategies. It helps to review other reports containing program recommendations in order to find a simple and concise format for communicating the information effectively (3). If necessary, you may want to appoint subcommittees to develop recommendations for specific occupational programs or services (5). To obtain a maximum use of the data collected, offer at least one recommendation or commendation for each program reviewed (4). Consultants may be hired to review (7) or supplement the existing data and information that is available (10). A comprehensive evaluation of a vocational education program should also include recommendations regarding key support services (such as career guidance, youth organizations, staff in-service training, placement services, remedial services as well as recommendations for individual occupational programs (14).

Comment C   The strategy for dissemination of the final report and recommendations is critical. These responses represent some key considerations. In addition to considering the political ramifications mentioned earlier, preliminary drafts should be made available to key individuals for their review (12). Specific reactions to proposed recommendations should be carefully discussed and analyzed relative to the data and other responses. Whenever possible, the chairperson or a representative of the committee should be available to assist other groups or individuals in accurately interpreting and using the information in the report (6).

Comment D   These responses are inappropriate considerations for this situation. A set of recommendations developed by one individual obviously circumvents the committee process and can hardly be considered as representing the views of a committee (2). A goal-free evaluation design might have been considered during the initial collection of data, but it has limited value in developing recommendations (13). As noted throughout the text, advisory committee are not intended to establish educational policy (15).

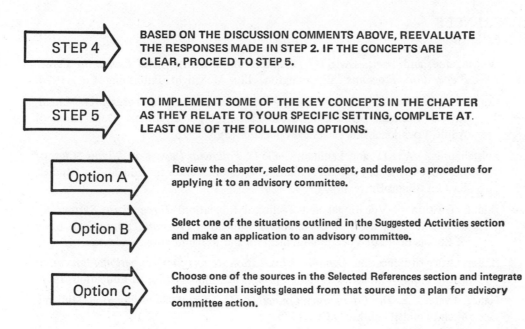

STEP 4 BASED ON THE DISCUSSION COMMENTS ABOVE, REEVALUATE THE RESPONSES MADE IN STEP 2. IF THE CONCEPTS ARE CLEAR, PROCEED TO STEP 5.

STEP 5 TO IMPLEMENT SOME OF THE KEY CONCEPTS IN THE CHAPTER AS THEY RELATE TO YOUR SPECIFIC SETTING, COMPLETE AT LEAST ONE OF THE FOLLOWING OPTIONS.

Option A Review the chapter, select one concept, and develop a procedure for applying it to an advisory committee.

Option B Select one of the situations outlined in the Suggested Activities section and make an application to an advisory committee.

Option C Choose one of the sources in the Selected References section and integrate the additional insights gleaned from that source into a plan for advisory committee action.

SUGGESTED ACTIVITIES

1. Contact your local director of occupational education to determine what program evaluation systems are used. Evaluate the role that advisory committees play in planning, conducting, and interpreting program evaluation information.

2. Obtain and review the following local leader guides for *Locally Directed Evaluation* (Illinois Office of Education, Department of Adult, Vocational and Technical Education, 100 North First Street, Springfield, Illinois 62777):

    No. 2: *Student Follow-up Survey*
    No. 3: *Employer Follow-up Survey*

3. Contact the executive director of your state's advisory council for vocational education and request any materials on program evaluation that they have prepared. Review and prepare a critique of the materials received.

4. Read the following chapters in *Evaluating Occupational Education and Training Pro-*

grams by Tim L. Wentling and Tom E. Lawson (Boston: Allyn and Bacon, 1975): Chapter 2: Designing an Evaluation System; Chapter 4: The Follow-up as an Evaluative Tool—The Student Follow-up; Chapter 5: The Follow-up as an Evaluative Tool—The Employer Follow-up; Chapter 9: Using Evaluation Results for Planning and Improvement.

5. Interview local occupational teachers and directors to discuss and obtain copies of instruments used in recent follow-up surveys. Analyze the commonalities and differences in information requested. Identify the purposes for the follow-up study.

6. Attend an advisory committee meeting and determine how much of the discussion is evaluative and how much informational in nature. Briefly describe how the committee's evaluative discussions might be further formalized and data based (if necessary).

7. Obtain a copy of a follow-up survey report. Study the report in detail and develop a dissemination plan. Your plan should lay out the most effective strategies for getting the recommendations fully implemented.

8. Participate as a team member in an advisory committee evaluation. Once the evaluation is completed, prepare a brief analysis of the committee's interactions during the planning of the evaluation. Offer some recommendations to the chairperson for improving this aspect of the evaluation process.

SELECTED REFERENCES

Borgen, Joe, and Davis, Dwight E. *Planning, Implementing, and Evaluating Career Preparation Programs.* Bloomington, Ill.: McKnight Publishing Co., 1974.

Connye M. Barrow et al. *Career Assistance and Placement Services Resource Manual, Report*—Contract Number RDC-A5-225. Springfield, Illinois: Department of Adult, Vocational and Technical Education, July 1976.

Felstehausen, Joyce L., and Lenihan, Genie O. *Followup Report on Illinois "Class of '73" Occupational Program Alumni.* Charleston: Center for Educational Studies, Eastern Illinois University, 1974.

Illinois Division of Vocational and Technical Education. *Three Phase System for Statewide Evaluation of Occupational Education Programs.* Springfield: State of Illinois Board of Vocational Education and Rehabilitation, undated.

Illinois Office of Education. *Composite Evaluation Report for Occupational Education in the State of Illinois, FY 1975.* Springfield: Illinois Office of Education, 1976.

Nance, Everette E. *The Community Council: Its Organization and Function.* Midland, Mich.: Pendell Publishing Co., 1975.

National Center for Research in Vocational Education. *Kentucky Advisory Committee Evaluation System.* Columbus: The Ohio State University, 1976.

U.S. Congress, Public Law 94-482, *Education Amendments of 1976* "Title II, Vocational Education." Washington, D.C.: Government Printing Office, 1976.

Wentling, Tim L. *Locally Directed Evaluation Guide 2: Student Follow-up Survey.* Springfield: Illinois Office of Education, 1976.

Wentling, Tim L. *Locally Directed Evaluation Guide 3: Employer Follow-up Survey.* Springfield: Illinois Office of Education, 1976.

Wentling, Tim L. and Lawson, Tom E. *Evaluating Occupational Education and Training Programs.* Boston: Allyn and Bacon, Inc., 1975.

8 The community public relations function

Community public relations has been viewed historically as a secondary role of the advisory committee. With declining enrollments and increasing operational costs, the public image of occupational and career education programs has become an extremely critical factor in program management. The public image of, in particular, occupational education programs has been affected by rapid growth and development over the past fifty years. Occupational education programs are now serving more than 15 million youths and adults. Over 40 percent of the high school students now enroll in at least one vocational course, when a few years ago the figure was less than 20 percent. With these changes the field has encountered new audiences both inside and outside the school that are unfamiliar with the role, organization, and missions of occupational and career education. Thus it becomes extremely important that educators and advisory committees be actively and continuously involved in enhancing the public's awareness of occupational and career education.

One of the major problems plaguing the field of educational public relations has been a lack of responsibility for action. Every group, including administrators, teachers, and school boards, agrees that effective communication with the general public is vital. However, each group tends to view public relations as the responsibility of someone else within the organization. Advisory committees are in a unique position to accept a leadership role in the community public relations function. By the nature of their role and composition, the advisory committee itself serves as a strong communications link between vocational education and the community. The advisory committee must stimulate an open and responsive dialogue between the educational institution and the community. The opinions and observations of advisory committee members are frequently highly regarded by other employers and community representatives because of their closeness to the educational program. Therefore the credibility of advisory committee members increases the impact of public relations efforts made by vocational educators.

To make the community public relations effort more effective, a major commitment of time and resources is required from the advisory committee. However, a needs assessment study of advisory committees in Michigan revealed that advisory committees are involved in only a limited way in efforts such as developing formal public relations plans, speaking to civic groups, or appearing in the local news media to discuss vocational education. The data reported by advisory committee members, administrators, teachers, and school board members suggest that

> Only 10 to 15 percent of the advisory committees represented were involved in community public relations activities. [38:43]
>
> Thirty-four percent of the responding school superintendents and board members felt their advisory committees were either ineffective or only slightly effective in their public relations activities. [38:45]

While Michigan may not be representative of the nation, it is apparent that much more needs to be done to stimulate advisory committees to engage in effective community public relations activities.

SCOPE OF COMMUNITY PUBLIC RELATIONS

A wide range of audiences and activities is critical to public relations efforts in occupational and career education programs. The advisory committee can engage in a number of activities related to planning and implementing a total public relations program. The scope of this public relations program can encompass some of the functions described in Chapters 3 through 9 (i.e., curriculum revision and updating, development of career guidance and placement services, facilities and equipment modification, program evaluation, and professional development activities). Each of these functions has a public relations and information component that needs to be examined. A comprehensive public relations program is built on a communications system that includes exchanging information with internal as well as external audiences.

Communicating with internal audiences

As noted earlier, often the weakest link in a public communications system is the lack of communication among faculty, staff, and students within the institution. A lack of consistent and complete understanding of the school's goals, programs, services, and future plans on the part of students, teachers, and administrators creates a communication problem. Encouraging frequent and meaningful communication between internal audiences is the essential first step to overcome this problem. An internal audience can be defined as any individual that has close, current involvement with the program(s) in question. For occupational and career education programs several groups might be described as internal audiences, such as students, teachers, administrators, guidance counselors, local and state school boards, advisory committees, student organizations, and state agencies [11]. The advisory committee can aid in identifying internal audiences and their information needs.

Communicating with external audiences

The primary attention and effort of public relations activities in occupational education is to disseminate information to such external audiences as the business community, parents, prospective students, and labor unions. Increased concern for communication with these groups has grown, in part, from the accountability movement. If schools are to be held accountable for the effectiveness of their programs in meeting learner and community needs, then they must have data-based and comprehensive public information systems. The effectiveness of these systems is especially important during periods of financial crisis. If the public is being asked to provide more funds for education, it deserves to know why additional funds are justified. An effective communications system is the only means for providing such justification.

The advisory committee can assist in developing an inventory or directory of all key external audiences within the community. Such external groups might include potential students; parents; government officials; civic, professional, church, and other community-based groups; leaders in labor, industry, and business; mass media (newspapers, radio, television); senior citizens groups; and the general taxpaying public.

COMMUNITY PUBLIC RELATIONS ACTIVITIES

In addition to the committee itself serving as a vehicle for sound public relations, it can directly promote occupational and career education programs by undertaking the four following types of activities: helping educators in planning, facilitating, conducting, and evaluating public relations efforts.

Planning activities

Initially the advisory committee should be briefed regarding the program's current public relations activities. The public relations plan should include

• The identification of internal and external audiences needing information about the program on a continuing basis

• A description of the type of information needed by each audience

- A list of current or potential problems that can be solved with improved public relations efforts
- A list or public relations goals and objectives for the coming year
- Specific activities and schedules for reaching these goals and objectives
- Evaluation procedures to assess the effectiveness of public relations activities and identify future problem areas

Facilitating activities

Facilitating can be described here as assisting educators informally to establish, maintain, or evaluate their public relations activities. In this role, advisory committee members can relay public opinion back to the staff, arrange publicity for appropriate activities (such as the local Skill Olympics student competitions), review and react to information brochures as they are being developed, or suggest new target audiences for public relations information (such as recently elected or appointed local officials).

Conducting activities

Advisory committee members can also be directly and integrally involved in the community public relations program. By virtue of their role on advisory committees they possess credibility in the eyes of the community at large, business, industry, labor organizations, and other external audiences. In addition, advisory committee members who are in managerial positions in businesses within the community usually have well-developed public relations skills (e.g., public speaking, preparation of advertising) that can be used to promote occupational and career education programs.

In the past, advisory committee members have conducted such public relations as making presentations to civic groups, providing interviews to local mass media regarding specific issues or program developments, developing promotional materials, and providing testimony at public or congressional hearings. Committee members, however, must not be overutilized. Remember that their basic responsibility is to advise educators as to program needs and directions. Providing advice and assistance relative to public relations is only one aspect of the total responsibility.

Evaluating activities

Advisory committee members can often provide substantive and candid evaluations of the program's image because they have been on the receiving end of public relations efforts. As employers, businesspersons, community agency representatives, or representatives of special groups such as ethnic minorities, advisory committee members can react to the public relations activities that are being planned or have been implemented.

When evaluating public relations efforts, the committee should consider the following essential questions: Is the public relations material (brochures, slide presentations, parent information packages) up-to-date? Have all of the appropriate audiences (target groups) been identified? How effective is the public information system in delivering a positive and complete description of the program to each target group? How can the public information system be improved? To what extent are internal groups (students, staff, administrators, advisory committees, school boards) working collectively and intensely in public relations efforts?

IMPLEMENTATION STRATEGIES

The success of a comprehensive public relations effort depends on the successful completion of a number of activities. This section will briefly describe activities that advisory committees have found to be highly productive in promoting community public relations.

Developing a public relations calendar

Initially, the advisory committee should assist school personnel with the planning of a public relations schedule for September through July. Long-range planning by the committee can coordinate important local community functions (such as trade shows) with promotional efforts for occupational and career education programs. Figure 8–1 presents a suggested public relations calendar that can serve as a model. Once developed and approved, the calendar should be distributed to all key personnel involved, including the local news media.

Reviewing news releases

In addition to suggesting topics for news releases, the advisory committee can be a valuable resource for reviewing and refining news releases. The lay members of the committee can eliminate educational jargon, react to the tone and level of the release, and offer suggestions for eliminating extraneous information as well as adding other important facts. School personnel should ask advisory committee members to review news releases on an individual rather than committee basis.

Public appearances

Advisory committee members are generally quite articulate and effective in public appearances on behalf of occupational and career education.

FIGURE 8-1. Suggested public relations calendar for vocational education programs

September Activities

Plan orientation program for new students and teachers.

Renew acquaintance with newspaper editors and reporters, radio and TV program managers. Send news releases on new equipment, program expansions, new projects.

Send materials explaining the program to parents of new students.

Complete plans for the student organization program for the year and publicize through newspapers and school paper.

Set up new advisory committees and plan schedule of meetings.

Participate in faculty workshop on public relations.

Begin planning for National Vocational Education Week (scheduled for February).

November Activities

Plan and conduct a radio or TV program explaining purposes, organization, and values of your program.

Prepare displays for public places to illustrate instructional content of your program.

Invite your state and federal legislators to visit and observe your program.

Plan bulletin board displays.

January Activities

Plan and conduct a student assembly program.

Publicize plans for adult vocational classes for second semester.

Participate and cooperate in career conferences.

Hold open house for the community.

Send articles about vocational education to trade papers and professional journals.

Speak to local service clubs, veterans organizations, etc., about values of vocational education.

Prepare newspaper articles on progress of vocational students.

March Activities

Provide information about vocational courses to students who may want to enter the program; make arrangements for tours of the department.

Send newsletter to graduates and former students.

Cooperate in planning exchange visits for teachers with industry, business, and labor groups.

Invite the superintendent to attend student organization meeting.

Work with school reporter on writing series of features about successful graduates of your program for local newspaper.

Collect occupational data and give to school guidance counselor.

Call photography class to take photos of your students in action.

May Activities

Make plans for participating and exhibiting at state and county fairs.

Contact local business, industry, employment agencies, etc., to help place graduates in suitable jobs.

Prepare annual reports.

Arrange for appropriate graduation ceremonies and publicity for graduates.

Hold banquet for parents or employers and show slides of year's activities.

Prepare exhibits of students' work for display in store window.

Evaluate results of year's public relations program.

July Activities

Attend summer school or workshop on public relations.

Attend state conferences.

Participate in county and state fairs.

Make plans for next year's public relations activities.

American Vocational Association. *Promoting Vocational Education: A Public Relations Handbook for Vocational Educators.* Washington, D.C.: American Vocational Association, 1978. Used with permission.

They have provided excellent presentations in different settings, from spot announcements for local radio and television stations to testimony before state legislatures regarding the need for additional funding. Advisory committee members might also make public appearances by being interviewed; by being a guest speaker at a civic, community, or professional association meeting; or by being a member of a discussion panel. The topics to be discussed by committee members in such public appearances vary extensively depending on the program, school district, or current issue being discussed. Topics can include, but are certainly not limited to, the need to support bond issues, the description of a successful student project or learning experience, the promotion of National Vocational Education Week, or the need to expand support services for handicapped and disadvantaged students.

The advisory committee should devote considerable time to planning the public appearances of its members. It should identify and discuss specific objectives and select the most appropriate medium or forum. Depending on the objectives of the specific presentation, the committee may decide to involve students, counselors, employers, or administrators to enhance the presentation.

Planning general program publicity

Public relations efforts can be strengthened considerably through the use of promotional materials. The common forms of program publicity include fact sheets, brochures, student recruitment packages, catalogs, displays, and slide/tape presentations. The advisory committee can assess the need for, plan, and review these materials. When specific materials are being considered, the advisory committee can provide input regarding the major themes, purposes, intended audiences, and alternative formats and strategies for field testing and distribution. Business leaders serving on advisory committees may be able to identify or contribute some professional publicity development expertise.

Sponsoring newletters

An effective internal communications system is critical to the overall community relations effort; therefore, students, staff, parents, and advisory committee members must be kept abreast of personnel changes, plans to implement new courses or programs, advisory committee activities, student organization activities, upcoming events such as local trade shows. An advisory committee can sponsor a regularly published newsletter as one means of improving and maintaining effective internal communications. Newsletters can also serve to recruit new students and advisory committee members and to maintain contact with program graduates.

Writing letters of appreciation

An important but frequently overlooked public relations strategy is sending letters of appreciation to individuals who have offered their assistance in an activity; for example, to donors of equipment, materials, and supplies; to individuals who have been directly involved in an instructional aspect of the program (such as a field trip or serving as a supervisor of co-op students); to students who have exhibited outstanding leadership or performance; to individuals who have spoken at open houses or other special events; or to elected officials who have supported a critical issue for occupational or career education. Letters of appreciation should sincerely express the appreciation of the advisory committee, students, and other individuals who were affected. The chairperson of the advisory committee and the course instructor are the most appropriate individuals to sign or cosign letters of appreciation. They should then send copies of the letter to the committee members and to other key personnel so that everyone is aware that the note of appreciation has been conveyed.

The advisory committee can also write letters of support in political situations. Letters to newspaper editors, elected government officials, and legislators can inform decision makers of current happenings in occupational and career education and can influence future legislation, funding appropriations, or state and federal regulations.

Reviewing public relations media

Reviewing draft versions of public relations material, such as brochures or film scripts, is an important task for the advisory committee. Because their views reflect the views of other employers, parents, labor groups, and students in the community, advisory committee members provide helpful suggestions prior to the final production of public relations materials. Advisory committees might evaluate descriptive brochures; slide/tape presentations; scripts for radio or television spots; and advertising for special events, posters, student recruitment packages.

Sponsoring tours and open houses

Throughout the year, sponsoring tours or open houses can be a very effective public relations activity. The advisory committee, along with the school staff, can assist in the planning and conducting of open houses and tours of educational facilities. Separate subcommittees can be formed to handle publicity, programs, decorations and refreshments, coordination, guest reception, and cleanup [107]. The overall planning committee should check scheduling to insure that the open house does not conflict with other school or major community events; design routes for tours throughout the building; serve as tour guides or recruit others to act as tour guides; coordinate displays, presentations, and demonstrations planned by instructional staff; and evaluate the effectiveness of the event once it is completed [11].

Promoting national theme weeks

National associations frequently sponsor theme weeks to focus attention on various programs. Each year, for instance, the American Vocational Association sponsors National Vocational Education Week during February. Theme weeks provide excellent public relations opportunities to create a renewed local awareness of occupational and career education programs. In conjunction with a national theme week, the advisory committee can sponsor spot radio or television announcements or newspaper stories, obtain proclamations from local or state officials (see Figure 8-2 for a sample), hold an open house, conduct a community forum on a current local issue affecting occupational or career education, or prepare displays for local businesses, industries, shopping malls, and other appropriate locations with the community.

THE COMMUNITY PUBLIC RELATIONS FUNCTION IN ACTION

In the early 1970s, the career education movement was discussed in many communities throughout the nation. The United States Commissioner of Education, Sidney P. Marland, introduced the concept in 1970. Many communities were excited by the concept and began massive public information efforts to acquaint their citizens with career education and its relevance to virtually all school programs.

One community in Arizona began with the local school board's

FIGURE 8–2. Sample format for proclamation-of-a-theme week

State of _____

MAYOR'S PROCLAMATION

WHEREAS,   The Congress of the United States and the State of _____ have recognized the growing and imperative need for Vocational Education and have provided broader concepts of vocational, career, and manpower education to prepare individuals for the world of work; and

WHEREAS,   Through the increased emphasis in reaching out to prepare individuals to enter employment, many new programs are now available to assist individuals in reaching their occupational goals; and

WHEREAS,   The American Vocational Association, by representative assembly, has established the second week of February as "Vocational Education Week" and is supported by (state) vocational groups in this endeavor; and

WHEREAS,   That week in February has been set aside by proclamation of the Governor of (state) as Vocational Education Week; and

WHEREAS,   The ultimate success of this endeavor rests with each and every individual who is concerned with providing training opportunities through a comprehensive educational curriculum for all students; and

WHEREAS,   Vocational Education serves secondary, post-secondary school youth, as well as adults, in preparing them for occupations in Agriculture, Business and Office, Marketing and Distribution, Vocational Home Economics, Trades and Industries, Health Occupations, Industrial Arts, Manpower, Technical Education and through the efforts of Vocational Guidance and Counseling by assisting individuals to reach their occupational goals:

NOW, THEREFORE, I, _____ , Mayor of the City of _____ do hereby proclaim February 12–18, 1978 as

VOCATIONAL EDUCATION WEEK

in the City of _____ and urge all citizens of this great community to visit their local Vocational Education schools and programs thereby making themselves better acquainted with the services offered by these dedicated institutions to the extent that each citizen can benefit from these services,

————————

     SEAL

————————

IN WITNESS WHEREOF, I have hereunto set my hand and caused the Seal of the City of _____ to be affixed this _____ day of February, 1978.

_____

Mayor

American Vocational Association. *Program Promotion Package.* Washington, D.C.: American Vocational Association, 1978. Used with permission of the American Vocational Association.

adoption of a policy statement supporting the infusion of the career education concept in the kindergarten-through-twelfth-grade curriculum. The board commissioned a general advisory committee and charged them with developing a public relations plan for informing the community of the importance of and need for career education. This general advisory committee included two board members, teachers from each of the schools within the district, two building-level administrators, parents of elementary, junior high, and high school students, a representative of the Spanish-speaking community, the president of the local chamber of commerce, officials from two local unions, and four local businesspersons.

After an initial meeting, the committee divided itself into two working groups. One group focused on communication strategies that would be critical for community awareness, while the second group concerned itself with schoolwide awareness. The overall plan developed by the committee emphasized the need to define career education; cite the national trend and its importance; describe what career education would do for students, parents, employers, and the community at large; outline the costs and the resources needed to implement the program locally; and provide additional in-service activities for school and community personnel regarding career education. The plan specified objectives and public relations activities for each of these concerns. Among the suggested activities were developing career education information packages to be mailed to parents, local employers, and community groups and organizations; preparing an audiovisual presentation on career education to be shown to local groups; and conducting a meeting on career education, open to the community.

After three months of study, the school board unanimously adopted the committee's public relations plan. At the same meeting, the board approved a budget allocation of $10,000 to implement the plan over the next fifteen months. As a result of this planned and concerted public relations effort, career education was well established as a fundamental educational concept that is shared by the school and community.

COMMUNICATIONS EXERCISE

THE COMMUNITY PUBLIC RELATIONS FUNCTION

The following communications exercise, by allowing you to apply your knowledge to a specific setting, can increase your understanding of the community public relations function. This exercise was designed and field tested as a self-instructional or small-group activity that stresses the application of concepts and ideas presented in this chapter.

 **THE FOLLOWING SECTION PROVIDES A BRIEF OVERVIEW OF A SPECIFIC SITUATION RELATED TO AN ADVISORY COMMITTEE. READ THIS SECTION COMPLETELY BEFORE PROCEEDING TO STEP 2.**

As the chairperson of the advisory committee for the drafting program, you have been selected to serve on the general advisory committee for the area vocational center. This general advisory committee, which is composed of the chairpersons of the eighteen programs at the center, has been asked to identify specific strategies for promoting the programs of area vocational centers. From the following worksheet, check those activities that could aid in promoting greater community support for involvement in the programs.

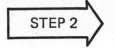

STEP 2

USING THE WORKSHEET BELOW, CHECK THE BOX(ES)
REPRESENTING THE ITEM(S) THAT MOST APPROPRIATELY
RESPOND(S) TO THE SITUATION DESCRIBED IN STEP 1.

Develop a calendar for public relations activities and releases to local news media. ____1	Approach the community in regard to sponsoring an awards program for outstanding students. ____2	Publicize programs at feeder high schools. ____3	Require each vocational teacher to join local community service group. ____4
Provide feedback to the community on special projects undertaken by students. ____5	Recommend a possible topic for newspaper releases. ____6	Assist in forming student chapters of professionally affiliated organizations. ____7	Recruit advisory committee members to speak on local television talk shows. ____8
Aid in the design of promotional advertising. ____9	Promote student/parent activities. ____10	Develop a listing of media contact persons. ____11	Offer suggestions regarding the development of short radio/TV spot announcements. ____12
Recommend a possibility of having an open house at the vocational center. ____13	Require each advisory committee member to speak at local civic club meetings. ____14	Develop follow-up stories regarding former students, for news release. ____15	Sponsor student displays at local shopping center. ____16

EVALUATE THE RESPONSES ON THE WORKSHEET BY COMPARING THE INDIVIDUAL RESPONSES WITH THOSE RECOMMENDED BELOW. READ THE APPROPRIATE COMMENTS AND CONTINUE ON TO STEP 4.

If you checked _____4, 14_____, read Comment A.
If you checked _____3_____, read Comment B.
If you checked _____1, 5, 6, 11_____, read Comment C.
If you checked _2, 7, 8, 9, 10, 12, 13, 15, 16_, read Comment D.

Comment A   Advisory committees cannot require teachers or advisory committee members to become involved in specific activities related to public relations. They can, however, encourage teachers and administrators to become involved in community activities in order to be close to issues and concerns that the community holds important regarding occupational and career education programs (4, 14). By becoming involved in educational programs, advisory committee members can have an extensive impact on the objectives and future directions of the program.

Comment B   One of the important external audiences for vocational education is the prospective student. To insure that all students are familiar with the available instructional programs prior to the time they become eligible to attend the area vocational school, programs must be well publicized in the home schools at the junior and senior high school level (3).

Comment C   As suggested throughout this chapter, the advisory committee can provide assistance in planning public relations efforts. The planning activities that would be appropriate here might include developing a public relations calendar and scheduling news releases (1), recommending possible topics for news releases (6), planning special community projects (5), and developing a directory of local media contact persons (newspaper, radio, television) (11).

Comment D   These responses represent possible activities for the advisory committee to undertake if they wish to get directly involved in public relations efforts. The time that advisory committee members can contribute to such activities is limited. Thus, it becomes essential that specific public relations activities be selected carefully. Among the more important activities are promoting contact with the local media (8), promoting student/parent activities (10), assisting with the development of public relations information (9, 12, 15), and becoming directly involved in community activities or discussion (2, 7).

BASED ON THE DISCUSSION COMMENTS ABOVE, REEVALUATE THE RESPONSES MADE IN STEP 2. IF THE CONCEPTS ARE CLEAR, PROCEED TO STEP 5.

TO IMPLEMENT SOME OF THE KEY CONCEPTS IN THE CHAPTER AS THEY RELATE TO YOUR SPECIFIC SETTING, COMPLETE AT LEAST ONE OF THE FOLLOWING OPTIONS.

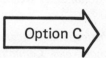

Option A   Review the chapter, select one concept, and develop a procedure for applying it to an advisory committee.

Option B   Select one of the situations outlined in the Suggested Activities section and make an application to an advisory committee.

Option C   Choose one of the sources in the Selected References section and integrate the additional insights gleaned from that source into a plan for advisory committee action.

SUGGESTED ACTIVITIES

1. Plan and conduct an advisory committee meeting for the purpose of developing a community public relations plan. The plan should outline specific target audiences, proposed activities, and a twelve-month schedule for completing the activities.

2. Obtain and review a copy of *Promoting Vocational Education* [11] from the American Vocational Association. Outline an appropriate public relations program for an occupational education program based on the procedures contained in Chapter 7.

3. Contact your state department of vocational education and state advisory council on vocational education for promotional and public relations materials. Build these materials into your local public information system.

4. Contact your state consultant for career education for promotional materials that can be disseminated locally to enhance the public's awareness of career education.

5. Assess the effectiveness of your school's internal communications system. If necessary, plan a committee effort to study and improve internal communications among teachers, students, administrators, counselors, advisory committees, and school boards.

6. Develop an evaluation checklist for assessing the effectiveness of public relations activities. Have your advisory committee review the checklist and use it to evaluate your occupational or career education program.

7. Identify contact persons for each of the local news media. Interview each individual to determine his or her level of knowledge and interest in occupational or career education. Develop a directory of interested contact people in the media and share it with other teachers, administrators, and advisory committees.

8. Collect and review educational news stories that have appeared recently in your local newspaper. Evaluate the articles to identify possible missing links in the school's public relations efforts.

SELECTED REFERENCES

American Vocational Association. *Program Promotion Package*. Washington, D.C.: American Vocational Association, 1978.

American Vocational Association. *Promoting Vocational Education: A Public Relations Handbook for Vocational Educators.* Washington, D.C.: American Vocational Association, 1978.

Anderson, Sherry L. *Key Concepts in Vocational Education: Public Relations for Vocational Education.* Lansing: Michigan Department of Education, 1976.

Herrscher, Barton R., and Hatfield, Thomas M. *College-Community Relations.* Washington, D.C.: American Association of Junior Colleges, 1969.

National Center for Research in Vocational Education. *Professional Vocational Teacher Education Module: Conduct an Open House,* Module G-7, Columbus: The Ohio State University, 1976.

National Center for Research in Vocational Education. *Professional Vocational Teacher Education Module: Develop a Plan for School-Community Relations,* Module G-1, Columbus: The Ohio State University, 1976.

National Center for Research in Vocational Education. *Professional Vocational Teacher Education Module: Give Presentations to School and Community Groups About the Vocational Education Program,* Module G-2, Columbus: The Ohio State University, 1976.

National Center for Research in Vocational Education. *Professional Vocational Teacher Education Module: Provide Brochures to Inform the School and Community About the Vocational Education Program,* Module G-3, Columbus: The Ohio State University, 1976.

National Center for Research in Vocational Education. *Professional Vocational Teacher Education Module: Provide Displays in the School and Community on the Vocational Education Program,* Module G-4, Columbus: The Ohio State University, 1976.

U.S. Office of Education. *Involving the Public in Adult, Vocational, and Manpower Programs.* Washington, D.C.: GPO, 1970.

9 The professional development function

The emergence of the advisory committee as a primary link in the educational/occupational/community partnership has produced a clearer delineation of the roles and responsibilities of the committee. In addition to the more widely accepted functions of curriculum advisement, student guidance and placement, and program evaluation, professional development has emerged as a new but integral role of the advisory committee. While, traditionally, the advisory committee evinced little interest or involvement in the professional development of teachers, administrators, or themselves as committee members, this is becoming a more critical function.

The development of this new function resulted from two forces; namely, the demand for greater educational accountability and the changing roles and responsibilities of all educational personnel. The seventies demonstrated a growing public demand that educational institutions be held accountable for their actions as well as for managing the financial resources committed to them. The factors bringing about this increase in the level of concern among citizens were declining enrollment, economic instability, collective bargaining, mass media, and the Watergate syndrome. In addition to these issues, various pieces of state and federal legislation contributed to this general trend. The Education Amendments of 1976, for example, mandated greater accountability for vocational education programs by placing specific funding conditions on state departments of education, requiring advisory committees and specifying annual program accountability reports. The move toward greater accountability has an impact on all phases of the educational system. While articles tended to focus on administrators, counselors, and teachers, it is inappropriate to single out any one group as being accountable; accountability is a broad concept that had to be shared by everyone

201

involved in the educational process, including the advisory committee.

A second force contributing to the expanded need for professional development was the changing roles of educational personnel. The factors that caused an increase in accountability also brought about an increased demand for a more clearly delineated set of responsibilities for educational personnel. State and federal legislation was again one of the most obvious areas of influence, as illustrated by the career education movement. Within a short period of time, a series of new concepts, approaches, and areas of emphasis related to career education were introduced. These concepts in turn suggested new and expanded roles and responsibilities for school personnel such as mainstreaming handicapped youth, eliminating sex bias and role stereotyping, and creating and implementing competency-based programs. Several states enacted laws that required educators to fulfill additional roles. The Career Education Incentive Act passed in 1977 also stimulated the development of new roles and responsibilities for educators.

In addition to the changing roles brought about by the career education movement, educational responsibilities toward serving disadvantaged and handicapped students in regular instructional programs has increased greatly. The Education for All Handicapped Children Act of 1975 required that greater numbers of handicapped students be educated in regular classes with their nonhandicapped peers and that handicapped students have access to the full range of educational opportunities, including vocational education, consumer and homemaking education, and industrial arts [163].

Other recent federal legislation expanded professional roles relative to serving bilingual and other special-needs students. The Comprehensive Employment and Training Act called upon educators to help address the problems of unemployed youth and adults. Still other legislation required educators to provide services and programs for displaced homemakers (females entering the labor force after the age of thirty-five). The list of state and federal legislation affecting the role of educators is long and further emphasizes the need for continued professional development of individuals involved with educational programs.

Additionally, many local educational agencies began to place greater emphasis on alternative forms of education with expanded work experience and cooperative education programs. The emergence of new concepts, like competency-based education and cognitive mapping, expanded professional requirements. With the expansion in scope and content of career and occupational education programs, the need for the continued professional growth and development of individuals involved with such programs becomes increasingly apparent. Adams [1:22] acknowledged this need for professional development by stating that

> Whether one is a teacher educator, supervisor, or teacher, one must sense in today's professional climate a compelling responsibility for personal growth and a commitment to contribute to one's own professional development and that of others. As America continues its accelerating pace of scientific and technological development with its related problems of unemployment, underemployment,

shortage of skilled manpower and displacement of workers, every professional person must accept changing roles and responsibilities so that contemporary society can build upon the best that every human has to offer.

With the need for professional development established via evidence of legislative and citizen demand for accountability and the changing roles and responsibilities of educators, this chapter describes the advisory committee's function in regard to professional development. While it is a relatively new, or at least a seldom discussed function of advisory committees, this chapter highlights the importance of this function and suggests numerous potential committee activities which exist within the framework of professional development. Emphasis is placed on the role of the advisory committee and suggested activities that may be employed by the committee.

SCOPE OF THE PROFESSIONAL DEVELOPMENT FUNCTION

The term *professional development* is a relatively new phrase that has gained rapid acceptance in the field of education. While the term is new, its meaning is generally accepted as a "planned and organized effort to provide teachers and other educational workers with the knowledge and skills necessary to facilitate improved student learning and performance" [153:3]. It is sometimes used synonymously with personnel development, but professional development is a more encompassing term. Many educators divide professional development into two components—preservice and in-service. Pre-service professional development is the academic work that a person has completed in a college or university prior to being employed as a teacher. In-service professional development is defined as instruction and supervision for employed educational personnel for the purpose of improving their professional abilities.

The advisory committee's major focus is on the in-service component of professional development, with some reference as to how the committee might have an impact on the pre-service component. The concept of professional development, however, extends beyond the school staff member. The professional development function of advisory committees focuses on two groups of individuals; the school staff members and the advisory committee members. The obvious role for advisory committees in this function is that of assisting teachers and other educational workers to improve their knowledge and skills for teaching the specific curriculum. The second role in this function deals with the professional growth and development of the advisory committee members themselves and, by extension, to other business and industry persons and citizens within the community.

Professional development of school staffs

The term *school staff* indicates that there are more than just teachers to consider. The teacher or program instructor would be the primary recipient of any professional growth and development opportunities that might be provided by an advisory committee. In addition to teachers, school and program administrators, such as the district superintendent, the high school principal, the career or vocational education director, and the department chairperson, could and should gain from professional development activities and opportunities provided or facilitated by the advisory committee. Others who might profit from this are members of the board of education, the curriculum director, the public relations specialist, the community education coordinator, the cooperative education coordinator, the placement specialist, and the classroom paraprofessional.

While there are many school staff members who could gain from the activities and programs provided by the advisory committee, the classroom teacher and the paraprofessionals are the most important group to reach. With the changing role of educators in mind, four major areas for professional growth and development can be identified: (1) skills and knowledge (competencies) to teach disadvantaged and handicapped students, (2) vocational guidance skills, (3) skills for locating and/or developing and utilizing community resources, and (4) skills and knowledge for curriculum development and improvement [58].

The career or occupational advisory committee can provide or facilitate the provision of in-service professional activities for all of the above areas. This does not imply that total skill and knowledge development in these areas could or should be provided by the advisory committee, but only that an advisory committee can provide certain aspects for each.

Other school staff members, such as paraprofessionals and counselors, should also be included in in-service programs whenever possible. More than just the instructional staff should be involved in the process of preparing students to acquire appropriate behaviors and marketable skills for the world of work. Involvement of these other school staff members and administrators will provide a closer link between business and industry and the educational community. The greater the knowledge and understanding of the program and student objectives by the administrative and support staff, the greater the potential for cooperation and coordination among the school personnel regarding the program and the students it serves.

Professional development of advisory committee members

If the advisory committee members are to function effectively, they must participate in activities that will increase their own professional growth. They must possess a thorough understanding of the school and its functions, the philosophy of career and occupational education, and the new laws that affect education and business and industry—for example, the Education Amendments of 1976, which mandate the elimination of sex-role stereotyping and sex bias in vocational education programs, and the Equal Employment Opportunity Act of 1972, which forbids employers from discriminating on the basis of sex, race, or national origin.

Advisory committee members should also see that the opportunity for professional growth is extended beyond themselves to their peers and colleagues. Committee members are representatives of the business, industries, and citizens of the community; therefore, certain knowledge and skills gained through serving on the advisory committee should be shared with others in the community. In this respect, the advisory committee member can be both the initiator and the recipient of in-service programs for themselves and those they represent.

Other audiences for professional development

Besides the school staff and the advisory committee itself, teacher educators could be affected by the professional development function. As teacher educators strive to maintain and update teacher preparation programs, it will benefit them to participate on a regular or ex officio basis with an advisory committee. Future teacher educators must have a thorough understanding of the role and functions of a career or occupational advisory committee and they must have the skills to organize and operate such a committee effectively. Teacher educators, themselves, need to obtain specific skills and knowledge regarding the effective use of advisory committees. Appropriate college personnel should make contact with local advisory committees that are active in the area surrounding the college or university. Field experiences for both university students and teacher educators may be arranged in this manner. Many of the suggested activities provided at the end of each chapter could be carried out in this real environment. In addition, a student teaching experience for those preparing to be teachers could require a minimum amount of work with an advisory committee. *The lack of proper preparation of potential teachers regarding the effective utilization of advisory committees has caused some educators to be reluctant to organize and operate such a committee in any meaningful way, thereby leaving a needless gap between the educational and business community.* The suggestions above are a few ways in which this problem may be overcome.

Occasionally advisory committees have expanded the concept of professional development of the school staff by considering program staffing to be one of their responsibilities. Included within this responsibility have been reviewing teacher selection criteria, suggesting recruitment policies, preparing job descriptions, recommending potential candidates, and reviewing teachers applications. These activities are not functions of an advisory committee unless the school administration specifically asks for assistance in these areas. A study conducted in Michigan [38] found these activities to be ranked very low in importance by teachers, administrators, and advisory committee members. While program staffing may be a part of the total professional development concept, it is only superficially related to the advisory committee professional development function.

PROFESSIONAL DEVELOPMENT ISSUES

There are several trends in career and occupational education that directly affect the role of both the educator and the advisory committee member.

These trends require new skills and knowledge on the part of the individuals involved and, as a result, create professional development issues that must be addressed. The four issues that are singled out in this chapter because of their special importance are (1) competency-based education, (2) disadvantaged and handicapped students, (3) sex-role stereotyping and sex bias, (4) technical updating. Legislation and changes in society are often responsible for initiation of trends in education; therefore, as legislation and social issues change, there is a corresponding shift in professional development needs.

Competency-based education

Compentency-based, or performance-based, education is an approach to career and occupational education programs in which *competency*, or the standard to which a certain *task* (specific activity performed by a worker or consumer) is performed [139], must be demonstrated at a minimal level by the student. Unlike many other educational concepts, competency based education is not dependent on a competitive approach. Rather, it encourages each student to develop to his or her full capacity at his or her own rate. Thus, competency-based education promotes the concept of open-entry/open-exit education. Students progress on the basis of whether or not they can perform the specific task at the stated standard, not on how well they can perform the task in comparison with other students.

After competencies of tasks have been identified, they are usually written in the form of *performance objectives*. A performance objective states a measurable behavior, the product to emerge from the performance, the conditions under which the performance will be conducted, and the criterion (standard) on which performance will be judged [139]. One of the most exciting aspects of competency-based education is that the public (students, parents, employers, advisory committee members, and citizens) can see exactly what the student must achieve in order to complete the program. This allows students to feel comfortable about what is expected of them, parents to gain concrete knowledge of exactly what their children are being taught in a specific class or program, and advisory committee members to determine when updating or other changes might be needed.

Advisory committee members can assist teachers in determining what the minimal competencies should be, ways in which students may acquire these competencies, and approaches for measuring student attainment of the required skills. Some businesses and industries have developed training programs for employees to acquire job-required skills. Teachers and paraprofessionals might participate in such programs to gain the knowledge and skills necessary to update their competencies and assist them in revising the curriculum. The committee can play an important role in sponsoring or facilitating such activities.

Disadvantaged and handicapped students

Making regular school programs and services available for the handicapped and disadvantaged student is a major concern of educators across the country. In the past, most of these students were placed in segregated classrooms, and only special-education teachers were prepared to teach such students. Today, legislation requires all teachers to develop and maintain skills to teach the handicapped and disadvantaged students. This is a particular challenge for career and occupational educational teachers as they work with students in career exploration, career decision making, career preparation, and in developing life role competencies.

School staff and advisory committee members should attend conferences and workshops provided by state and local education agencies. Attendance at such meetings is especially important for both groups if they are to understand fully the implications of current legislation and gain strategies for implementing legislative mandates. The needs of all students must remain the foremost concern of the committee as it makes program recommendations; therefore, the committee must have a thorough understanding of the needs of these students. Just as teachers need to gain skills and knowledge for teaching the handicapped and disadvantaged student in their programs, counselors need to understand state and federal mandates for including these students in regular programs and how to guide them, for example, in career decision making. It is equally important that employers realize the potential of hiring such individuals in their businesses and industries. Appropriate professional development programs and activities can help all committee members, teachers, and employers gain the needed competencies for teaching and working with the disadvantaged and handicapped.

Sex-role stereotyping and sex bias

The elimination of sex-role stereotyping and sex bias in educational programs and materials is another of the many professional development issues brought about by legislative requirements. It is particularly difficult to eliminate sex-role stereotyping and sex bias because these values and attitudes are predominant in society; in fact, many individuals have difficulty identifying their own sexist attitudes and behaviors. Even though legislation demands the eradication of such stereotyping and bias in educational programs, it will continue to be difficult for educators to carry out this requirement.

Advisory committee members can be instrumental in assisting educators to identify and eliminate sexist actions and materials in career and occupational programs. In addition, their awareness of the problem and their ability to identify such practices can easily be extended to the community and to the businesses and industries within the community.

School staff and advisory committee members might gain knowledge and skills to eliminate sex bias and sex-role stereotyping in career and occupational programs through a multitude of available workshops, materials, and audiovisual media. Members of the group who are more knowledgeable in regard to this topic may share with the others techniques and strategies to make educational programs, counseling, and employment environments sex fair. Great sensitivity should be demonstrated in this area.

Technical updating

Regardless of the amount and type of professional development activity, the question of technical updating is never fully resolved. This is a primary concern of teachers in local occupational educational programs and their advisory committees. As technology continues to change and advance, the skills and knowledge of those preparing individuals for the work force must also change and advance. These technological changes must be reflected in the curriculum, student performance objectives, instructional materials, and equipment, as well as in the instructor's competency to teach them. In order to facilitate changes in the performance objectives, instructional materials, and so on, teachers must possess the updated technical knowledge and skills.

Providing teachers with opportunities to gain these new competencies is the area within the professional development function in which advisory committees can be most effective. Advisory committee members can provide access to internships, specialized schools, and business and industry training programs. Committee members can also work with the school administration in promoting the concept of professional development among teachers and other school staff members and in making specific recommendations as to ways in which professional development activities can be promoted.

PROFESSIONAL DEVELOPMENT ACTIVITIES AND STRATEGIES

The teacher is the primary recipient of in-service or professional development activities provided or facilitated by the advisory committee. Prior to actually providing or making professional development activities available, the committee should assist in conducting professional development needs assessment, which can be either committee based (designed for the purpose of providing the professional development of the committee members) or community based (designed for school staff and others not serving on the advisory committee).

Professional development needs assessment

It is usually the responsibility of school personnel to develop and conduct a professional development needs assessment. Generally, such needs assessments are conducted on a schoolwide basis and ascertain the felt or perceived needs of teachers. The school administration analyzes the results of the assessment, sets up a list of priorities, and makes plans to provide professional development programs for the needs most commonly identified by those participating in the assessment. This approach has two possible shortcomings: first, the professional development programs provided may not meet the needs of some staff members; second, school staff members are often not aware of their needs for professional growth. This occurs particularly when new concepts and trends in education evolve, and educators are not made aware of them or what they mean in light of their instructional role.

Advisory committee members can help individual teachers identify professional growth needs. One of the major roles they can play in this respect is to promote and encourage the concept of professional growth and development, which should be seen as a positive, continuous type of career and personal development. To prevent the creation of negative attitudes and resistance to participation in in-service or professional development activity, it should not be presented as a form of criticism to the teacher.

Another aspect of the needs assessment concept is focused on the advisory committee members themselves. Committee members should be encouraged to conduct an assessment of their own needs, both as a group and on an individual basis, based on their role as advisory committee members. For example, the committee as a group may identify areas of professional growth needed by all involved; however, the chairperson may identify additional needs that are unique to his or her role. Once the needs for both the instructional staff and the advisory committee members have been identified, the advisory committee can look for ways in which it might be involved in meeting those needs.

Committee-based activities and strategies

Advisory committee members have professional development needs that should be met so they may more effectively carry out their role. The following are some strategies and activities that might be used for committee-based professional development.

Advisory committee orientation. As a new advisory committee is organized or as new members join the committee, an orientation as to the role, function, and responsibilities of its members is necessary. This orientation is a form of professional development of committee members and may be provided by the school staff alone or with the assistance of experienced advisory committee members.

To orient a committee member to the role and functions of the advisory committee, he or she might have a close working relationship with a school staff member prior to the first meeting of the advisory committee, or the committee could provide the new member with some orientation and in-service instruction regarding the functions and activities at each meeting. (See Chapter 10 for further details.) Still another approach is for the committee to develop and conduct a special orientation workshop for all new advisory committee members. Individuals in the community who have served on an effective advisory committee in the past could be asked to assist in conducting such a workshop. If there are members of the state advisory council in the area, they might be asked to provide their support in conducting the orientation workshop. Teacher educators and state department of education personnel might also be enlisted to assist in this effort. School personnel from neighboring school districts, who are establishing new advisory committees or selecting new members for committees, may want to plan a joint orientation program and include their new members as participants in the workshop. A tentative workshop agenda is provided in Figure 9–1; however, local school staff and others planning the workshop should remember that adaptation of the agenda to fit local time constraints and the readiness level of the participants is a must. Chapter 10 provides suggestions for advisory committee orientation.

State plan for vocational education.   Participation in the development of the state plan for vocational education or the state plan for career education is another way that members serving on an occupational and career education advisory committee could gain professional growth and development. Advisory committee members should attend public meetings and hearings held by state officials during the formation of the state plan in an effort to enhance their own development and increase their understanding of the statewide directions.

Long-range planning.   Assisting school staff in the development of district or regional long-range plans for career or vocational education is still another professional growth experience that can be undertaken by advisory committee members. Participation in this process can provide committee members with an understanding of the school structure, the vocational and/or career education philosophy, and the most recent legislative requirements regarding educational programs. It might also have significant value as a guide for the committee in planning its own activities.

Leadership seminars.   As discussed in Chapter 11, leadership is a vital component of a successful advisory committee. Members may want to conduct or participate in a workshop or seminar that will help them develop or refine leadership skills. This type of activity is of particular importance to committee chairpersons. Business and industry, chambers of commerce, universities, and professional education associations offer a variety of leadership development workshops and seminars in which advisory committee members may want to participate.

Professional education associations.   One of the most effective professional development opportunities available to advisory committee members may be attending a state or national professional education association conference. By attending various sessions, committee members can gain a better understanding of educational programs and their objectives; a better understanding of the interrelationship of local, state, and federal education agencies; and an awareness of new trends, issues, and concerns. Some suggestions for possible state and national conferences include

- State/national career education association conference
- State/national vocational technical education association conference
- State placement association conference
- State special needs association conference

FIGURE 9-1. *Sample agenda for a committee orientation workshop*

1. Welcome	School official and a member of the business community
2. Introductions and get-acquainted activity	Workshop facilitator
3. Goals of the workshop	Workshop facilitator
4. What is an advisory committee?	
Overview	*Use filmstrip or slide/tape*
Definition	
Brief history or background	*Use overhead transparencies, handouts, posters*
Need	
5. What is the role of this advisory committee?	
Purpose and goals	School staff
Functions (small groups)	Past committee members
6. Relationship to state and national advisory councils	State advisory council member or staff person
7. Specific state rules, guidelines, or requirements	Local vocational or career education director or state department of education staff member
8. Advisory committee planning	School staff member who will be working directly with advisory committee
9. Advisory committee evaluation	Workshop facilitator
10. Workshop evaluation	Workshop facilitator

- State sex equity in education association conference
- State career guidance association conference
- State curriculum association conference

School staff should invite advisory committee members to attend such conferences. If needed, and if possible, schools should pay some or all of the advisory committee members' expenses to such a conference. This does not have to become a routine or expected activity for committee members, but the increased enthusiasm and support it can produce for school programs may be worth the investment.

Informing other members of the business and industry community. Advisory committee members can carry out the professional development function by providing in-depth training and sharing information with their colleagues in the community. As an example, most state departments of education require or strongly recommend that local districts conduct a follow-up study of individuals who are currently employing or have employed program graduates. The advisory committee might sponsor a breakfast, luncheon, or other activity to bring together employers of program graduates.

Members of the advisory committee could explain the follow-up effort to the community employers, could actually walk them through the survey instrument, and could outline how the results of the follow-up study would be used by the advisory committee and local school district staff to advise and improve the program. Similar topics could be presented and discussed at other functions; often Rotary or Kiwanis clubs are looking for someone to make such presentations at their regular meetings. The goal is for the advisory committee member to share some *in-depth* information about the program or some component of it. This activity is related to the community public relations function presented in Chapter 8; however, more than just exposure or awareness of the program is sought here.

Community-based activities and strategies

The following are suggested activities and strategies for the professional growth and development of school staff and other individuals not serving on the advisory committee.

Teacher internships. The most obvious and probably the most effective way for teachers to upgrade their technical skills is for them to work periodically as employees in the occupation for which they prepare students. Advisory committees can identify the latest technological developments within an occupation and conduct informal surveys of businesses and industries within the community to determine how many have adopted or plan to adopt the new technology. The school staff, with the assistance of the advisory committee, can evaluate the program curriculum to determine how and when the curriculum might be revised to include the new technology, what new equipment and materials might be needed, what community resources are available, and how the program instructor might obtain the new skills.

Advisory committee members can sponsor and encourage other business and industry representatives in the community to sponsor internship programs. Internship programs can encourage classroom teachers in the occupational programs to update their technical skills by spending a period of time working as an employee in a local company. Such an internship might be a summer experience in a specific technical area, it could be a series of short-term experiences throughout the year in which broad-based experiences are provided, or it might even be a part of a formal exchange program in which company employees assume various roles in the school program. Whatever the form, teachers should be encouraged to take advantage of such opportunities to update their technical and professional skills.

Another approach to the internship program might be to focus on the career and vocational counselor. A handbook produced by the National Association for Industry-Education Cooperation [76:12] describes such a program:

> The purpose is to provide an in-depth exposure to a variety of job skills and to gain experience in performing and observing various types of job conditions. This on-the-job scene exposure to employee situations will provide a kind of experience usually lacking in college courses leading to counselor certification. A closer working relationship between counselors and community firms is an added benefit of this activity.

Professional occupational association. Through attendance at occupational association conferences, school personnel can gain information and knowledge about the occupation, the need for workers, the requirements of workers, and the trends of the future. Conference attendance is an excellent strategy for professional development of school staff. In the past, this strategy has created renewed enthusiasm on the part of teachers as well as providing them with many ideas and materials to use in the occupational or career education program.

Community resource workshops. Development of community resources is an area needing continued expansion. Teachers and other school staff must continually be aware of potential community resources and have the skills to develop those resources. Chapter 5 provides details on community resource identification and development and an agenda for a community resource workshop.

THE PROFESSIONAL DEVELOPMENT FUNCTION IN ACTION

The professional development function has great potential for enhancing the educational/occupational/community partnership. Unfortunately, professional developed is *not* often identified as an advisory committee function. Professional development should not be viewed as an isolated function but rather as one that is an integral part of all other functions. As school personnel and advisory committees work together, it may be beneficial to remember that the quality of the program cannot be greater than the quality of the individuals planning and conducting the program. In turn, the effectiveness of an advisory committee cannot be greater than the effectiveness of its members.

The Genesee Skill Center in Flint, Michigan, may be used to illustrate instances in which advisory committees have been involved in the professional development function. The following is a brief description of professional development activities involving advisory committees and school staff.

Advisory committee members for the automotive program in the skill center periodically plan and conduct updating sessions regarding the latest equipment and developments in the automotive industry. In the past, advisory committee members brought in actual equipment and demonstrated its use; they provided a slide/tape presentation showing new developments on how to operate a particular piece of equipment; and, whenever possible, they provided printed resource material to those attending the session. In addition to inviting all appropriate instructors at the skill center, they invited other automotive instructors from school districts within the region to attend. At times they have also invited mechanics and garage dealers to attend the updating program. As a result, not only is technical upgrading provided but communication is improved as a large number of educators and members of the business and industry community meet together for a common purpose.

Students are also often invited to attend these technical upgrading programs, which is an excellent way of achieving greater linkage between the school and community. Students gain an opportunity to meet employers and workers in the occupation for which they are being educated, and employers have a chance to meet students who are potential employees. Employed mechanics attending the session may begin to view the local school district as a place for occupational updating; while students may note the return of workers for updating and be encouraged to do the same in the years after they complete the program and are employed.

The health program provides another example of advisory committee involvement in the professional development function at the Genesee Skill Center. The center staff teaching in the health program meets once a week. Every two or three weeks the school staff invites a member of the health occupations advisory committee to meet with them at their regular meeting. Through this exchange, committee members and school staff develop a working relationship and a two-way approach to professional development takes place: the school staff can gain technical information and the advisory committee member can gain a better understanding of the program, the students to be served, and the needs of the school.

A third example of the professional development function at this same school is unique in that it integrates a professional development component into the annual advisory committee appreciation dinner. School personnel plan a program that provides for professional development of the committee members. They explain why advisory committees are important and give an overview of what the various committees have done. Within this presentation, school personnel (or experienced advisory committee members) are able to reemphasize the role of committee members and identify specific activities to improve on the year's accomplishments.

COMMUNICATIONS EXERCISE

THE PROFESSIONAL DEVELOPMENT FUNCTION

The following communications exercise, by allowing you to apply your knowledge to a specific setting, can increase your understanding of the professional development function. This exercise was designed and field tested as a self-instructional or small-group activity that stresses the application of concepts and ideas presented in this chapter.

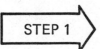 **STEP 1** **THE FOLLOWING SECTION PROVIDES A BRIEF OVERVIEW OF A SPECIFIC SITUATION RELATED TO AN ADVISORY COMMITTEE. READ THIS SECTION COMPLETELY BEFORE PROCEEDING TO STEP 2.**

As chairperson of the advisory committee for the health occupations program in an area skill center, you are to provide leadership in helping the committee members identify their professional development needs. There are nine members of the committee, and this is the first year it has been in operation. None of the members has served on an occupational education advisory committee before. How would you go about identifying the professional development needs of the committee members?

STEP 2

USING THE WORKSHEET BELOW, CHECK THE BOX(ES) REPRESENTING THE ITEM(S) THAT MOST APPROPRIATELY RESPOND(S) TO THE SITUATION DESCRIBED IN STEP 1.

Analyze current legislation. _____ 1	Invite a consultant to analyze the committee's ability to function as a group. _____ 2	Contact a health-related occupational association for information regarding current trends. _____ 3	Provide a news release describing the professional development program for advisory committee members. _____ 4
Encourage those who have special roles or responsibilities within the committee to identify needs related to those responsibilities. _____ 5	Ask the instructional and administrative staff of the school to identify the professional development needs of the committee. _____ 6	Review national and state studies regarding advisory committee needs. _____ 7	Adopt or adapt a plan used by a nearby local committee. _____ 8
Identify the technical skill needs of the instructional staff. _____ 9	Develop a survey questionnaire to be completed by each member of the committee. _____ 10	Establish priorities based on the results of the survey. _____ 11	Contact another advisory committee to see how it has gone about identifying professional development needs. _____ 12
Allow each member to identify individual needs that differ from the priority needs resulting from the survey. _____ 13	You, as chairperson, determine the needs. _____ 14	Develop a plan to meet the needs identified. _____ 15	Visit health facilities within the community. _____ 16

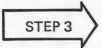 **STEP 3**   EVALUATE THE RESPONSES ON THE WORKSHEET BY COMPARING THE INDIVIDUAL RESPONSES WITH THOSE RECOMMENDED BELOW. READ THE APPROPRIATE COMMENTS AND CONTINUE ON TO STEP 4.

If you checked 2, 5, 7, 10, 11, 12, 13 , read Comment A.

If you checked 1, 3, 8, 15 , read Comment B.

If you checked 4, 6, 9, 14, 16 , read Comment C.

Comment A   These are all good first steps to identify the professional development needs of advisory committee members. A survey questionnaire or checklist (10) might be developed by contacting another advisory committee (12) to learn how it identified the professional development needs of its members and also to obtain a list of the needs that were actually identified. The use of national and state studies (7) will also be helpful in identifying items to include on the survey checklist.

Since an advisory committee cannot spend all of its time on in-service activities for its members, it should establish priorities among the identified needs (11) and select the first two or three. In addition, each member should give serious consideration to his or her individual needs—those needs that differ from the needs of the group (13). The members having specific roles or responsibilities on the committee should be encouraged to consider what information or skills they need to fulfill their roles better (5). Since the committee must be able to function effectively as a group, it may be appropriate to invite a consultant to observe the group and make recommendations regarding areas of need in developing group interaction and communication skills (2).

Comment B   The activities represented here are alternative actions that might be considered when identifying the professional development needs of advisory committee members. For example, advisory committee members may need more information and understanding about certain aspects of current legislation (1). Analyzing and understanding current legislation may also be a need in itself. Professional associations may be able to provide committee members with current information on trends about which members need to know more (3).

After identifying the needs, the next step is to develop a plan to meet the needs (15). A plan used by another advisory committee could be adopted or adapted (8).

Comment C   None of the actions represented here are appropriate for identifying the professional development needs of committee members. Providing a news release is not helpful in identifying the needs (4). The instructional and administrative staff may be able to provide assistance but should not be asked to identify the needs (6), nor should the committee chairperson assume such authority (14). Identifying the technical skill needs of the instructional staff has nothing to do with identifying advisory committee needs (9). Visiting health facilities might be a nice activity for the committee, but it does not focus on identifying professional development needs (16).

The professional development function   **219**

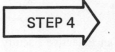

STEP 4 BASED ON THE DISCUSSION COMMENTS ABOVE, REEVALUATE THE RESPONSES MADE IN STEP 2. IF THE CONCEPTS ARE CLEAR, PROCEED TO STEP 5.

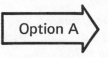

STEP 5 TO IMPLEMENT SOME OF THE KEY CONCEPTS IN THE CHAPTER AS THEY RELATE TO YOUR SPECIFIC SETTING, COMPLETE AT LEAST ONE OF THE FOLLOWING OPTIONS.

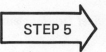

Option A Review the chapter, select one concept, and develop a procedure for applying it to an advisory committee.

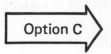

Option B Select one of the situations outlined in the Suggested Activities section and make an application to an advisory committee.

Option C Choose one of the sources in the Selected References section and integrate the additional insights gleaned from that source into a plan for advisory committee action.

SUGGESTED ACTIVITIES

1. Develop a brief paper for your board of education justifying the need for professional development programs and activities for school staff.

2. Outline a procedure for presenting the professional development function to an advisory committee. Be sure to consider the type of advisory committee you are addressing.

3. Assist a local school district in developing and implementing a procedure to assess the individual professional development needs of teachers and other school staff.

4. Design a procedure for providing for the technical upgrading of occupational program instructors. Work with school administrators to gain approval for individual instructors to participate in these technical upgrading activities.

5. Determine the orientation needs of the members of a newly formed advisory committee and prepare a workshop agenda. Include names of appropriate individuals to conduct the workshop and collect or develop all necessary support materials (brochures, handbooks, excerpts of legislation, state guidelines).

6. Contact ten to fifteen local advisory committees to determine what types of professional development activities they have been involved in or they have conducted or facilitated for school staff. Prepare a brief synopsis of each activity.

7. In cooperation with an advisory committee, develop a plan to locate sites for internships or arrange for access to business and industry training programs.

8. If you are an advisory committee member, attend an educational professional association conference. If you are a school staff member, attend a business/industry professional association conference. Try to gain a better understanding of the educational program or the occupation. Look for ways to enhance the linkages and coordination in the educational/occupational/community partnership.

SELECTED REFERENCES

Bergquist, William H., and Phillips, Steven R. "Components of an Effective Faculty Development Program," *Journal of Higher Education,* 46 (March/April 1975): 177–211.

Doty, Charles K., and Gepner, Ronald, eds. *Post-Secondary Personnel Development,* Vol I., Trenton: New Jersey Department of Education, 1976.

Industry-Education Councils: A Handbook. Buffalo, N.Y.: National Association for Industry Education Cooperation, undated.

Morgan, Samuel D. *Proceedings of National Leadership Development Seminar for State and National Advisory Councils on Vocational Education,* Blacksburg: Virginia Polytechnic Institute and State University, June 1976.

National Center for Research in Vocational Education. *Staff Development Guidelines and Procedures for Career Education.* Columbus: The Ohio State University, 1975.

National Center for Research in Vocational Education. *Staff Development Program for Promoting More Effective Use of Community Resources in Career Education.* Columbus: The Ohio State University, 1975.

National Center for Research in Vocational Education. *Staff Development Program for the Implementation of Career Education (Teacher's Guide): A Group Approach.* Columbus: The Ohio State University, 1975.

National Center for Research in Vocational Education. *Staff Development Program for the Implementation of Career Education (Teacher's Guide): An Individual Approach.* Columbus: The Ohio State University, 1975.

PART III

ORGANIZATION AND MANAGEMENT OF ADVISORY COMMITTEES

In Parts I and II the essential characteristics that form the base for advisory committee action were provided. To implement these underlying concepts, an essential organizational and management plan is required. The chapters in Part III focus on specific aspects of this process, provide practical examples and illustrations to assist in this process, and suggest other learning activities that can be completed to facilitate this task.

The implementation strategies, techniques, and guides suggested in this section will not guarantee success. They do, however, provide a framework in which advisory committees can be utilized to enhance the quality of the educational program. Chapter 10 delineates the major areas to focus on when planning, developing, and organizing the committee. Chapter 11 provides guidelines to personal behavior, to interpersonal relationships, and to leadership approaches for integrating these concepts within the group dynamics process. Chapter 11 also suggests actions to be avoided and practices to be followed in working with committee members. Chapter 12 illustrates what impact planning has on the various roles of the advisory committee. It provides a detailed description of planning and how planning determines the role of the committee with regard to the program it serves. Chapter 13 highlights the importance of and the process of evaluating the advisory committee. Focus is placed on the committee's own organization, how it operates, and the degree of success or impact that it has.

10 The establishment of an effective advisory committee

The preceding chapters described the specific functions performed by advisory committees. These functions form the base for advisory committee action and provide the underlying concepts that support the conceptual framework for advisory committee activity. An effective organizational structure is essential to make these concepts operational. Only through a highly planned and organized process can the committee serve its purposes, can members furnish the input necessary for effective program development, and can individuals provide the required leadership. Therefore, this chapter explains how to establish an effective advisory committee. Focus is placed on planning, organizing, and developing a committee.

An advisory committee is distinctive from other groups in that it is composed primarily of volunteers, serves totally an advisory role, and, for the most part, functions outside of the formal educational structure while at the same time having a direct impact on this structure. From an operational perspective, however, the advisory committee is like any other managerial group, depending on the same key concepts of organizing, operating, planning, and evaluating. Naturally, the application of these concepts will vary widely with the advisory committee, just as advisory committees differ in scope, purpose, and function.

While broad generalizations can be made about any organization, a realistic appraisal of the advisory committee reaffirms the fact that there is no one best method of organizing group activity. Organizational efforts are shaped by such factors as the purpose of the committee, the tasks to be performed, and the knowledge and capabilities of those serving on the committee. Similarly, there is no universal system for planning the activities of the committee, nor is there one leadership style that is applicable to guide advisory committee action. The situational factors and various interrelationships operating on and within the committee greatly influence its formal and informal structure. There are, however, several guiding principles for organizing an effective advisory committee.

PLANNING FOR THE ESTABLISHMENT OF AN ADVISORY COMMITTEE

The planning that takes place prior to the formation of an advisory committee follows the same general principles as those applied to the development of a new or the revision of an existing program. The key planning concepts are described in Chapter 12. These preliminary activities provide an opportunity to assess the situation and the problems and to develop a strategy to overcome the problems and attain the specific committee goals.

Before organizing a committee, the situation should be assessed so there is a thorough understanding of the factors that may affect the committee; some basic preliminary planning should occur to ensure that the various roles, responsibilities, and purposes are clearly understood; the approval process should be understood and ways of facilitating this process developed; and a plan should be developed for each of these areas to ensure the smooth establishment of the committee.

Assessment of the situation

A prerequisite to forming an advisory committee is to obtain a thorough understanding of the character and purpose of the committee. If this assessment is not handled properly, errors may result that could seriously hamper the success of the committee after it has been established. In order to avoid, for example, a feeling of "cramming the committee down their throats," there must be a feeling of need and an understanding of the community. Teachers, parents, and citizens must understand the various factors that might have an impact on the committee. The following points and questions should be considered at this early stage:

1. Those responsible for establishing the committee should have a thorough understanding of the functions of an advisory committee and the responsibilities of its members.

2. The teachers and administrators involved in the effort should be knowledgeable about the community and the existing program.

3. Information on career opportunities, placement possibilities, changing employment patterns, and interests in vocational offerings should be available.

4. There should be a clear understanding of the procedures to be followed and of the chain of command in the school system to avoid bypassing some segment of the administrative hierarchy.

5. There should be a clear understanding of the history and status of advisory committees within the community. For example:

- What are the existing attitudes of administrators and board of education members?

- Are there existing career or occupational advisory committees? If so, how were they formed?

- Can any deficiencies be determined related to how existing committees were formed or how they are operating?

- If advisory committees existed at one time, why are they no longer in existence?

6. Determination should be made of the extent that advisory committees are used in other segments of the school, community, or region.

Preliminary organizational planning

The manner in which these early organizational efforts are handled may play a significant role in determining how well the plan for the committee will be accepted. The form of the proposals may affect the initial reactions of key administrators; and these early impressions may have a lasting impact and may result in long-standing roadblocks or unnecessary delays. Vagueness, uncertainty, and ambiguity at this time may be detrimental to the future of the committee. Therefore, attention should be given to the following:

1. The appropriate administrator(s) should be informed early that the organization of an advisory committee is being considered.

2. A written statement should be prepared describing the rationale for the advisory committee and outlining how the committee might assist in improving or strengthening the program and the relationship between the school and the community.

3. A brief, written statement describing the proposed committee in the following terms should be prepared:

   - The purpose of the committee

   - The responsibilities and duties of the committee

   - The organizational structure of the committee and the methods of selecting and the length of terms of the committee members

   - The relationship of the committee to the program and the school

4. An outline of the procedures to be followed in organizing the committee should be developed. Consideration should be given at this time to the possibility of involving a small group of citizens and school officials in this process.

Approval to form the committee

The culminating act, after the information resulting from the initial assessments and preliminary planning activities has been collected and prepared, is the process of gaining approval for the formation of the advisory committee. This process is critical because it is usually the first formal presentation, outside of the department or school unit, concerning the establishment of the committee. Normally the board of education is the administrative unit that takes the action to organize the committee; but this may vary according to the size and complexity of the community. This presentation should explain the need for forming the committee and describe the educational benefits to be derived by the community. The teacher or administrator responsible for the proposal should be prepared to answer questions such as the following: Why should the advisory committee be formed? What is the purpose of the committee and within what framework will it operate? How will the committee be organized? How will it benefit the school and community?

Usually, on the recommendation of the administration, the board will approve a resolution establishing the committee and the procedures for organizing it. The resolution usually takes the form of a statement of purpose and becomes the charter under which the committee operates. This charter serves as the legal framework within which the committee is authorized to work. Figure 10–1 illustrates a sample charter that might be used for gaining authorization for a general vocational advisory committee. Although the charter will vary depending on the nature of the board of education and the scope and purpose of the committee, such authorization should focus on the role of the committee, the rights of the board, and the ways in which the committee is expected to contribute to the improvement of the program.

Implementation plan to form the committee

The development of the basic plan of work is the first task that must be faced in preparing to form an advisory committee. Since the plan may be under constant refinement, it need not be totally completed before some of the activities are undertaken. However, the sooner the details of the plan are finalized, the better the chances that a logical sequence may be followed and pitfalls may be avoided.

The plan may simply be a detailed outline identifying the major questions that need to be answered or the specific tasks that need to be accomplished. Figure 10–2 illustrates such an outline plan for establishing an agricultural advisory committee. Figure 10–3 provides a more structured approach to this task since a PERT network is used to illustrate the interrelationships between starting a new program in a community college and, at the same time, forming an advisory committee. This is a graphic illustration of the relationships between forty-six tasks (depicted by circled numbers) and the time (indicated by solid lines) required to accomplish the total project (in this case, to form the advisory committee). The dotted lines do not indicate activity but are used to reveal the relationships between one event and another. The arrows indicate the sequence of events. The numbers on the list correspond to the circled numbers and describe the tasks to be completed. There are complex

FIGURE 10-1. *Sample charter for the establishment of a general vocational education advisory committee*

The school board of _____ on this _____ day of
_____, 19 ___, authorizes the establishment of a continuing committee to be known
as the General Vocational Education Advisory Committee.

The General Vocational Education Advisory Committee is intended to supplement and stimulate other types of citizen participation.

The purpose of the General Vocational Education Advisory Committee is to serve as an arm of the school board by providing advice and counsel to the board.

The General Vocational Education Advisory Committee serves at the pleasure of the school board which reserves the right to dissolve the committee at any time for any purpose.

The General Vocational Education Advisory Committee is expected to contribute to the improvement of the school division's vocational education program by:

1. Assisting with annual and long range planning.
2. Advising on current and long range labor market trends.
3. Conducting occupational/community surveys as related to the vocational education needs of the community.
4. Advising the school division's administration and school board concerning course content and program development.
5. Assisting in finding on-the-job and full-time placement of students.
6. Facilitating communications that create good public relations between the school and the community.
7. Providing a consulting service to the school board and administration in the areas of equipment and facility planning.
8. Providing assistance to the school board and administration through assigned activities associated with program staffing.
9. Assisting in program review activities and/or program evaluation.
10. Identifying and assessing community resources that will offer support to the instructional program.

In authorizing the organization of the General Vocational Education Advisory Committee, the school board pledges cooperation in the committee's work. The General Vocational Education Advisory Committee will be expected to operate within the guidelines set forth.

Walter S. Ramey. *A Guide for the Organization and Operation of Local Advisory Committees for Vocational Education.* Richmond: Virginia State Department of Education, 1975, pp. 49-50. Used with permission.

FIGURE 10-2. Possible steps in forming an advisory committee.

Steps	How to Accomplish
1. Teacher must be sold on the use of an advisory council.	1. Study and learn of the duties and functions of an advisory council.
	2. Visit advisory councils in operation. Watch them perform.
	3. Talk to administrators where a successful advisory council is in operation.
	4. Check yourself to see if you have a personality that will not conflict with people offering suggestions and advice to you.
	5. Check section on advantages of organizing a council
2. Secure administrator's approval.	1. Explain the function of an advisory council.
	2. Point out local needs and advantages of the advisory council.
	3. Be able to cite specific examples of schools where they have an advisory council operating.
	4. Be able to show him/her how the advisory council will be an asset to him/her as well as to the school and you.
	5. Ask for assistance in preparing final plans for presentation to board of education.
	6. Check the final plans with the administrator.
3. Secure administration permission.	1. Present plans of organization to the board.
	2. Give specific purposes of the organization.
	3. Point out that the advisory council is strictly advisory on problems. It is not a pressure or lobby group.
	4. Make it plain to the board that the council is responsible to them and can be discharged or discontinued at any time.
	5. Explain that the board may designate one of its members to sit in on all council meetings.
	6. Offer to be present to help to present the plan to the board if they desire your presence.

4. Secure council nomination.

1. Prepare list of people in the community as a pool from which members will be selected by:

   Director and superintendent decide on one name to start the list. Contact this person and ask him/her to suggest another individual. Keep this procedure going until a list of 18–20 names are compiled.

2. Take superintendent along when compiling this list if possible.

5. Select council members.

1. Superintendent and Director prepare suggested list of council members and submit to board of education.

2. Board of Education may elect members to the council.

3. Keep list of nominees not selected on file to fill future vacancies.

4. A rotation system is useful for members.

6. Notify elected members.

1. Secretary of the board of education write personal letter of notification of election.

2. Letter to be signed by president of board.

7. Personal contact with elected members.

   (*This step is important.*)

1. Director should visit each member and congratulate him/her and get his/her acceptance.

2. Be able to answer member's questions on the overall program.

3. Check on preferable time of first meeting.

8. Call first meeting.

1. Mail reminder cards. Call day before meeting.

2. Avoid conflict as much as possible.

3. Impress on members the importance of attendance at the first meeting.

9. Hold first meeting.

1. Explain the job of the advisory council.

2. Elect temporary chairperson, secretary and appoint nominating committee.

3. Appoint committee for drawing up constitution.

4. Discuss some live, pertinent topic so members feel they have accomplished something.

5. Decide on definite meeting time and place.

"Advisory Council." A paper provided by Francine Kremsdorf, Career Development Systems, Parsippany, New Jersey for Wayne Career Education Program, Wayne, N.J., April 1977, pp. 5–6. Used with permission.

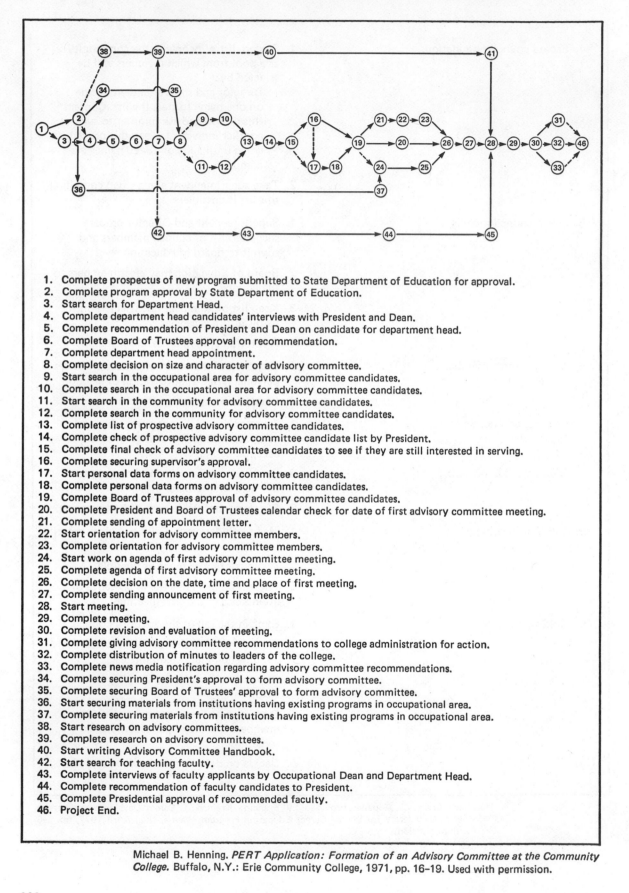

1. Complete prospectus of new program submitted to State Department of Education for approval.
2. Complete program approval by State Department of Education.
3. Start search for Department Head.
4. Complete department head candidates' interviews with President and Dean.
5. Complete recommendation of President and Dean on candidate for department head.
6. Complete Board of Trustees approval on recommendation.
7. Complete department head appointment.
8. Complete decision on size and character of advisory committee.
9. Start search in the occupational area for advisory committee candidates.
10. Complete search in the occupational area for advisory committee candidates.
11. Start search in the community for advisory committee candidates.
12. Complete search in the community for advisory committee candidates.
13. Complete list of prospective advisory committee candidates.
14. Complete check of prospective advisory committee candidate list by President.
15. Complete final check of advisory committee candidates to see if they are still interested in serving.
16. Complete securing supervisor's approval.
17. Start personal data forms on advisory committee candidates.
18. Complete personal data forms on advisory committee candidates.
19. Complete Board of Trustees approval of advisory committee candidates.
20. Complete President and Board of Trustees calendar check for date of first advisory committee meeting.
21. Complete sending of appointment letter.
22. Start orientation for advisory committee members.
23. Complete orientation for advisory committee members.
24. Start work on agenda of first advisory committee meeting.
25. Complete agenda of first advisory committee meeting.
26. Complete decision on the date, time and place of first meeting.
27. Complete sending announcement of first meeting.
28. Start meeting.
29. Complete meeting.
30. Complete revision and evaluation of meeting.
31. Complete giving advisory committee recommendations to college administration for action.
32. Complete distribution of minutes to leaders of the college.
33. Complete news media notification regarding advisory committee recommendations.
34. Complete securing President's approval to form advisory committee.
35. Complete securing Board of Trustees' approval to form advisory committee.
36. Start securing materials from institutions having existing programs in occupational area.
37. Complete securing materials from institutions having existing programs in occupational area.
38. Start research on advisory committees.
39. Complete research on advisory committees.
40. Start writing Advisory Committee Handbook.
42. Start search for teaching faculty.
43. Complete interviews of faculty applicants by Occupational Dean and Department Head.
44. Complete recommendation of faculty candidates to President.
45. Complete Presidential approval of recommended faculty.
46. Project End.

Michael B. Henning. *PERT Application: Formation of an Advisory Committee at the Community College.* Buffalo, N.Y.: Erie Community College, 1971, pp. 16–19. Used with permission.

formulas in the PERT process that may be used to project time estimates of when the project may be completed. If the PERT process is used as simple timeline—as presented here—it facilitates organization by sequencing the tasks that need to be completed and by demonstrating the relationship between specific tasks. The PERT process can also be used as an effective tool in presenting the plan.

ORGANIZING THE ADVISORY COMMITTEE

The determination of an appropriate organizational structure, the nature of the committee, and the techniques utilized in organizing the committee rest totally within the control of personnel in the educational system. In some cases the board of education may exercise more control over how the committee is organized; but these operational details are usually left to the discretion of the teacher or administrative person directly affiliated with the program. Some of the typical areas of focus in this respect include the selection and appointment of committee members; the delineation of committee responsibilities, structure, and membership; the decision about the format of committee meetings; and the development of procedures, bylaws, and/or a committee constitution. Although techniques and strategies to organize an advisory committee may vary, the following sections provide a general framework to guide this process.

Selection of committee members

The steps followed in forming a committee can have a direct bearing on the effectiveness of the committee. Since forming an advisory committee is a cooperative venture between the school and the community, those forming the committee must take care to ensure that appropriate members are selected and that this process is accomplished in a professional manner that avoids any possible confusion or embarrassment. One method of selecting members is to have one representative from the school and one from an industry or an association select individuals after consulting with recognized leaders in the field to be served. Another procedure is to have the representatives selected by organized groups within the community so the individuals can serve as delegates and actually speak on behalf of the parent group. Some schools have found it effective to call a community meeting and ask for open nominations from which the final membership is selected.

While any of these approaches may be appropriate under specific conditions, the use of a selection committee is recommended. Normally, such a committee is composed of three or four members, with one being a member of the school staff. The other members should be well-respected citizens, knowledgeable about the program and the community, and available to serve on a three- or four-year basis. As an ad hoc committee, the group functions sporadically and for a short duration. Its prime responsibilities are to determine the characteristics and components of the community; secure the names of representative individuals; and interview, screen, and recommend the individuals best qualified to serve.

Regardless of the selection method used, a list of qualified candidates representative of the community should be developed, and sufficient information concerning the individuals must be obtained to ensure that the criteria for membership are fulfilled. This information can be obtained in an interview and summarized as indicated in Figure 10–4. Prior to conducting the interview, the list should receive a preliminary approval to eliminate anyone who is not acceptable to the approving group or individual.

Committee member qualities. One of the primary goals in the selection of an advisory committee is to secure active participation by those individuals in the community who are able and willing to contribute most to the success of the career or occupational education program. Since one of the most important considerations is the selection of personnel to serve on the committee, discretion must be exercised to ensure the selection of individuals with an ability and willingness to contribute and cooperate. There are at least three overall criteria that should be kept in mind when selecting individuals for membership. First, members must have had successful firsthand experience in the area in which the committee will serve. They should be persons with the respect and confidence of their associates, know their jobs thoroughly, and have a broad understanding of various careers in the area. Second, members should be in a position to devote adequate time to the committee so close contact can be maintained with the school, and they should be energetic and enthusiastic. Third, members should be of high character and demonstrate desirable personal qualities such as intelligence, integrity, courage, and an unselfish spirit. Members should exhibit a strong sense of responsibility, civic-mindedness, and a willingness to cooperate with various segments of the community.

Shinn [150:252] summarized these qualities by recommending that committee members be selected on the basis of the following qualifications:

- be presently engaged in or connected with the work community in positions directly related to your program;
- be interested in and enthusiastic about your program's activities;
- be willing to give of their time to attend regularly scheduled meetings, make visitations, and serve on advisory committee appointed committees.
- have a wide variety of educational and work experience background;
- be willing and capable of providing positive input at meetings.

Committee representational factors. In addition to desirable personal qualities, committee members must be representative of the total school and community area they serve. Balance must be maintained to ensure that all points of view are represented, that recommendations do not favor a particular corporation or segment of the community, and that all phases

FIGURE 10-4. Prospective advisory committee interview form

Name _____

Home Address _____

Name of Business _____

Position _____ Phone _____

Address of Business _____

Type of Business _____

Approximate Number of Employees: Men _____ Women _____

Does your company have representatives on other advisory committees?

               Yes _____ No _____

When is the best time for you to meet on the committee?

               Time

     Breakfast   _____

     Lunch   _____

     Afternoons _____

     Evenings   _____

Would you need transportation to attend meetings? Yes _____ No _____

COMMENTS: _____

_____

_____

_____

_____

of the program are treated in a consistent manner. Before forming the advisory committee, the selection committee should develop a profile of the community in respect to the areas that need representation—i.e., large, medium, and small businesses or industries; labor and management; employment agencies; graduates from the program; civic leaders; and school staff. The seven major representational factors used by the Dakota County Area Vocational Technical Institute [45] provide working guidelines for the selection of members:

1. *Management/Worker Balance*
   A good balance between worker and manager is desirable on a committee.

2. *Size/Type of Firms/Businesses*
   Many sizes and types of firms frequently hire persons in the same occupational area with different expectations. Plan your committee so you can illuminate the differences and similarities between them.

3. *Geographic Differences*
   If your community includes urban, rural, and suburban populations, you should account for this.

4. *Organized Labor*
   If your occupational area is one in which there is an organized union, they should be represented on the committee.

5. *Associations*
   In many professions, businesses, or industries there are associations formed to represent the viewpoints of their members.

6. *Students*
   Students both past and present can make a contribution to an advisory committee in light of their knowledge of the program. At the secondary level particularly, a parent can speak from a particularly advantageous viewpoint.

7. *Sex, Age, and Minorities*
   In many occupational areas there is great concern with recruiting new workers without sex, age, or minority bias. A committee member familiar with viewpoints of the opposite sex, a particular age group, or minority viewpoints can be an important asset.

Special attention must be placed on other agencies in the community—such as CETA, vocational rehabilitation, or other social agencies—that have paralleling interests or programs to those operated by the school. Similarly, the views and needs of the handicapped and disadvantaged must also be represented on the committee.

Appointment of committee members

If the selected committee member responds positively to the letter of invitation, the highest administrator or school board chairperson should send a formal letter of appointment to the new member. Figures 10-5 and 10-6 illustrate possible letters that may be sent. The sending of these letters formalizes the process, ensures prestige to the committee, clarifies

FIGURE 10-5.   *Sample letter of invitation*

```
Ms. Jane America
Bank Manager
Withit Bank and Trust
Your Town, Indiana

Dear Ms. America:

Because of your experience and demonstrated competency in the field of
(General Committee—vocational education; Program Committee—vocational pro-
gram area), the Board of (Name of School) believes that you could perform a
valuable service to the school and community, as a citizen member of the (Title
of Committee) Advisory Committee of (Name of School).

The advisory committee is composed of outstanding business and civic leaders
in the community and is directed toward achieving closer cooperation between
business and education in providing vocational training for young people
and adults in our community.

I would appreciate it if you would give this invitation to serve on the (Name
of Committee) Advisory Committee your consideration and inform me of your
decision in the next few days.  Your acceptance of committee membership will
aid in the vocational program of (Name of School).

Sincerely,



Administrator and/or
  Chairperson of Board
```

Indiana State Advisory Council on Vocational Education. *Local Advisory Committee Handbook.* Indianapolis: Indiana State Advisory Council on Vocational Education, 1976, p. 12. Used with permission.

FIGURE 10-6. Sample letter of appointment

Dear _____

    The _____ is pleased to inform you of your appoint-
ment to the Vocational Education Advisory Council. We wish to thank you for
your indication of your willingness to serve on this advisory council.

    The ultimate objective of the advisory council is to improve and expand
opportunities in vocational education. Your active interest and participation
will be influential in helping to make this community a better place in which
to live and work.

    We realize that your time is limited, and we will make every effort to
have meetings and other business prompt, precise, and purposeful. Initially,
meetings will be held once a month, and after the council is functioning they
may be held less frequently. The period of service may be from one to three
years. This will be determined at one of the early meetings.

    Your first meeting as a member of the advisory council is scheduled for
_____ at _____ P.M. at the _____.
A copy of the tentative agenda for the first meeting is enclosed.

    We hope that you will be able to attend. Please inform us as quickly
as possible whether or not you will be able to attend our first meeting.

    If you have questions regarding the appointment, please do not hesitate
to call me at (phone number).

                                       Sincerely yours,

                                     School Administrator

Alabama Division of Vocational Education. *Guide for Organizing and Utilizing Local Vocational Education Advisory Councils.* Montgomery: Alabama State Department of Education, 1977, p. 12. Used with permission.

FIGURE 10-7. *Sample certificate of membership*

THE STERLING PUBLIC SCHOOL DISTRICT
STERLING, NORTH DAKOTA

Certificate of Membership

This is to Certify That

_____

has served as a member of the advisory committee for the
VOCATIONAL OFFICE EDUCATION PROGRAM
of the Sterling Public High School for the year 19____ to 19____
We gratefully acknowledge the services of the above named.

PRESIDENT, BOARD OF EDUCATION   SUPERINTENDENT OF SCHOOLS   VOCATIONAL TEACHER

Board for Vocational Education. *The Vocational Education Advisory Committee.* Fargo: North Dakota State Advisory Council for Vocational Education, undated, p. 17. Used with permission.

the service role the member is to perform, and sets the stage for a harmonious relationship. Once the new member accepts the appointment, it is common practice to send a separate package of materials including an advisory committee handbook, a framed certificate of membership (Figure 10–7), and minutes from the previous year.

Orientation of committee members

The orientation process for new members starts as the individuals are being selected and appointed to the committee. Much of this may occur in the process of convincing the individual of the importance of serving on the committee or when describing the program and the role of the advisory committee. Adequate attention, however, must be focused on this task because the haphazard orientation of new members can result in a committee that does nothing or one that extends beyond its intended purpose. A locally prepared handbook can be helpful; but if one is not available, the following items should be brought up with each new member individually or at the first meeting of the committee; (a) an overview of the total educational program, (b) a discussion of the career and occupational programs, (c) the role of the advisory committee, (d) recent accomplishments of advisory committees, (e) the responsibilities and duties of committee members, (f) a list of advisory committees and of their members, and (g) the organizational structure and meeting plans.

Advisory committee meetings

The first meeting of a newly formed advisory committee or the initial meeting of the year for an established committee is important if the committee is to make a constructive addition to the educational program. The series of preliminary and orientation activities should culminate in this meeting. The teacher or director responsible for the meeting must plan it well and should hold it within thirty days of the committee appointment date or after the beginning of the school year. Since not everything can be covered, the goals of the committee leader in this first meeting should be to familiarize the committee with the key facets of the program, acquaint committee members with the purpose and duties of the committee, plan meetings for specific purposes, and develop a regular schedule for committee activities.

Preparation for the meeting. The effectiveness of the first meeting depends on the amount of time devoted to planning the meeting, which, in turn, will depend on the experience of the members, the length of time the committee has been in operation, the focus (social and/or business) of the meeting, and the manner or style (formal or informal) utilized by the teacher or program director. The following should be included on the agenda of the first meeting:

- Review of the minutes of the previous meeting
- Committee reports
- Teachers' reports
- Unfinished business
- Communications
- New business
- Suggestions from members
- Plans for the next meeting

Physical and organizational preparations can directly affect the meeting. The meeting room should be well lighted, well ventilated, and appropriately furnished. Those in charge of the meeting should make proper reservations, provide directions to the room or building, answer parking questions, order refreshments, and make available appropriate materials, supplies, and equipment.

Agenda for the meetings. The individual being advised, in cooperation with the chairperson, prepares the agenda and sends it to each member before the meeting. It normally includes from three to five new items of discussion. The agenda should not include routine, operational questions that can be handled through personal contact or by a telephone call. In its meetings, the committee should focus its attention on areas in which advice is needed. Ample time must be provided for input; the meeting is a time for school personnel who are committee members to listen.

The first meeting is the one exception to this guide since the school personnel usually have full responsibility for it. Normally, the responsible teacher or director plans, organizes, and conducts this meeting. This should be pointed out so new members can properly assess their role on the committee. Since this meeting differs from subsequent meetings, some major areas need special attention.

Boyd [23:8-9] summarized these as follows:

1. Welcome and remarks by the school personnel.

2. Introduction and biographic information about members of the committee

3. Statement of the role of the committee and how it is expected to be of assistance to the school

4. The names and brief biographic information of key school officials and teachers

5. A brief sketch of the history and background of the school

6. The nature and objectives of the school

7. The nature and objectives of the specific program

8. A brief outline of problems of the school and specific program

9. Future plans for expansion of the school or a specific program

10. Standards specified in Federal acts for vocational education and the State plan for vocational education

11. Organization of the committee
    a. Selection of chairperson and secretary
    b. Selection of dates and time for meetings

12. Other items

13. Adjournment

How this initial meeting is conducted will determine the number of topics that can be covered. Figure 10-8 suggests a social/business approach for this first meeting and a postponent of some topics to a later meeting. In this way, a sharper focus can be maintained; and the members can feel more comfortable about the meeting and their contributions to it.

Minutes of meetings. The reporting of discussions and actions taken by the committee serves as a valuable resource for the committee. The minutes from the meeting provide an official record of the activities of the committee and are used as a means of providing regular reports to committee members and those associated with the committee, as a historical record, as a source to orient new members, and as a basis for forming official recommendations made by the committee.

At the end of each meeting, the secretary and chairperson should

FIGURE 10-8. Sample agenda for the first meeting of a general vocational education advisory committee

September, 19___

Time	Item	Responsible
6:30	Social hour Refreshments by occupational food service students	Vocational Student Organizations
7:00	Meeting called to order Introduction of members, school officials, teachers, and dignitaries	Director of Vocational Education
7:15	Guest speaker	
7:40	Charge to committee	Chairperson of the School Board
7:45	Remarks	Superintendent of Schools
7:50	Overview of vocational education Vocational education programs (visual) Advisory committee concepts Vocational education advisory committee charge	Director of Vocational Education
8:20	Problems needing study	
8:35	Establish date, time, and place of next meeting Agenda for next meeting Election of officers Adoption of bylaws Planning year's agenda	
8:45	Call for adjournment	
8:45–9:30	Conducted tours by vocational students	

Walter S. Ramey. *A Guide for the Organization and Operation of Local Advisory Committees for Vocational Education.* Richmond: Virginia State Department of Education, 1975, p. 26. Used with permission.

FIGURE 10-9. Sample agenda for the first meeting

6:30	Social hour Refreshments or meal	
7:00	Meeting called to order	Director of Vocational Education or School Representative
7:05	Welcome	School Administrator
7:10	"The Role of the Advisory Council"	Guest Speaker
7:30	The vocational education program	Local Director or School Representative
7:45	Overview of the total educational program	School Official
8:00	Election of officers	
8:15	Appointment of bylaws committee	Chairperson
8:20	Establish date, time, and place of next meeting	Chairperson
8:30	Call for adjournment	Chairperson

Alabama Division of Vocational Education. *Guide for Organizing and Utilizing Local Vocational Education Advisory Councils.* Montgomery: Alabama State Department of Education, 1977, p. 5. Used with permission.

FIGURE 10-10. *Sample agenda for a regular meeting of a carpentry craft advisory committee meeting*

7:30 Call to order	Chairperson
Approval of minutes	Secretary

Report of the subcommittee on safety practice observed in the school shop and in work on class project:

      Discussion of report and recommendations

Report on additional tools and equipment needed for the class:

      Report on status of equipment and tools on hand,

                              _____ , Instructor

      Discussion and recommendations

Plans for class project for school year:

      Report of tentative plans _____ , Director

      Discussion and recommendations

Other business

10:00   Adjournment

Missouri Advisory Council on Vocational Education. *Handbook for Local Advisory Committees.* Jefferson City: Missouri Advisory Council of Vocational Education, 1977, p. 17. Used with permission.

review the minutes and delete any unimportant material or add material that may have been omitted from the first draft of the minutes. Once the minutes have been edited and typed, the secretary should distribute them to all committee members and to those school officials who have the authority to implement the recommendations of the committee. For future reference, the secretary should maintain a complete file of the minutes and of all other documents related to the committee. The minutes should include the date, time of meeting, time of adjournment, place, name of presiding officer, those in attendance, and dates of future meetings. In addition to summarizing the regular business and discussion, the minutes should provide a detailed account of motions, recommendations, and significant points of discussion. Figure 10–11 suggests an overall format for the accurate reporting of committee minutes.

Scheduling of meetings. The committee should schedule meetings only when pertinent questions, issues, or recommendations need to be discussed or when key reports are to be made. Usually this is once a month, depending, of course, on the nature of the committee and the manner in which the committee is utilized. Meetings should be scheduled

FIGURE 10-11. Sample format for the minutes of a business education advisory committee

Date: _____ 19___ Place: _____ Time: _____

Members Present: _____

_____

_____

Members Absent: _____

Others Present: _____

MINUTES:

The Chairperson, (Name), opened the meeting and called for reading of the minutes of previous meeting.

The coordinator reported on the status of new classes: efficient reading, IBM tabulation and keypunch training, and preparation for Civil Service exams.

A discussion followed of possible new classes to meet the expressed needs of the community, and the Chairperson called for recommendations for classes, textbooks and teacher qualifications. Approved were: workshop course for medical secretaries; reorganization of advanced typing laboratory; adoption of a new shorthand text.

The coordinator reported on the plans to host the State meeting of FBLA/VOCA.

The committee voted to meet semimonthly instead of monthly.

The coordinator took the group on a tour of the remedial reading laboratory.

Meeting adjourned at (Time).

Respectfully submitted,

Secretary

Coordinator
Original for committee files and copies for each member and interested administrator.

Arizona Division of Vocational Education. *Advisory Committees.* Phoenix: Arizona State Department of Education, undated, p. 16. Used with permission.

well in advance so committee members can effectively plan their time. The time and day of the meetings should be agreed on at the first meeting or at the time the committee appointments are made. Monthly reminders, indicating the date, time, place, and purpose of the meeting, should be sent out well in advance of the meeting. Each member should also be informed and supplied with any data or special materials that may be discussed at the next meeting. If possible, the member should be reminded of the meeting by phone the day before the meeting and told approximately how long the meeting will last.

Committee structure and membership

The differences among communities, the scope of the committee activity, the nature of leadership, and the complexity of the program all suggest why the organizational structure of committees will vary. Figures 10–12, 10–13, and 10–14 illustrate three of the many alternatives available.

Chapter 2 suggested guidelines for the size of committees operated by career and occupational education personnel. While a size of twelve to fifteen was suggested for general advisory committees and five to eight for program committees, there are no prescribed numbers for membership. To determine how many members are desirable for a committee, consider the purpose of the committee, the size of the program, the size of the community, and which groups are to be represented. Group decision making can be difficult if the membership is too large; the use of subcommittees for specific assignments is a way of avoiding this potential problem.

Most schools appoint members to the committee on a regular, staggered schedule to ensure continuity, while at the same time providing an opportunity for replacing committee members. The method of rotation should be devised at the time the committee is created. A suggested method of rotation is to replace one-third of the committee each year after the committee has been in operation for two full years. Since the usual term of membership is three years, under this approach, one-third of the members of a newly created committee are appointed for two years, one-third for three years, and one-third for four years. This method provides for both continuity and the introduction of new members.

Committee organization

The organization of the committee must provide a system for transmitting committee recommendations to the official who is empowered to act on these suggestions and a procedure for the day-to-day operations of the committee.

The committee should maintain a general flow of information throughout the year by the sharing of committee minutes and periodic discussions between members of the committee and the school personnel. The committee may transmit its recommendations informally or formally. If it does so informally, the committee should develop a procedure to keep

FIGURE 10-12. *Example vocational-technical advisory committee organization*

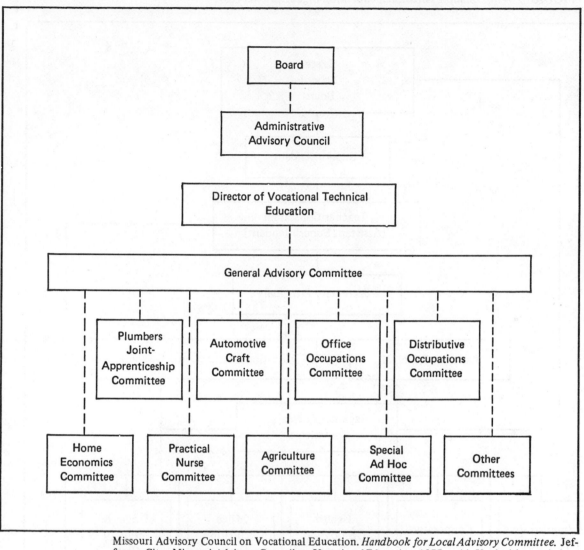

Missouri Advisory Council on Vocational Education. *Handbook for Local Advisory Committee.* Jefferson City: Missouri Advisory Council on Vocational Education, 1977, p. 11. Used with permission.

FIGURE 10-13. *Example occupational advisory committee structure*

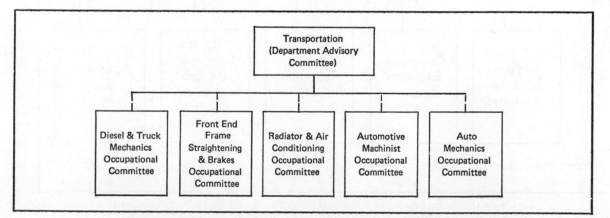

Provided by Bud Haan, Averill Career Opportunities Center, Saginaw, Michigan, March 1977. Used with permission.

FIGURE 10–14. Sample vocational education organizational chart

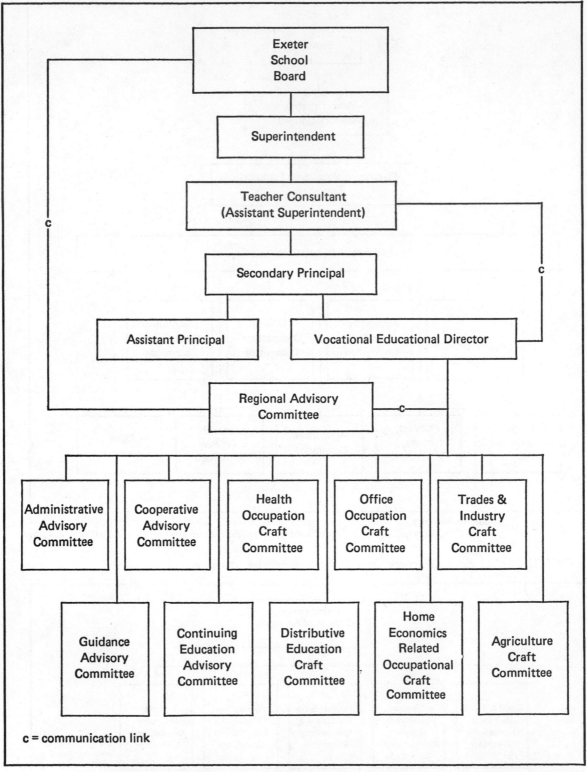

New Hampshire Division of Vocational Education. *Making the Most of Your Advisory Committee.* Concord: New Hampshire State Department of Education, undated, Appendix D. Used with permission.

all involved administrative personnel informed. Good judgment and a sensitivity to the seriousness with which the chain of command is taken often mean that roadblocks that could materialize out of misunderstandings never appear. The committee should present major recommendations formally in written form. To avoid any possible confusion, the chairperson of the committee or school representative may wish to be present when these recommendations are made to the board or to the top administrative officers. Each school, community, and board will have to work out its own details for approving and acting on the advice of the committee.

For its day-to-day operations, three officers are usually sufficient to meet the internal needs of the committee: chairperson, vice-chairperson, and secretary. Depending on the size of the committee, the committee may sometimes form an executive committee.

Committee chairperson. The chairperson should be from the community and should be elected by the committee from its membership. The selection of the chairperson is critical because much of the success of the committee will depend on her or him. The individual must be sensitive to the views of the members; be able to listen critically; exercise good judgment, fairness, and reasonableness; and be able to work closely with the school liaison. The chairperson will be expected to spend more time than the other committee members on the affairs of the committee and must be well informed and well prepared.

From the beginning, the committee members must be aware of the school's need for committee assistance and of the respect they, as committee members, command. Likewise, the chairperson should be recognized by school leaders as the head of the committee. The chairperson must be an active leader with all of the usual duties and prerogatives. The hard-to-define and difficult-to-establish successful working relationships within a committee can be shattered by the feeling that the chairperson is only a figurehead.

The responsibilities of the chairperson are to

1. Establish meeting dates and call the meeting to order
2. Plan the meeting agenda with the individual(s) receiving advice from the committee,
3. Develop a sociable, relaxed, and rewarding atmosphere conducive to productive discussion and dialogue,
4. Plan committee activities and provide sufficient background information as needed,
5. Maintain the necessary personal contacts with members and school personnel,
6. Approve all announcements, notices, and other information sent to committee members,
7. Preside over all meetings, lead discussions, and bring closure on key points of discussion.

In performing these roles, the chairperson should avoid being the final authority on all subjects, putting pressure on the group to agree with his or her personal views, chairing subcommittees, and discussing questions or issues that are outside the purpose of the committee.

Committee vice-chairperson. The vice-chairperson works closely with the chairperson on all tasks and may serve as the facilitator for many of the activities of the committee. In addition to performing specific tasks assigned by the chairperson, the vice-chairperson serves in the absence of the chairperson and acts as the program chairperson for the committee. As a potential chairperson, the vice-chairperson should also be selected carefully.

Committee secretary. This position requires a person who is tactful, patient, hardworking, and willing to adjust to the committee. It is suggested that a school representative serve as secretary for the committee, to act as the liaison between the school and the community and to maintain a close working relationship with members of the committee. The secretary can also assist the chairperson in setting the tone of the committee activity. The duties of the secretary are to

1. Prepare and mail agenda, announcements, minutes, and other information to committee members and others associated with the program,
2. Prepare and forward necessary correspondence,
3. Provide statistical information about the school and disseminate progress reports,
4. Explain committee actions (along with the chairperson) to school personnel,
5. Be alert, imaginative, and sensitive to points of view and suggestions from the committee,
6. Motivate appropriate school officials to implement and respond to committee recommendations.

Executive committee. In the case of general advisory committees or large committees, it is common to form an executive committee to help facilitate the work of the larger committee. In such cases, the executive committee coordinates the activities of the main committee with other committees in the system, it plans programs, and it prepares meeting agenda. The executive committee should be authorized by the committee of the whole to conduct business as designated by the larger committee. It is usually composed of the elected officers of the main committee.

Committee member responsibilities

Committee members have certain rights and certain responsibilities. Their rights include

1. Having a letter signed by some educational official requesting that they serve on the committee,

2. Knowing exactly what is expected of them in the way of advice, assistance, cooperation, time, and support,

3. Being provided initially and on a continuing basis with information concerning the career and occupational education program developments,

4. Being invited to attend local and state meetings concerning career and occupational education,

5. Receiving special invitations to attend educational functions pertaining to the program,

6. Being kept informed of special studies affecting the program and the educational system.

In return, committee members are expected to

1. Attend meetings regularly, participate in committee discussions, and serve on subcommittees,

2. Study carefully any problem or question before the committee and seek the counsel and recommendations of constituents in the community before committing themselves to a final conclusion,

3. Respect the rights of fellow members by not reporting or discussing the opinions of other members outside the committee. The opinions and conclusions of the committee on which there is a consensus may be discussed informally.

4. Study and advise on school matters as a part of group action. No individual member of the committee has any rights or privileges that are not possessed as a member of the community. When involved in other public activities, the member must be careful to avoid the possible confusion as to whether he or she is speaking as an individual or as a member of the committee.

Special responsibilities for school personnel and student members

In addition to the duties and responsibilities already outlined for committee members and officers, school representatives and student members of the committee have a unique role because of their close, direct ties with the school.

School representatives. As members of the school staff, educational personnel can expect to be called on to do more than other committee members. For example, they should be prepared to offer clear explanations, from the school's viewpoint, of problems that come before the committee or to obtain answers by the next meeting. They may be asked to do research, provide information, or prepare special reports. They may also be involved in making special arrangements for facilities and equipment to be used by the committee. If nothing else, the general impressions, personal relationships, and respect they convey and demonstrate can have a direct impact on the effectiveness of the committee and on how the committee is viewed by its school colleagues.

Student committee members.   While it is common for only one student to serve on each advisory committee, that student's role is extremely important. Students are the ones directly affected by the recommendations of the committee. Normally, the student member is an officer in a student organization or is an active member in such a group. Student committee members have the same rights and responsibilities as other committee members. Typically, students assume an active role in committee activities and can provide a realistic perspective of the program. Student members must be properly introduced so any possible uneasiness they may feel in interacting with other committee members may be avoided.

Committee handbook

A committee handbook can be a useful tool in orienting new committee members, organizing the committee, providing an overall view of committee activities, and providing specific direction to those serving on the committee. A looseleaf notebook or folder system is suggested so new materials can be easily added. Some of the key sections of this resource might include the following:

- Letter of introduction to the handbook
- Advisory committee directory
- Method of selecting members and officers
- Responsibilities of committee officers
- Functions of the advisory committee
- Former actions and committee minutes
- Philosophy of the school, career, and occupational programs
- School and program organizational chart
- Program objectives and descriptors
- Brochures describing the program
- Information about youth activities
- Floor plans of the career and occupational education facilities
- Summaries of federal and state legislation
- Related provisions of the state plan for vocational education

Advisory committee constitution and/or bylaws

The committee has the responsibility to develop an appropriate organizational structure. To provide a guiding structure for this process, the committee develops or adopts a constitution and/or bylaws. School personnel should take the lead in this process so as to reduce the time devoted to this task. Committee members who have had previous experiences in this area can be of great assistance. Adopting a prepared set of bylaws without taking the time to study them properly, however, can pave the way for dissension within the committee at a later date. The school representative should explain the committee's assignment, the committee's structure, and the committee's relationship to the program. Each item of the proposed bylaws should be discussed and modified, deleted, or approved by a majority vote of the committee.

Some possible formats for advisory committee constitutions and/or bylaws are provided on the following pages.

FIGURE 10-15. Advisory committee constitution and bylaws

ADVISORY COMMITTEE CONSTITUTION

Section A. Purposes and name

ARTICLE I   (Persons and agencies to whom the advisory committee is to be advisory.) The above named advisory committee shall exist only during such time as it may be authorized by the Board of Education.

ARTICLE II   (Operating field of Advisory Committee.) The above named Advisory Committee shall operate in those fields directly included in the program for which it has been appointed, and shall limit its activities to matters which directly concern the program.

ARTICLE III   (Purpose and duties of the Advisory Committee.) The purposes and duties of the above named advisory committee shall be to:

1. Study the needs of the industry which may be related to the work of the department.

2. Aid and guide the department in those activities which will lead toward progress.

3. Help in developing a program for the department that will better fit the industry.

4. Offer recommendations for the improvement of the instruction offered and the instructional facilities available.

5. Assist in evaluating the success of the courses offered, in the light of the objectives previously selected.

6. Correlate the work of the department with that of other unions, labor, management, and Chamber of Commerce, with which the advisory committee and committee members may have close relationships.

7. Assist the department in resisting inappropriate and unreasonable demands from the community.

8. Study the programs in other communities with the idea of encouraging the use of those practices which may be applicable to the Local School.

9. Revise the objectives of the department as warranted by study and experience.

10. Serve as an avenue of communication between the department and industry.

11. Estimate or measure annually the progress made toward accepted objectives.

Section B. Membership

ARTICLE I   Number of Advisory Committee members. The number of committee members will be 3 (minimum) and 7 (maximum) plus ex officio members.

ARTICLE II   Members shall be selected to represent a cross section of industries served by the department.

ARTICLE III   The active advisory committee will submit names of prospective committee members to the Superintendent or Board of Education.

ARTICLE IV   Each appointment of an advisory committee member shall be for three years, except when the appointment is to fill an unexpired term.

ARTICLE V   At least two-thirds of the members will be retained each year with none serving more than three successive years, and that one year will expire before any outgoing member may be reappointed for a full term after serving the unexpired term of a member who has left the committee.

ARTICLE VI   One-third of total membership shall be appointed each year.

ARTICLE VII   The term of a new committee member shall begin on September 1.

ARTICLE VIII   An individual will automatically lose membership in the committee if he/she fails to attend two successive meetings without presenting, in advance, to the chairperson of the committee a valid reason for his/her absence.

ARTICLE IX   The instructor in charge will be expected to be present at each committee meeting. The director shall be encouraged to attend each meeting.

ARTICLE X   The teachers of department shall attend committee meetings at the request of the Advisory Committee.

ARTICLE XI   Advisory Committee Chairperson shall represent the group at the official meeting requested by the director.

Section C. The Constitutional Changes

ARTICLE I   The constitution, articles, and bylaws may be amended or added to by a two-thirds majority vote of active members at any regular committee meeting.

BYLAWS

Section A. Meetings

ARTICLE I   Regular meetings of the Advisory Committee will be held during the school year.

ARTICLE II   The advisory committee or its executive committee may call special meetings of the advisory committee.

ARTICLE III   Written notices of committee meetings shall be mailed to all members at least 30 days before each meeting by the committee secretary.

ARTICLE IV   Meetings shall not be more than six hours long unless a majority of the committee members vote to continue a particular meeting for more than six hours.

ARTICLE V   Officers of the committee and the instructor in charge will meet prior to committee meetings to prepare the agenda.

ARTICLE VI   As the need for standing and special committees arises, such committees may be appointed by the chairperson.

Section B. Officers and their duties

ARTICLE I   The officers shall be: a chairperson, a vice-chairperson and a secretary.

ARTICLE II   Chairperson, vice-chairperson shall be elected annually by majority vote of the committee members at the annual meeting. The secretary shall be the instructor in charge of the department.

ARTICLE III   The chairperson shall be elected from among those members who have served on the advisory committee for at least one year.

Chairperson duties shall be:
a. to preside at the meetings of the advisory committee.
b. to serve as chairperson of the executive committee.
c. to appoint special committees which may include persons other than committee members.

ARTICLE IV   The vice-chairperson shall perform the duties of the chairperson in his/her absence.

ARTICLE V   The secretary shall:

a. keep records of the attendance of members at meetings.
b. keep a record of discussion and recommendations.
c. maintain a permanent record file of advisory committee activities.
d. distribute minutes of committee meetings and copies of other committee documents to committee members, teachers, and others who may be concerned. He/she shall have the assistance of the school staff and the use of school facilities in performing these functions.

ARTICLE VI   The executive committee shall consist of the chairperson, vice-chairperson, and secretary, and the instructor in charge as an ex officio member. It shall:

a. act on urgent committee matters between committee meetings.
b. prepare agenda for committee meetings if requested to do so by the advisory committee.
c. call special meetings of the advisory committee as they are needed.

North Dakota State Board for Vocational Education. *The Vocational Education Advisory Committee*. Fargo: North Dakota State Advisory Council for Vocational Education, undated, pp. 14–16. Used with permission.

FIGURE 10-16. Constitution for Lewis County Area Occupational Center, Glenfield, New York

ARTICLE I—ORGANIZATION NAME

The name of the organization shall be: Advisory Council for the Lewis County Area Occupational Center.

ARTICLE II—PURPOSE

The purpose of this council shall be to act in an advisory capacity in all matters pertaining to the improvement of the Occupational program as it relates to secondary school students, out-of-school youth and adults of the community and to assist the Director of Occupational Education in this pursuit.

ARTICLE III—MEMBERSHIP

Prospective members shall be recommended to the Jefferson Lewis Board of Cooperative Educational Services, for their appointment, by the Director of Occupational Education. The membership shall include, but not be limited to, persons:

1. Familiar with vocational needs and problems of management and labor in the region.
2. Familiar with programs of occupational education at the postsecondary and adult levels.
3. Familiar with the manpower needs and requirements of the region to be served.
4. Familiar with the special educational needs of the physically and mentally handicapped.
5. Representative of community interests, including persons familiar with the special needs of the population to be served.
6. Representatives (2) of the students attending the Occupational Center. Their terms shall be for one year.

ARTICLE IV—TERM OF MEMBERSHIP

Members shall serve a term of three years and the effective date of membership shall be July 1, except as indicated in Article III, Section 6.

ARTICLE V—ATTENDANCE

Each Advisory Council member is expected to play an active role on the council. Failure to attend two consecutive meetings shall be interpreted as a resignation. Such members shall however have the privilege of requesting the council to waive this requirement.

ARTICLE VI—OFFICERS AND RESPONSIBILITIES

Officers of the council shall include:

1. *Chairperson* who shall:
   a. Schedule meetings
   b. Preside over such meetings
   c. Appoint all necessary committees
2. *Vice-Chairperson*
   Shall perform the responsibilities of the Chairperson in the latter's absence.
3. The *Executive Secretary*
   Shall conduct the official correspondence and develop, distribute and maintain the records of all council proceedings.

Each officer shall be elected for a one year term prior to each July 1.

ARTICLE VII—FREQUENCY OF MEETINGS

The advisory council shall meet a minimum of five times per calendar year. Meetings shall be conducted during September, November, January, March and June.

Additional meetings may be called at the discretion of the Chairperson.

ARTICLE VIII—AGENDA

The Chairperson and the Director shall develop an agenda and include a copy of it with a notice of each preceding meeting.

ARTICLE IX—CONSTITUTION AMENDMENTS

Amendments of this constitution shall be made upon notification by mail of the total membership of the proposed change no later than 30 days prior to the voting date.

A majority vote of the total membership in an affirmative manner will be necessary to effect such change.

"Constitution for Lewis County Area Occupational Center," a paper provided by Myrle Bauer, Jefferson Vocational-Technical Center, Watertown, New York, undated. Used with permission.

*FIGURE 10-17.   Barstow regional adult and vocational education council
(BRAVE)*

(Approved October 14, 1976)

I. *Purpose of the Council*

The purpose of the Council, in order to avoid unnecessary duplication as cited in Section 6268.10 of the California State Education Code, is to meet and review vocational and adult education courses and programs and make recommendations which promote optimum articulation and integration of existing and future vocational and adult educational programs within the area served by the Council.

II. *Geographic Boundaries of the Council*

The geographic boundaries of the Council cover the mutual areas served by the Barstow Community College District and the Barstow Unified School District.

III. *Time of Meetings*

The Council will meet on a regular basis at least once every two months.

IV. *Members*

There shall be eleven (11) members of the Council.

  A. *Composition of Membership and Selection*

    1. Representative of the Comprehensive Employment and Training Act selected by the Prime Sponsor (one member).

    2. Representative of a Private Post-Secondary School, limited to officers and employees of that institution (one member).

    3. Secondary School representation based upon nominations and elections outlined in Section 11616 of the California State Administrative Code, Title V (four members).

    4. Community College representation based upon nominations and elections outlined in Section 11616 of the California State Administrative Code, Title V (four members).

    5. Representative of the San Bernardino County Superintendent of Schools selected by its Board of Education (one member).

  B. *Term of Office*

  Members of the Council shall serve terms of two years.

  C. *Voting Rights*

  Each member of the Council, including the chairperson, has one vote.

  D. *Quorum*

  A quorum shall consist of a majority of the membership. The concurrence of six members of the Council shall be necessary to the validity of any of its Acts.

  E. *Attendance Policy*

  The Council shall recommend to the appointing power the resignation of any member who is absent from three consecutive meetings. In cases of extenuating circumstances, after three consecutive absences, a member may request and be excused from meetings by a majority vote of the Council.

F. *Resignations*

A member may resign by filing a written resignation with the appointing power and with the Council chairperson.

G. *Alternates, Proxy Voting*

Substitute or alternate members and proxy votes are prohibited.

H. *Vacancy*

Vacancies occurring in incompleted terms shall be filled by the initial appointing power. Appointing power is defined as:

Secondary School	The District Board
Community College	The Community College Board
C.E.T.A.	The Prime Sponsor
Private Post-Secondary	Election by eligible Private Post-Secondary Schools
County Representative	The County Board of Education

V. *Officers*

There shall be a chairperson and a vice-chairperson.

A. *Election and Term of Office*

Officers shall serve a one-year term or until a replacement is selected and shall be elected by a majority of the Council. Elected officers shall serve from July 1 to June 30 and may be re-elected.

B. *Time of Election*

Elections will be held at the Council's May meeting.

C. *Removal*

Any officer elected or appointed by the Council may be removed by a two-thirds vote of all members whenever in the judgment of the membership the best interests of the Council would be served.

D. *Vacancy*

A vacancy in any office for any reason may be filled by the Council for the unexpired portion of the term.

E. *Chairperson—Duties*

The chairperson shall preside at all meetings of the Council and may sign all letters, reports, and other communications. In addition, the chairperson shall perform all duties incident to the office of chairperson and such other duties as may be prescribed by the membership from time to time.

F. *Vice-Chairperson—Duties*

The duties of the vice-chairperson shall be to represent the chairperson in assigned duties and to substitute for the chairperson during time of absence. The vice-chairperson shall perform such other duties as from time to time may be assigned by the chairperson or by the Council.

VI. *Executive Secretary to the Council*

The Executive Secretary shall cause to be kept the minutes of the meetings, both regular and special, of the Council and shall transmit to each member, and to such other persons as the Council may deem appropriate, true and correct copies of the minutes of such meetings; see that all notices are properly given; be custodian of the Council records; keep a register of the addresses and telephone numbers of the Council which shall be furnished to the secretary; and perform all duties as may be assigned by the Council or by the chairperson.

The secretary to the Council has no voting rights or privileges.

VII. *Committees*

A. *Advisory Committee*

A Vocational and Continuing Education Advisory Committee shall be appointed by the Council.

1. *Duties*

The Advisory Committee shall develop recommendations on existing programs, provide liaison between the programs and potential employers, and assist in the development of a plan for the short-term improvement of vocational and continuing education; and other duties as assigned by the Council.

2. *Membership*

The committee shall be composed of not more than eighteen members, consisting of a single-member representation from each of the following agencies:

a. Regional occupational centers and regional occupational programs.
b. A state university or college or campus of the University of California.
c. A field office of the Employment Development Department.
d. One or more representative from each of the following categories:
   1. Handicapped;
   2. Disadvantaged;
   3. Teachers;
   4. Business and Industry;
   5. Labor, the Joint Apprenticeship Committee, and Labor management;
   6. Any significant racial or ethnic minority, or both, in the region;
   7. Students.

3. *Term of Office*

Each member of the Advisory Committee shall serve a term of three (3) years. Vacancies shall be filled by the Council for the remainder of the term of the vacant position.

4. *Meetings*

The Advisory Committee shall meet periodically with the Council and may serve as an ad hoc committee on appropriate assignments of the Council.

5. *Attendance Policy*

The Advisory Committee shall recommend to the Council resignation of any member who is absent from three consecutive meetings. In cases of extenuating circumstances, a member may request and be excused from meetings by a majority vote of the advisory committee.

B. *Other Standing or Special Committees*

Other committees may be formed by the chairperson of the Council.

VIII. *Amendments to the Bylaws*

These bylaws may be amended by a vote of six (6) members of the Council.

"Bylaws for Barstow Regional Adult and Vocational Education Council," a paper provided by Mark J. Fabrizio, Barstow Unified School District, Barstow, California, undated. Used with permission.

SUGGESTED ACTIVITIES

1. Prepare a brief document describing the history and current status of the use of advisory committees in your school system.

2. Outline a procedure for assuring that school personnel responsible for establishing advisory committees have a thorough understanding of their functions.

3. Define the administrative heirarchy within your school system, and delineate any special procedures that should be followed in communicating with the administration regarding advisory committee establishment and activities.

4. Prepare a statement describing a proposed committee, including the purpose, responsibilities, and duties of the committee: its organizational structure: and its relationship to other school functions.

5. Outline a procedure that could be used for the orientation of newly selected committee members.

6. Determine the number of individuals to serve on the advisory committee of your school or program as well as the factors or areas to be represented by each member.

7. Gather and prepare appropriate documents to be assembled in a package of materials for each advisory committee member.

8. Prepare an agenda and make appropriate plans for the first meeting of a newly formed advisory committee.

9. Develop an outline for an advisory committee handbook and collect and prepare draft material for each section.

10. Prepare a preliminary constitution or set of bylaws that can be discussed by a committee.

SELECTED REFERENCES

Alabama Division of Vocational Education. *Guide for Organizing and Utilizing Local Vocational Education Advisory Councils.* Montgomery: Alabama State Department of Education, 1977.

American Vocational Association. *The Advisory Committee and Vocational Education.* Washington, D.C.: American Vocational Association, 1969.

Basualdo, Eugenio A. *Advisory Committees in Vocational-Technical Programs.* Memphis: State Technical Institute at Memphis, 1976.

Borgen, Joseph A., and Davis, Dwight E. *Planning, Implementing, and Evaluating Career Preparation Programs.* Bloomington, Ill.: McKnight Publishing Co., 1974.

Boyd, James E. *Organization and Effective Use of Representative Advisory Committees.* Cincinnati: Great Oaks Joint Vocational School District, 1975.

Burt, Samuel M. *Industry and Vocational-Technical Education.* New York: McGraw-Hill Book Co., 1967.

Carlisle, Howard M. *Situational Management.* New York: American Management Association, 1973.

Cochran, Leslie H.: Phelps, L. Allen: and Skupin, Joseph F. *A Guide for Effective Utilization of Advisory Committees.* Lansing: Michigan Department of Education, 1974.

Cook, Desmond L. *Program Evaluation and Review Technique: Applications to Education.* Washington, D.C.: GPO, 1966.

King, Sam W. *Organization and Effective Use of Advisory Committees.* Washington, D.C.: GPO, 1960.

McInnis, Douglas, W. "An Appraisal of the Organization and Function of Advisory Committees in Community College Occupational Education in the State of Washington," Doctoral Dissertation, Washington State University, 1971.

National Center for Research in Vocational Education. *Professional Vocational Teacher Education Module: Organize or Reorganize an Occupational Advisory Committee,* Module A-4. Columbus: The Ohio State University, 1975.

North Carolina Department of Community Colleges. *Organization, Function, and Operation of Advisory Committees.* Raleigh, N.C.: Department of Community Colleges. 1972.

Ramey, Walter S. *A Guide for the Organization and Operation of Local Advisory Committees for Vocational Education.* Richmond: Virginia State Department of Education, 1975.

Riendeau, Albert J. *Advisory Committees for Occupational Education: A Guide to Organization and Operation.* New York: McGraw-Hill Book Co., 1977.

11 The operation of a successful advisory committee

The accomplishments of any group depend, to a large degree, on the quality of leadership and whether the group is capable of operating effectively as a team. The advisory committee is no exception to this general rule; regardless of how well a committee may be organized, its effectiveness depends on the satisfactory integration of ingredients essential to basic group behavior.

While the preceding chapters have delineated specific goals, purposes, functions, and activities essential to operating a successful advisory committee, this chapter adds another ingredient—namely, guidelines to personal behavior, interpersonal relationships, and leadership approaches that will integrate these concepts within the context of a group dynamics process. This chapter is divided into three sections: first, a set of operating guidelines to be followed in planning, organizing, and leading committee activities; second, a group of precautions, potential pitfalls, and ways of avoiding negative reactions and criticisms; and third, a series of recommendations as a means for recognizing contributions made by advisory committee members.

In the process of implementing these suggestions, an atmosphere of trust and security must remain foremost. There must be an attitude of mutual confidence and respect in which each member feels free to express particular points of view openly on any pertinent issue. The group climate can have a vital effect on the committee and directly determines the vigor with which the group tackles its problems. If the group climate is one of tension, group interaction may be stifled. On the other hand, if members can be motivated to listen with interest to different viewpoints, even though they may not agree with these viewpoints, a climate conducive to effective committee action can be established [131].

OPERATING GUIDELINES FOR COMMITTEE ACTION

To learn to operate an advisory committee successfully, one might study leadership styles in order to develop a theoretical model for committee activity; one might study the theories of motivation; or one might draw key concepts from various theories of organizational behavior. None of these approaches, however, addresses the specific questions associated with the day-to-day operation of a successful advisory committee.

Simply stated: How do you get group members to work together effectively? For success, guidelines should be provided for the conducting of person-to-person relationships as well as for the operational practices that shape the overall group dynamics process.

Effective committee leadership

Personal relations form the basis for any leadership process. While the concepts and ideas that are presented in a discussion are an integral part of the leadership process, successful leadership depends on the leader's ability to deal with the reactions of individual personalities and to handle divergent points of view in a positive manner. Since each situation varies and calls for different reactions and responses, there are no set rules that can guarantee success in this process; but there are several guides that may be followed in respect to leadership qualities, traits, and actions. While these suggestions are directed at leaders of advisory committees, they form the basis for action for all committee members.

Leadership qualities. As in any group or organization, the leader needs to comprehend fully the factors that might affect the actions of the individuals involved. The three basic qualities of effective leadership are empathy, self-awareness, and objectivity. Simply knowing about the importance of these qualities will not ensure their development in a leader, but an understanding of these qualities can contribute to sound leadership and to a diagnosis of areas needing improvement.

- *Empathy* is the ability to look at things from another person's point of view. If committee leaders are to guide, motivate, or provide information, they need to be able to project themselves into the other person's position. Although no one can be expected to understand exactly the feelings or position of another, if you are empathetic you sense almost intuitively another person's reactions to a given situation.

- *Self-awareness* is an equally important requisite for leadership. To gain an accurate picture of yourself, you must be objective. Most individuals are not totally aware of their own preferences, weaknesses, or habits or of what impression a particular action may make on another individual. As a result, your self-image may differ from the way others perceive you. Not only is knowing yourself an important quality for leadership, it is essential for having a better understanding of others.

These self-perceptions can directly affect how individuals react to what is said or how it is said, thereby establishing potential motivation and communication problems.

• *Objectivity* is a third quality that is crucial to good leadership and effective person-to-person relationships. While empathy and self-awareness foster personal identification with other people, a good leader must also be objective in making decisions. An effective leader will be detached and will react to the behavior of others in an analytical rather than emotional way. The feelings of others must be understood, but impartiality must be maintained. By being open-minded and fair and maintaining a high level of objectivity, committee members will be able to assess different points of view in a constructive and cooperative manner.

Leadership traits. An integrated approach to group leadership combines the major advisory committee functions with the basic leadership qualities and a number of leadership traits. Working effectively with others requires many skills and insights. The listing of traits that follows is not complete, nor are the traits mutually exclusive. They do, however, create a framework for providing leadership for committee action [143].

• *Be Flexible.* Because of the complexity of various committee situations, the committee leader must maintain a high degree of flexibility to changing demands. Flexibility should not be confused with uncertainty or ambivalence.

• *Be Fair.* Committee members should be ready to accept new ideas or proposals. The committee leader must not show preference to certain individuals or to specific points of view.

• *Be Courteous.* An effective leader remains courteous and avoids offending other committee members.

• *Be Interested.* A committee leader must demonstrate interest and arouse it in others by showing enthusiasm about the topics under discussion.

• *Be Rational.* To work effectively with others, the leader must demonstrate a sound application of problem-solving principles.

• *Be Patient.* The leader should give the committee an appropriate amount of time to consider topics and answer important questions and should assist and encourage members who have difficulty expressing themselves.

• *Be Diagnostic.* The effective leader has the ability to diagnose objectively the emotional and rational needs produced by the committee situation.

• *Be Attentive.* The committee is composed of individuals with different backgrounds and specific expertise. The committee members and especially the leader of the group should listen for the full meaning of each comment that is made.

Leadership actions. As the committee develops into an effective group, it will assume its own character. Specific steps cannot be suggested to ensure that this developmental process occurs in the most productive manner. The following leadership actions, however, can help:

- Start on time
- Stick to the agenda
- Clearly state the problems to be considered
- Invite discussion, but do not encourage debate
- Keep attention focused on the problem at hand
- Secure participation from each member
- Retain a sense of humor
- Show appreciation for contributions
- Preserve an informal atmosphere
- Avoid playing the "school teacher"
- Keep discussions alive until all points are covered
- Direct group thinking, but provide an atmosphere conducive to discussion
- Summarize from time to time
- Record all ideas and conclusions
- Stop on time

Effective operational practices

Effective operational practices form the second basis for effective committee action. When properly integrated, good operational practices and desirable leadership traits form an overall approach to coordinating and guiding the tasks of the committee. As with effective committee leadership, there are no set rules that can ensure the successful operation of an advisory committee. Based on a study in New Jersey, however, Buontempo and Klavon [26] found that there are certain features characterizing effective advisory committees for career or vocational education. They concluded that (1) advisory committees are effective when there is a clearly stated organizational structure—for example, committee duties and purposes, lines of authority or responsibility, and relationships with the staff need to be clearly understood; (2) committees should give careful attention to their policies and procedures to ensure prompt and meaningful action, free interchange of ideas, effective subcommittee action, and regular feedback and a sense of accomplishment; (3) committee members should know how and why they were selected, choose a chairperson thoughtfully, and ensure that there are procedures for effective periodical evaluation; (4) the committee should deal with real problems, gain firsthand knowledge of the program, and openly participate in committee activities.

From a cursory review of publications from state departments of education, the following practices could be added to this list: (1) Develop a clearly written statement of the objectives, duties, and authority of the advisory committee. (2) Have the teacher or coordinator assist the committee in organizing and developing the ground rules and in electing its officers. (3) Maintain an informal conference or discussion approach rather than a more formalized *Robert's Rules of Order* approach. (When taking formal action, however, these *Rules* should be followed.) (4) Keep adequate records or minutes of all committee actions. (5) Send copies of all minutes to those parties and groups interested in the deliberations of the committee. The following points compiled by Riendeau [143:68–70] represent a comprehensive grouping of effective advisory committee practices*:

1. Provide a handbook for each member explaining the purpose, operation, bylaws, goals, and objectives of the advisory committee, and the functions lay members are expected to perform.

2. Provide parking permits for lay members to facilitate attending committee meetings at the school.

3. Schedule advisory committee meetings at a time convenient for lay members to attend.

4. Send a reminder letter along with a preliminary agenda of the coming meeting to each member about two weeks before a scheduled meeting and invite suggestions for inclusion on the agenda.

5. Run the committee meetings on an organized time schedule and hold to this schedule.

6. Make follow-up reports promptly to the advisory committee regarding action on recommendations made by the committee members.

7. Encourage the lay members to visit the school whenever possible, particularly the classes with which the committee is involved.

8. Provide lay members with maps of the campus to assist them in locating parking, meeting rooms, etc.

9. Send a letter over the signature of the school's leading administrator, officially notifying each lay member of his or her appointment to the advisory committee.

10. Encourage individual meetings with advisory committee members when an administrator or representative of the school requires special information.

11. Keep lay members informed about current and pending state and federal legislation that will affect the school's occupational program.

12. Inform the lay members about the pertinent actions and activities of the state board for vocational education.

13. Assign the responsibility for taking minutes to a school representative at each committee meeting.

14. Provide refreshments at each committee meeting.

*Albert, J. Riendeau. *Advisory Committees for Occupational Education: A Guide to Organization and Operation.* New York: McGraw-Hill Book Company, 1977. Used with permission.

15. Inform the lay members about special studies affecting the educational program of the school.

16. Invite instructors to sit in occasionally on committee meetings on the subject they teach.

17. Ask the lay members for recommendations and comments for improving the effectiveness of the committee and its meetings.

18. Invite the lay members to school functions such as graduation, open house, special exhibits, athletic events, and plays.

19. Establish and maintain a climate of informality at committee meetings, encouraging a full interchange of information.

20. Encourage school administrators to reward committee's efforts when particular goals have been achieved.

21. Inform the lay members about the actions and activities of the state advisory council for vocational education.

22. If possible, attend industry programs when invited by lay members.

23. Continually inform the lay members about events concerning vocational education at the local, state, and national levels.

24. Conduct telephone conversations with lay members when confirming facts or seeking advice.

25. Plan an annual breakfast or dinner for all committee members and invite a distinguished speaker.

26. Invite committee members to serve as guest lecturers in order to demonstrate special techniques or skills, or to discuss current practices in a particular occupation.

27. Work through committee members to arrange a conducted tour of industrial facilities for school field trips.

28. Inform the lay members about the actions and activities of the school's general advisory council.

29. Schedule committee meetings regularly.

30. Mail each member a copy of the minutes of the committee meeting as soon after the meeting as possible.

31. Make a reminder call to each member during the morning of the scheduled committee meeting.

32. Hold meetings in a room that provides comfortable and quiet surroundings.

33. Recognize the efforts of a lay member who contributes outstanding service to the program by any or all of the following methods: a letter to this person's superior, a letter to his or her family, a letter of commendation, a release to the school and local newspaper, or a mention of it in major speeches.

34. Put a name plate on donated equipment showing the contributing member's name and firm.

35. Encourage instructors to visit and tour the facilities of industries to which their teaching relates.

36. Keep committee rosters current and updated. Outdated rosters can be a source of embarrassment.

37. Check to see that no committee appointments are politically motivated.

38. Check to see that the qualifications of all potential lay members are carefully reviewed by appropriate school officials to ensure a good working committee.

39. Whenever possible, have the advisory committee include a student, a graduate, and a member of an ethnic or racial minority group.

40. Schedule the term of membership for a definite period of time, with provisions for a regular system of replacement.

41. Avoid unnecessary detail work for the committee members, who are busy individuals serving on a voluntary basis.

42. Have in attendance at all committee meetings a representative of the occupational education department.

43. Have supervisors and/or coordinators of vocational education programs attend all committee meetings on their particular programs.

44. Have the school maintain a complete file of minutes of all committee meetings. Copies will be distributed to all committee members and alternates.

45. Plan to hold at least one luncheon meeting per year at a good restaurant, if convenient, for the members of the committee.

PITFALLS COMMONLY ASSOCIATED WITH ADVISORY COMMITTEES

A properly organized and operating advisory committee can serve as a unifying agent in the educational/occupational/community partnership. It can make the school more sensitive to the community and the community more aware of the career and occupational offerings. It is unrealistic, however, to assume that there are no difficulties or pitfalls that might be associated with an advisory committee. In any activity that involves people working together, there is always a possibility for misunderstandings, personality conflicts, and differences in leadership and organizational styles. The increased availability of resource materials, the development of workshops, and the integration of instruction on advisory committees into teacher education programs may alleviate many of these problems.

Operational hazards

Although there is no prescription for these potential hazards, an awareness of and sensitivity to them during the process of planning, organizing, and operating an advisory committee may, in itself, ensure their nonexistence.

• A committee that is unrepresentative of the community or segments of the program may result in a loss of confidence, skewed recommendations, or an inaccurate reflection of the community.

• Members that "use the committee" as a means of venting hostile feelings, seeking publicity, or gaining power or prestige may significantly limit the effectiveness of the committee.

- A committee that extends beyond its normal scope of responsibility into such areas as labor-management controversies, partisan politics, fund raising, personnel matters, or the day-to-day operation of the program may reduce the prospects for community and school support.

- Actual or perceived lack of administrative support or unresponsiveness to committee recommendations may result in a lessening of the individual commitment of committee members.

- Ineffective organization, leadership, and communications may result in an inoperative committee and an unwillingness of the laity to serve on the committee.

- The committee may be misused because of lack of understanding of its role, its value, or how it can be used effectively.

- A committee can die of inactivity. Poorly planned or infrequently held meetings may cause little to be accomplished, unimportant questions to be worked on, or little carryover from one meeting to another.

- Morale problems for the school staff and dissension between the staff and the committee may develop if the committee is requested to perform school staff functions or to execute rather than recommend policy.

- Overburdening committee members and making unreasonable demands on their time may limit their willingness to serve on the committee or call into question issues that were not properly studied.

- Committee members may feel that they are being manipulated or that they are rubber-stamping decisions that have already been made.

- An inability to take into consideration different points of view, to deal positively with a member's suggestions, or to respect the particular interests and concerns that members represent may result in internal conflicts.

- Committee members may represent personal interests or deal with short-range needs rather than providing the community with an overall perspective of future needs.

- Apathy or complacent attitudes in relationship to committee activities may keep discussion at a superficial level.

- Committee members may not properly understand their roles and responsibilities, which may make them produce inappropriate recommendations or make them feel that they are only a "paper committee."

- If the committee is inadequately informed, it may produce inaccurate pronouncements, opinions, or recommendations.

- "Loading" or handpicking the committee with known supporters may limit the effectiveness of the committee and may affect how the community perceives the committee's actions.

- If school personnel take action in areas assigned to an advisory committee without first consulting the committee, mass resentment and negative reactions may result.

Leadership hazards

The committee leader should also avoid numerous pitfalls when working individually with committee members and when conducting committee meetings. The person responsible for such activities must demonstrate positive leadership skills while at the same time helping to develop a cooperative spirit among committee members.

- If the chairperson tries to dominate the discussion or to bring pressure on the group to agree with a personal view, it may turn the members off or cause a negative reaction.

- If school personnel use clichés or educational jargon, a lack of understanding or confusion on the part of other committee members may result.

- If a chairperson leaves a discussion hanging or does not bring to conclusion a particular issue, a feeling may be produced in the committee that little is ever accomplished and that the committee is wasting its time.

- A leader who establishes a personal level of expertise as the final authority on questions may adversely affect the interaction and cooperative attitude of committee members.

- Committee members who consistently demonstrate distracting mannerisms, such as adjusting clothing, cleaning a pipe, polishing nails, or combing hair, may be stating their disinterest in the activities of the committee.

- A leader who does not encourage active participation by all members may set the stage for the monopoly of the discussion by a few, thereby limiting the broad-based character of the group.

- An individual who continually interrupts other committee members or puts down other committee members, individuals in the community, or the school system may lose credibility within the group and lessen the impact of any contributions that may be made.

Regardless of the care taken in selecting committee members, there is always a possibility that a "meeting detractor" may be selected to serve on the committee. The chairperson must be tactful but firm when dealing with members who wander from the subject, complain rather than discuss, heckle speakers, hold side discussions, present misinformation, and take adversary positions.

RECOGNIZING ADVISORY COMMITTEE MEMBERS

Committee members must be recognized for the time and effort they devote to working with educational personnel. It is impossible to compensate individual members for the invaluable service they provide. The impact that committees have on the instructional program and the benefits that students derive from these programs cannot be measured. When an advisory role is not filled, however, the program and the community cannot benefit from the essential exchange between educators and individuals in the community. Most importantly, if the program does not fulfill its potential, the individual student is denied the amount of assistance that could and should be available.

The most significant reward advisory committee members gain is the personal satisfaction of having contributed expertise, experience, and hard work; of being a part of a community education team; and of seeing a program improve and expand. Committee members can take pride as they see their input, advice, and recommendations shape the educational program. Although this sense of accomplishment cannot be measured, it motivates busy individuals in government, business, industry, and labor to donate their time to advisory committees.

From the beginning when the committee is formed, efforts should be made to establish mutual respect between school representatives and the advisory committee. School representatives must have an appreciative attitude toward the committee. Educators must not patronize non-educator committee members nor underestimate their interest and understanding of educational matters if confidence and cooperation are to be expected from advisory committee members.

While an advisory committee member's most important reward is the personal satisfaction of serving, the imaginative educator can adapt the following examples as a basis for providing gratitude, recognition, and appreciation:

1. Publish the names of advisory committee members in school or college publications, catalogs, brochures, the committee handbook, and releases to newspapers.

2. Schedule a dinner or informal cookout for committee members, administrative personnel, and faculty members in the program.

3. Ensure that announcements and reports made by administrators include reference to committee service, suggestions, and recommendations.

4. Extend invitations to committee members to school events and activities.

5. Send a letter of appreciation to each committee member (see Figure 11-1).

6. Send a letter of appreciation to the advisory committee's supervisor.

7. Present a framed certificate of appreciation (see Figure 11-2) or a plaque at a public meeting.

8. Prepare a display or bulletin board containing a listing of current advisory committee members.

9. Distribute a news release indicating the work of the committee along with a listing of the members.

FIGURE 11-1. Sample letter of appreciation

```
Mr. Julian A. Carpintero
Production Manager
Victoria Tools and Dies
5042 Liberty Avenue
Memphis, TN      93418

Dear Mr. Carpintero:

Thank you for your cooperation with the Tool and Die Design Program.  Your
role has been instrumental in the success of the program.  Thanks to your
efforts, all the graduating students have been placed in jobs related to
their field of study.  The scholarship award program and the cooperative
work-study program that you helped to implement are now being used as a model
by other craft advisory committees in this school.

I am convinced that a continuation of a superior program in Tool and Die
Design at its present level is possible only with the support of a know-
ledgeable and enthusiastic advisory committee.

May I extend to you the good wishes of this institution for your continued
success and dedication.


Very sincerely yours,



Bradley J. Rhodes, Chairperson
Board of Trustees
```

Eugenio A. Basualdo. *Advisory Committees in Vocational-Technical Programs.* Memphis: State Technical Institute at Memphis, 1976, p. 48. Used with permission.

10. Extend special privileges, such as parking permits or passes to athletic games and events, to committee members.

11. Present a resolution of appreciation to the appropriate governing body (see Figure 11-3).

12. Schedule a regular meeting that will be attended by the chief school administrator.

FIGURE 11-2. Sample certificate of appreciation

THE STERLING PUBLIC SCHOOL DISTRICT
STERLING, NORTH DAKOTA

Certificate of Appreciation

This is to Certify That

_____

has served as a member of the advisory committee for the

VOCATIONAL OFFICE EDUCATION PROGRAM

of the Sterling Public High School for the year 19_____ to 19_____
We gratefully acknowledge the services of the above named.

PRESIDENT, BOARD OF EDUCATION   SUPERINTENDENT OF SCHOOLS   VOCATIONAL TEACHER

North Dakota State Board for Vocational Education. *The Vocational Education Advisory Committee.* Fargo: North Dakota State Advisory Council for Vocational Education, undated, p. 18. Used with permission.

FIGURE 11-3. Sample resolution of appreciation

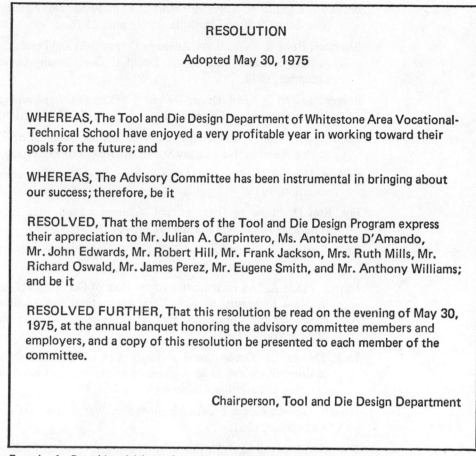

RESOLUTION

Adopted May 30, 1975

WHEREAS, The Tool and Die Design Department of Whitestone Area Vocational-Technical School have enjoyed a very profitable year in working toward their goals for the future; and

WHEREAS, The Advisory Committee has been instrumental in bringing about our success; therefore, be it

RESOLVED, That the members of the Tool and Die Design Program express their appreciation to Mr. Julian A. Carpintero, Ms. Antoinette D'Amando, Mr. John Edwards, Mr. Robert Hill, Mr. Frank Jackson, Mrs. Ruth Mills, Mr. Richard Oswald, Mr. James Perez, Mr. Eugene Smith, and Mr. Anthony Williams; and be it

RESOLVED FURTHER, That this resolution be read on the evening of May 30, 1975, at the annual banquet honoring the advisory committee members and employers, and a copy of this resolution be presented to each member of the committee.

Chairperson, Tool and Die Design Department

Eugenio A. Basualdo. *Advisory Committees in Vocational-Technical Programs.* Memphis: State Technical Institute at Memphis, 1976, p. 46. Used with permission.

SUGGESTED ACTIVITIES

1. From a current article on leadership, select a key concept and apply it to the advisory committee setting.

2. Select a standard questionnaire, like "Management Style Diagnosis Test" (Organizational Tests, Ltd., Box 324, Fredericton, N.B., Canada), and complete a self-assessment of your leadership style.

3. Identify the main leadership trait in which you need improvement and outline a process for making the necessary changes.

4. Develop a list of ways in which you can demonstrate the leadership qualities of empathy, self-awareness, and objectivity.

5. Select one of the organizational hazards and outline a plan you would follow to correct, improve, or avoid the situation.

6. Discuss the use of advisory committees with individuals in the community who have had experience in using such committees and prepare a list of pitfalls that should be avoided.

7. Outline an informal process to be followed in dealing with one of the "meeting detractors."

8. Write a sample letter of appreciation that could be sent to members of an advisory committee with which you are involved.

9. Complete a self assessment of your personal relationships with others and list those areas in which you need improvement.

10. Review resolutions that have been passed by your board and then prepare a resolution of appreciation for your committee.

SELECTED REFERENCES

Basualdo, Eugenio A. *Advisory Committees in Vocational-Technical Programs.* Memphis: State Technical Institute at Memphis, 1976.

Behymer, Ruby J. "Vocational Advisory Committees and Perceptions of Members Regarding Selected Functions." Doctoral Dissertation, University of Missouri-Columbia, 1977.

Borgen, Joseph A., and Davis, Dwight E. *Planning, Implementing, and Evaluating Career Preparation Programs.* Bloomington, Ill.: McKnight Publishing Co., 1974.

Buontempo, Gregory, and Klavon, Michael. *Making the Most of Your Advisory Committee.* Trenton: New Jersey State Department of Education, undated.

Carlisle, Howard M. *Situational Management.* New York: American Management Association, 1973.

Ely, Ron H. "How to Organize and Maintain a Productive Advisory Committee." *American Vocational Journal,* 52 (March 1977): 37–39.

King, Sam W. *Organization and Effective Use of Advisory Committees.* Washington, D.C.: GPO, 1960.

Lahren, James A. "An Examination of the Role of Occupational Advisory Committees in State University of New York Agricultural and Technical Colleges as Perceived by the Committee Members." Doctoral Dissertation, State University of New York at Buffalo, 1970.

Link, Dwight E. "Occupational Advisory Council Interactions: Their Relationship to Council Age and to Perceptions of Effectiveness as Reported by Participants." Doctoral Dissertation, University of Illinois, 1973.

Lippett, Gordon L., ed. *Leadership in Action.* Washington, D.C.: National Education Association, 1961.

Mial, Dorothy, and Mial, H. Curtis, eds. *Forces in Community Development.* Washington, D.C.: National Education Association, 1961.

Nagel, James E. "Characteristics of Effective Vocational Education Occupational Advisory Committees in Secondary Schools of the United States." Doctoral Dissertation, The University of North Dakota, 1973.

Newman, William H., Summer, Charles E., and Warren, E. Kirby. *The Process of Management,* Third Edition. Englewood Cliffs, New Jersey: Prentice-Hall, Inc., 1972.

Riendeau, Albert J. *Advisory Committees for Occupational Education: A Guide to Organization and Operation.* New York: McGraw-Hill Book Co., 1977.

Sorensen, Robert P. "Perceived Priorities and Achievements of Occupational Advisory Committee Functions in the Wisconsin Vocational, Technical and Adult Education System." Doctoral Dissertation, University of Wisconsin at Madison, 1974.

Sumption, Merle R., and Engstrom, Yvonne. *School-Community Relations.* New York: McGraw-Hill Book Co., 1966.

Whitten, Benjamin, et al. "The Effective Functioning of Local Advisory Committees." *American Vocational Journal* 52 (January 1977): 30–35.

12 The planning of advisory committee action

Planning may be defined as the determination of a course of action to achieve a desired result. To plan means to think out the general form and detail of work so that the job can be accomplished with direction and economy. It is a process of thinking before doing, and therefore, involves imagination, foresight, and sound judgment. Within the context of an advisory committee, planning means identifying and evaluating occupational needs, determining program or course objectives, establishing policies, and making a continuous effort to find new and better ways of accomplishing the goals of the program.

From a management perspective, planning is a key component that—along with organizing, leading, motivating, controlling, and evaluating—forms the basis of any organizational framework. Management planning involves the development of forecasts, objectives, policies, programs, procedures, schedules, and budgets. These elements are interrelated but, as Allen [8:26] points out, they have a distinctive nature of their own.

> . . . sound planning calls for separation, at least mentally, of the determination of goals, and of policy statements that govern the conditions under which the goals are to be reached, decision as to what sequence of activities must be followed to accomplish the goals, the preparation of time schedules, decision as to how standardized work is to be performed, and estimates of the units of money, time, materials, and so forth that will be required to reach the goals.

This chapter demonstrates the importance of planning and the impact of planning on the various roles of the advisory committee. It also provides specific examples of the application of these planning concepts to the real setting.

Planning is part of each of the major advisory committee functions.

277

Whether planning is short term or long range, it is a continuing activity that attempts to anticipate and shape the future through intelligent action, rather than being a series of tasks or projects to be implemented. Planning is difficult on an individual basis and even more complex when it becomes a group process, as is inherent in the advisory committee structure. The committee purpose and the aspirations of its members may differ widely. The needs, priorities, and strategies may vary considerably. But to fail to plan means to be unprepared, to have given inadequate attention to alternatives, and to have made little conscious effort to determine the course of the committee.

THE ADVISORY COMMITTEE PLANNING CONTINUUM

Whether the committee uses a planning continuum to develop its own actions or applies it to program planning, the same series of events occurs. It may give the appearance of a step-by-step process or one in which there are isolated phases, but planning is cyclic, with each phase interacting directly or indirectly with each of the other phases. Figure 12–1 illustrates these interrelationships and suggests that the normal flow of events follows the circular path around the perimeter with alternative paths possible at any point. The committee would normally start by developing an *awareness* of the existing programs or committee purpose, move to an *identification* of goals or problems, complete an *assessment* of needs and directions, identify or establish *priorities*, develop plans or strategies for a *program of work*, express concerns or recommendations in a *report*, and then start a new cycle.

In practice, however, it is not uncommon for the committee to pursue various options. For example, a needs assessment may reveal new information that suggests the identification of new goal statements thereby reversing the cycle. Or the establishment of priorities may result in committee recommendations that suggest new goals and strategies for implementing a program of work. Although the phases may be discussed individually for greater clarity, they are simply components of a continuum and can be applied to the committee itself as well as to its actions in dealing with career and occupational education programs.

The awareness phase

The initial task of a committee is to gain a full understanding of its role by reviewing the assignment, purpose, or direction of the committee; studying previous actions of the committee or other committees in the system; and discussing alternatives that the committee might pursue. This phase need not be formal nor time consuming but should focus on creating a comprehensive awareness of the functions of the committee. From this point, it is common for members of the committee to discuss some of the more detailed or operational aspects of the committee such as procedural questions and parameters within which the committee operates.

FIGURE 12-1. The advisory committee planning continuum

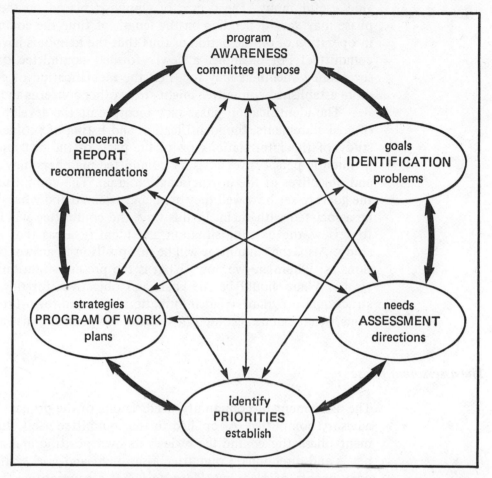

The committee's task of gaining awareness in respect to its role with the career-related program follows the same format as that utilized by the committee in reviewing its internal structure. Typically, the committee will gather materials describing the program in an effort to gain an overall perspective of the program. This is usually a more time-consuming process than reviewing the committee's internal structure and might include discussions on various aspects of the program with individuals associated with the program, as well as tours through the facilities. Committee members should gain a thorough understanding of the kind of offerings, the various levels, and the structure of the program; however, they must not be overburdened with every detail of the program. In this awareness phase, an overall understanding rather than a working knowledge of the program is primary.

The identification phase

The identification phase is the same whether it is applied to the committee itself or to the program it serves. As with the awareness phase, the identification phase need not be a long, drawn-out process, but it should clearly delineate goals and problem areas. Vagueness in either phase can hamper the capability of the committee to function effectively or to provide useful input. The degree of emphasis placed on the identification phase may vary depending on the length of time the committee has been in operation or on the period of time that the members have served on the committee. For example, a newly formed committee or one that has several new members may focus on the identification of goals, whereas a more established committee might stress other concerns and problem areas.

The identification phase may incorporate the development or review of goal statements, the identification and listing of problem areas, or the study of the interrelationships of the parts of the program. From a programmatic perspective, advisory committee members may study the goals and objectives of the instructional program. The committee may analyze the goals to see how well they are being attained and what problems might be associated with them. In this way, the committee will be in a position to review the existing situation and identify areas that deserve further study. Also, the committee will be in a position to answer such basic questions as: Where are we now? What is the present situation? Where should we be? What should be the goals and objectives for this part of the instructional program? What information is needed for future recommendations? What can be accomplished within the present constraints?

The assessment phase

The assessment of community needs is one of the primary purposes of an advisory committee. As applied to the committee itself, during the assessment phase the committee reviews its own position and assesses its own needs and directions. Committee assessment and goal setting are essential components of planning. Planning is not a competitive task but an individualized process through which a committee, school, or district may appraise its current level of activity and establish short-term or long-range aims. Normally planning is accomplished through a team approach rather than on an individual basis or through the use of an outside consultant. The team—usually composed of administrators, teachers, the committee chairperson, and other representative members of the committee—utilizes information revealed in the awareness and identification phases to develop an instrument that lists the major functions and supporting activities of the committee. Figure 12–2 illustrates one approach that might be followed first to assess the current level of activity and then to set goals for a specific length of time. The solid line in this illustration represents the group's effort to measure the level of committee activity; the dashed line represents the goals that were established. As illustrated, the group may suggest no change (item 3A, D, E, F), increased effort (item 2A, B, C, D) or decreased emphasis (item 7B) for the committee.

The priorities phase

The priorities phase of planning is the simplest to describe. It is by no means, however, the least important, because the judgments reflected in

---

LOCAL ADVISORY COMMITTEE ACTION PLAN

PART 1—EXAMPLE ASSESSMENT AND GOAL SETTING

Action Plan Development Team:

School: Local High School

Date: 9-1-74

Peter Smith , Principal

Mary Jones , Voc. Dir.

Sam Soski , Voc. Teacher

Larry First , Adv. Comm.

(name)   (position)

Purpose:

Local Action Plan Assessment for:
(type of program)
Drafting

This instrument is intended to provide an avenue for self-assessment regarding the utilization commonly performed by advisory committees, in addition it will assist in process of establishing goals for the effective utilization of advisory committees.

(A) — Occupational Committee √

(B) — General _____

(Check one.)

Code

——— Present Assessment

– – – – Six-Month Goal Projection

Function

Percent of Utilization

0   25   50   75   100

1. *Occupational Surveys*
   A. Use of the local manpower planning handbook
   B. Consultation with Michigan employment security commission
   C. Use of occupational outlook handbook
   D. Surveys community needs
   E. Use of community survey data

2. *Course Content Advisement*
   A. Identification of occupational competencies
   B. Development of program goal statements
   C. Review of topical outlines
   D. Review of performance objectives

3. *Student Placement*
   A. Organization of employer-student conferences
   B. Notification of job openings
   C. Writing recommendation letters for students
   D. Employment of graduates
   E. Review of follow-up studies
   F. Liaison with MESC

Function	Percent of Utilization

Percent of Utilization
0 25 50 75 100

4. *Community Public Relations*
   A. Speaking to civic groups
   B. Input at program funding activities
   C. Input at public hearings
   D. Promoting the program via the media
   E. Development of promotional materials

5. *Equipment and Facilities*
   A. Review of equipment and facilities
   B. Survey of equipment and industry
   C. Suggesting equipment replacement
   D. Calculation of depreciation allowances
   E. Soliciting equipment donations

6. *Program Staffing*
   A. Review of teacher selection criteria
   B. Suggesting recruitment policies
   C. Recommending potential candidates
   D. Review of teaching applicants

7. *Program Review*
   A. Evaluation of student performance
   B. Evaluation of teacher performance
   C. Use of annual state department review questionnaire
   D. Suggestions for program improvement
   E. Comparing accomplishments with stated objectives
   F. Making periodic reports to administration

8. *Community Resources*
   A. Arranging field trips
   B. Recommending potential co-op work stations
   C. Identifying community resources
   D. Obtaining personnel for classroom presentations
   E. Obtaining consultants for teachers

Leslie H. Cochran, L. Allen Phelps, and Joseph F. Skupin. *A Guide for Effective Utilization of Advisory Committees.* Lansing: Michigan Department of Education, 1974, pp. C-4 and C-5. Used with permission.

this process form the basis for all actions taken by the committee. The practice of identifying, establishing, and reviewing priorities requires the committee's foremost attention and close interaction with all other aspects of the career and occupational education program.

A committee may identify its priorities by working totally within its own framework, by inviting individuals to present additional perspectives to the committee, or by forming subgroups composed primarily of non-committee members to provide other insights. The information collected in the assessment phase serves to reveal current and projected levels of committee action. Perceptions and insights developed in the awareness and identification phases, previous experiences from the committee or other committees, and input from others associated with the program may serve to shape the recommendations. It is the responsibility of the committee to determine which areas of concern have the greatest significance and require initial effort or sustained attention. The time constraints placed on the committee further emphasize the need to establish priorities.

The program-of-work phase

The program-of-work phase demonstrates how the committee will structure its efforts. The program of work serves as a guide for the allocation of committee time and resources, provides a format to facilitate progress, and serves as a benchmark for the committee to use when evaluating its accomplishments.

The number and type of items that emerge in a plan may vary, of course, according to the scope, nature, purpose, and level of activity of the committee. The activities of the committee may also be influenced by the problems or concerns reflected in the school and community, the character of the program, and the facilities that are available. Figure 12-3 provides several sample items that might appear in such a plan. As another example, some of the following topics might appear in a program of work for agriculture*:

1. The role of the vocational agriculture department in the school and in the community:

    a. What are the purposes of the vocational agriculture department?
    b. To what extent is the department achieving these purposes? (Use of evaluation material.)
    c. How many in-school youth, Young Farmers, and adult farmers are reached at present with organized, systematic instruction?

2. An evaluation of the agricultural situation in the community, including the unmet needs of agriculture.

*Guide for Establishment and Conduct of Local Advisory Committees for Vocational Agriculture Departments. San Luis Obispo: California State Polytechnic College, Vocational Education Productions, undated, pp. 15-16. Used with permission.

FIGURE 12-3. *Sample items for first-year program of work*

Objectives	Activities	Dates
A. The committee will become organized to function on a continuing basis	1. Develop rules for operating the committee	Sept.–Oct.
	2. Elect officers	Sept.–Oct.
B. The members of the committee will become familiar with the instructional program	1. Identify the existing goals of the program	Sept.–Nov.
	2. Review the parts of the program: a. classroom/lab instruction b. work experience c. youth organization d. adult education e. teacher professional development	Sept.–Nov.
	3. Evaluate the outcomes of the program in relation to the goals	Dec.–Jan.
C. The committe will assist with the development of short and long-range goals for the program	1. Determine long-range employment trends	Nov.–Dec.
	2. Identify anticipated technological changes	Nov.–Dec.
	3. Prepare a statement of goals for the program for the next five years	Jan.
D. The committee will identify areas of concern	1. Identify potential problem areas by comparing long-range goals with outcomes of the present programs	Feb.–Nov.
	2. Identify existing problem areas with the assistance of the teacher	Feb–Nov.
	3. Select one or more areas of concern, examine the problems, and make recommendations to the board of education	Nov.–June
E. The committee will prepare an annual report of activities and accomplishments to be submitted to the board of education	1. Describe major activities and accomplishments of the program	May–June
	2. Describe major activities and accomplishments of the committee	May–June
	3. State recommendations and/or suggestions for improvement of both the program and the committee	May–June

National Center for Research in Vocational Education. *Professional Vocational Teacher Education Module: Maintain an Occupational Advisory Committee,* Module A–5. Columbus: The Ohio State University, 1975, pp. 20–21. Used with permission.

3. The occupational placement and opportunities in agriculture available to young men and women in the community.

4. The supervised practice and programs of the all-day students. This could well be followed by a field trip to observe the agricultural programs of representative students.

5. The development of a chapter program of work for the Future Farmers of America. Meetings should be held with the executive committee of the chapter and with the entire chapter. This particular phase may be assigned to a sub-committee of the advisory committee.

6. The development of plans for cooperation with governmental agencies and non-farm groups dealing with agricultural problems.

7. The development of suggestions pertaining to the buildings and facilities needed in the local department.

8. The promotion of annual meetings for the following purposes:

   a. A get-acquainted social program for the advisory committee members, their families, the students, teachers, and other agriculture-interested persons in the community.
   b. Joint meeting with the board of education as occasion requires.
   c. An evaluation of the committee's work done during the last year.
   d. Assistance in planning and implementing any summer programs being undertaken by the vocational agriculture department.
   e. Planning of the program for the next year.
   f. Visitation of classes in the all-day, Young Farmer, or adult levels to improve the program.

Each of these examples suggests beginning points for the development of the plan of work. Specific illustrations on how to develop a plan of work are provided later in this chapter. There should be flexibility in the plan since not all concerns that may need to be brought to the attention of the committee may be known at the time the plan is adopted.

A committee cannot accomplish all of its goals and activities in one year. Long-range planning covering several years can help to coordinate the yearly activities. The goals of this long-range plan should be to focus on improvement of the overall program, provide systematic and continuous progress, and assist in the ongoing evaluation of all major program activities.

The report phase

During the culminating report phase, the committee has the opportunity on an annual basis to describe its activities, express concerns, summarize evaluations, and present recommendations. The report phase, however, encompasses more than the simple providing of insights at the end of the year. As is characteristic of the other phases, the report component interacts on a regular basis with each of the other phases.

Reporting may take the form of informal insights or discussions shared with administrators or teachers in the program; of a memo outlining findings from an evaluative effort in any of the phases; of a newspaper article, radio talk, television interview; or of open discussions with other segments of the committee. In another case, it may be totally internalized within the committee and simply shift discussion to another phase. The annual report assumes special importance because it summarizes the activities of the committee and the accomplishments of the instructional program. The report may include general recommendations not previously included in other communications; but it is relatively brief, usually three to four pages in length. The following information may be included in the annual report [110:43-44]:

1. Statement of purposes or reasons why the board of education established the occupational advisory committee

2. Summary of the major activities and special accomplishments of the instructional program (from the teacher's report), such as:
   a. objectives and/or goals of the program which were met
   b. student enrollment data
   c. activities such as special field trips, resource persons
   d. descriptions of new or revised courses
   e. important youth organization activities
   f. adult education activities
   g. major professional development activities in which the teacher participated

3. Summary of the major activities and accomplishments of the advisory committee, such as:
   a. overview of a committee's program of work
   b. number of meetings held, and attendance rate
   c. special activities; resource persons utilized, ad hoc sub-committees, etc.
   d. special reports and/or recommendations made to the teacher, administrators, and/or board of education

4. Recommendations to the board of education reflecting ways and means that the program goals and/or the committee's goals might be better met

5. Recognition of individuals and/or groups that made special contributions to the success of the instructional program

6. Statement of appreciation from the committee to the board of education for the opportunity to serve on the advisory committee

Regardless of the form, reporting serves as a mechanism by which the committee may communicate findings, concerns, and recommendations to other individuals associated in some way with the program.

ACTION PLANNING FOR GOAL IMPLEMENTATION

The success of planning depends on the degree to which it facilitates good judgments, aids in the attainment of objectives, serves as a guide for action, enhances the wise use of time and resources, and serves as a communication device for those involved in or associated with the plan.

The program-of-work phase of planning fosters these goals by providing the formal mechanism with which the committee can delineate its plans. In this respect, it is the final evaluative measure of committee actions. In addition, the program of work is the bridge between the present situation and what is needed or projected for the future.

The actual action plan may take the forms illustrated in Figure 12–4, 12–5, 12–6, and 12–7. It may be a simple checklist or outline of tasks to be accomplished. More commonly, however, such plans include considerable detail regarding goals, objectives, strategies of goal attainment, criteria and measurement techniques, and areas dealing with timetables and priority listings.

FIGURE 12–4. Sample plan of work

LOCAL ADVISORY COMMITTEE ACTION PLAN
PART 3—STRATEGY EXAMPLE

School: Local High School

Date: 9-1-74

Action Plan Development Team:

(name)	(position)
Peter Smith	Principal
Mary Jones	Voc. Dir.
Sam Soski	Voc. Teacher
Larry First	Adv. Com.

Action Plan Goals	Strategy for Goal Attainment	Goal Attainment Criteria/ Measurement Technique	Projected Timetable Initiation	Completion	Priority
I. Select an advisory committee for drafting program.	1. Solicit names of prospective members from community groups and local industries with prospective members.	Were names and titles obtained?			
	2. Send letter of invitation to prospective advisory committee members.	Did advisory committee member accept the invitations?	9-15-74		1
	3. Discuss individually the function and role of the committee.	Were individual discussions held?			
	4. Send follow-up letter of appreciation for involvement together with timetable of advisory committee meetings.	Are the times and dates of advisory committee meetings acceptable to majority of members?	10-01-74	10-12-74	
II. Conduct an organizational advisory committee meeting.	1. Arrange for meeting place.		10-15-74		2
	2. Send out announcement of meeting with proposed agenda and return postcard.		10-22-74		
	3. Have agenda printed.	Was agenda ready?	10-25-74	10-27-74	
	4. Set up room.	Was room prepared in time?	11-01-74	11-01-74	
	5. Call meeting to order, handle introduction and introduce "Do We Really "Care" (sound/slide program).				
Supportive *Guide* Resources	6. Have committee select a chairman.	Did committee select a chairman?		11-01-74	
Section B—Implementation Resources. "Do We Really Care?" Sound/slide or filmstrip	7. Conduct organizational committee meetings.	Was the meeting conducted? Were appropriate organizational details taken care of?		11-01-74	

Leslie H. Cochran, L. Allen Phelps, and Joseph F. Skupin. *A Guide for Effective Utilization of Advisory Committees.* Lansing: Michi
Department of Education, 1974, pp. C–9 and C–10. Used with permission.

FIGURE 12-5. *Vocational education advisory committee activity planning guide*

| Functions* | | | | | | | | Goals | Objectives | Strategies | Evaluation |
OS	CA	SP	PR	EF	PS	PR	CR				

*OS—Occupational Surveys
CA—Course Content Advisement
SP—Student Placement
PR—Public Relations

EF—Equipment and Facilities
PS—Program Staffing
PR—Program Review
CR—Community Resources

Walter S. Ramey, *A Guide for the Organization and Operation of Local Advisory Committees for Vocational Education.* Richmond: Virginia State Department of Education, 1975, p. 68. Used with permission.

FIGURE 12–6. Sample program of work for a general advisory council on vocational education

Goal	Objectives	Activities	Committee Assigned	Year 19 19	19 19	19 19
1. To provide local educational agencies with advice in promoting and developing vocational education opportunities	(a) To advise on the development of long-range and annual plans for vocational education.	1. Review annual and long-range vocational education plan.				
		2. Hold public meeting on vocational education.				
		3. Assist board with development of program evaluation procedures.				
		4. Assist in the development of apprenticeship training related to educational courses.				
		5. Review of existing board policies on vocational education.				
		6.				

(b) To advise regarding new and future vocational program needs.

1. Assist and participate in surveying local industry manpower needs.				
2. Provide visual aids, magazines, and books concerning industry.				
3. Sponsor industry-school seminar.				
4. Testify in support of vocational education financial needs at local and state government bodies.				
5. Assist in making studies of new and emerging occupations in local industries.				
6.				

Alabama Division of Vocational Education. *Guide for Organizing and Utilizing Local Vocational Education Advisory Councils.* Montgomery: Alabama State Department of Education, 1977, pp. 16–17. Used with permission.

FIGURE 12-7; *Sample checklist of craft advisory committee plan of work*

	1976–77	1977–78	1978–79
A. Student Recruitment, Selection, and Placement			
1. Number of Speeches at:			
a. Feeder schools			
b. Youth Clubs			
c. Civic clubs			
d. Other organizations			
2. Developing tests used for student selection			
3. Reviewing tests used for student selection			
4. Number of Students Placed on:			
a. Part-time jobs			
b. Cooperative arrangements			
c. Summer jobs			
5. Number of graduates placed on jobs			
6. Number of scholarships raised for students			
7. Number of student follow-ups			
B. Program of Instruction			
1. Curriculum revisions			
2. Reviewing laws affecting the program			
3. Pieces of equipment obtained			
4. Supplies obtained			
5. Visual aids or charts obtained			
6. Evaluation of book(s) used for the program			
7. Shop safety checks			
8. Evaluation of shop layout			
9. Establishing a library of:			
a. books			
b. magazines			
c. movies			
d. visual aids			
10. Library additions:			
a. books			
b. magazines			
c. movies			
d. visual aids			
11. Selection of instructional projects			
12. Field trips arranged			

C. *Public Relations*	1976–77	1977–78	1978–79
1. Presenting the program to:			
a. Unions			
b. Labor			
c. Employers			
d. Magazines			
e. Local news media			
2. Attending and speaking in favor of vocational education at:			
a. State board meetings			
b. Local board meetings			
c. Other			
3. Mounting support campaigns among:			
a. Labor			
b. Management			
4. Guests brought to:			
a. Career day			
b. Open house			
c. Other school activities			
5. Providing means to advertise the program			
6. Presenting the program on:			
a. Television			
b. Radio			
7. Promoting the program in companies			
D. *Teacher Assistance*			
1. Lecturing in classes			
2. Interpreting laws			
3. Arranging part-time work for instructors			
4. Arranging substitute teachers			
5. Organizing youth contests			
6. Serving as youth contest judges			
7. Helping in the budget			
8. Helping establish teacher qualifications			

Eugenio A. Basualdo. *Advisory Committees in Vocational-Technical Programs.* Memphis: State Technical Institute at Memphis, 1976, pp. 44–45. Used with permission.

SUGGESTED ACTIVITIES

1. Develop an outline to be followed in introducing the importance of and role of the committee in planning its activities.

2. Prepare a package of materials that may be used by the committee in developing an awareness of the role of the committee and the program it serves. This should include descriptive information about the program and details outlining how to accomplish this task.

3. Establish a procedure to be followed that will assist the committee in the identification of goals and problem areas.

4. Develop an instrument or procedure that may be used by the committee in assessing its current level of activity and setting goals for the future.

5. Outline the areas to be addressed and the format to be followed in a meeting in which individuals in the community will be invited to speak on priority areas in the program. Contact the appropriate representatives and schedule the meeting.

6. Devise a plan to be followed in developing a program of work for the committee.

7. Develop a list of activities and concerns that should be included in a short-term or long-range program of work.

8. Prepare a planning format to be followed by the committee, and develop a plan for the coming year.

9. Develop a set of guidelines to be followed by the committee in assessing its activities.

10. Outline a plan to ensure that other agencies and organizations in the community are involved in the committee planning process.

SELECTED REFERENCES

Allen, Louis A. *Management and Organization.* New York: McGraw-Hill Book Co., 1958.

Borgen, Joseph A., and Davis, Dwight E. *Planning, Implementing, and Evaluating Career Preparation Programs.* Bloomington, Ill.: McKnight Publishing Co., 1974.

Buontempo, Gregory, and Klavon, Michael. *Making the Most of Your Advisory Committee.* Trenton: New Jersey State Department of Education, undated.

Burt, Samuel M. *Industry and Vocational-Technical Education.* New York: McGraw-Hill Book Co., 1967.

Cochran, Leslie H.; Phelps, L. Allen; and Skupin, Joseph F. *A Guide for Effective Utilization of Advisory Committees.* Lansing: Michigan Department of Education, 1974.

Cook, Desmond L. *Program Evaluation and Review Technique: Applications to Education.* Washington, D.C.: GPO, 1966.

King, Sam W. *Organization and Effective Use of Advisory Committees.* Washington, D.C.: GPO, 1960.

National Center for Research in Vocational Education. *Professional Vocational Teacher Education Module: Maintain An Occupational Advisory Committee,* Module A-5. Columbus: The Ohio State University, 1975.

National Center for Research in Vocational Education. *Professional Vocational Teacher Education Module: Conduct a Student Follow-up Study,* Module A-10. Columbus: The Ohio State University, 1976.

Newman, William H.; Summer Charles E.; and Warren, E. Kirby. *The Process of Management: Concepts, Behavior, and Practice,* Third Edition. Englewood Cliffs, N.J.: Prentice-Hall, 1972.

Ramey, Walter S. *A Guide for the Organization and Operation of Local Advisory Committees for Vocational Education.* Richmond: Virginia State Department of Education, 1975.

Riendeau, Albert J. *Advisory Committees for Occupational Education: A Guide to Organization and Operation.* New York: McGraw-Hill Book Co., 1977.

Touche Ross and Company. *Vocational Education Local Manpower Planning Handbook.* Lansing: Michigan Department of Education, 1972.

13 The evaluation of the advisory committee

One of the most important roles of an advisory committee is that of program assessment and review. It is an ongoing process that gives citizens in the community an opportunity to assess program goals and objectives, make recommendations concerning the curriculum, and suggest improvements that will enable the career-related programs better to meet the occupational needs of the community. Through this process, members of the community serve in the role of outside consultants to school personnel by providing a continuous source of input from the community itself.

Program assessment and review have direct application to each of the functions described in Chapters 3 through 9. Evaluation, however, is not a process limited to the review of the specific goals, functions, and activities that form the core of the educational program. The advisory committee must also focus attention on its own organization, how it operates, and the degree of success or impact that it has. By its very nature, the advisory committee must have a dual focus. There is little said about the assessment process as it relates to the committee itself. Evaluation of the committee's regular activities, however, is essential. Without this twofold evaluation, the role of the committee is severely limited for if only an outward review is made of programs, the possible inefficiency or lack of focus of the committee's activities will not be seen and will, therefore, restrict the usefulness of the committee. The fact that only on rare occasions have committees served this dual role may further suggest why there is generally a nonsupportive research base concerning the effectiveness of committees in fulfilling their responsibilities.

Although the assessment process has received only limited attention, there are several compelling factors that suggest the important role to be performed by the committee in evaluating its goals, organization, and activities. First, the advisory committee is an integral part of the career education and occupational education programs. As such, it is only natural for the advisory committee to be involved in the evaluation process as it is involved with the various components of the program. Second, the field of evaluation has experienced significant growth during the last few years. New philosophies and concepts have accompanied this development. As a result, evaluation has shifted from a narrow, final task to an ongoing process that has direct impact and implications for each phase of the program. Third, the new emphasis on advisory committees and the fact that they are mandated by federal legislation has, of course, given new emphasis to their use and to an evaluation of their effectiveness. Fourth, since the advisory committee plays an important role in program evaluation, it is a natural expectation that the committee, also, would be evaluated. Evaluation is important not only as a measure of the committee's contributions but because of the effect it may have on the perceptions toward evaluation held by individuals involved in the program.

The Virginia State Department of Education [141:33] placed the following emphasis on committee evaluation:

> A general vocational education advisory committee is, within itself, an evaluator of the school division's vocational education program. Before any advice can be offered, the committee must engage in collecting, analyzing, and evaluating data that will provide a basis for the giving of advice. In the same way, the committee must apply these principles to itself to determine its effectiveness and overall contribution to the school division.
>
> In establishing a yearly agenda, or program of work, the advisory committee is in reality setting goals for itself. The local director of vocational education can assist the committee in this task by offering suggestions that will help members see the appropriate steps to be taken toward the accomplishment of the goals. These steps can be stated as performance objectives. Not only will this provide direction for the committee, it will improve the communicative processes. As each objective is attained, the committee will grow in stature and enthusiasm, and their efforts will be recognized by the school and the public.
>
> By instituting this concept early in the formative stages of organization, the committee will see itself as a body with a purpose and tasks to be performed. This procedure will also assist the committee in the preparation of its annual report to the school board and in coordinating efforts with the state advisory council if this is deemed desirable by the locality.

THE GROUP EVALUATION PROCESS

It is difficult to delineate a procedure for evaluating a group because of the variables inherent in the group process and in the evaluation process. Individually, these processes have emerged as two areas that permeate all educational theory. When combined, the group and evaluation processes produce, in effect, a unique setting that draws elements from each and emerges as a more encompassing group evaluation process.

The group process

Any process can be characterized as having four basic elements—action, a continuous change in time, progress over time, and a goal or result. It involves a set of dynamic, ongoing, everchanging interdependent events and relationships. A change in any one of the ingredients affects all of the other ingredients. A group can be defined as being a unit of two or more individuals who interact in a manner whereby each influences and is influenced by others in the group.

From this definition emerges the concept of "groupness," which stresses the importance of the relationships that exist between the individual members of the group. In this respect, a group may be portrayed as having the following characteristics:

1. A number of people sufficiently small for each to be aware of and have some reaction to each other.

2. A mutually interdependent purpose in which the success of each is contingent upon the success of the others in achieving this goal.

3. Each person has a sense of belonging or membership, identifying himself with the other members of the group.

4. Oral interaction (not all of the interaction will be oral, but a significant characteristic of a discussion group is reciprocal influence exercised by talking).

5. Behavior based on norms and procedures accepted by all members. [24:12]

In oversimplified terms, an advisory committee or group may be thought of as having its own way of thinking, separate from those of the individual members. While a "group mind concept" is not implied, a group does possess an identity of its own apart from the identities of its members. What this suggests is that while specific guidelines may be provided for the group's actions, it is the responsibility of the group leader to adjust to the character of the group.

The group process also draws heavily on systems theory and systems of behaviors. As a process or system, the group's existence is dependent on structure, function, and evolution. Structure is defined as the pattern of relationships among components at any given point in time; function is the recurring day-to-day relationships among components through time; and evolution is the continuous changes of structure and function through a period of time. Similarly, the way in which the behaviors of the group are combined produces another set of phenomena inherent in the process. Fisher [56:24] summarized this complex process by defining the group as

a collection of individuals whose communicative behaviors—specifically, acts, interacts, and double interacts—become interstructured and repetitive in the form of predictable patterns. To the extent that the communicative behaviors or group members are interstructured, the attributes used to characterize a group may be assumed to exist.

In evaluating the advisory committee, these basic elements of the group process must be given careful consideration.

The evaluation process

The evaluation process, like the group process, is composed of complementary and diverse elements. As applied to the advisory committee itself, evaluation must consist of more than examining the attainment of objectives, evaluating the results of committee actions, and assessing the techniques employed by the committee. It is more than a simple procedure because it is a management tool that is people centered.

Within this framework, there are several key concepts that deserve special attention. First, evaluation must not only measure behavioral changes in individuals but must ensure the proper balance in the number and type of individuals reached, must judge the extent to which the results deal with needs, and must oversee the care with which the resources of the committee are used. Second, the process combines a description of the results that occurred with an evaluation of the results. Third, it must influence ongoing developments in the committee, thereby providing immediate benefits. Fourth, evaluation can be a powerful working tool. It is not an end in itself nor something to engage in because it is intrinsically good, rather it is a way to get things accomplished. Fifth, as a continuous process, it is focused on everyday processes, diagnostic reviews, and more systematic endeavors as required by the committee.

In a general sense, evaluation is a process of obtaining and delineating information whereby the merits of alternative decisions can be judged. Like any other process, it is composed of many elements. As an example, the Context, Input, Process, Product (CIPP) Evaluation Model divides decisions into four classes called planning, structuring, implementing, and recycling decisions.

> Since there are four kinds of decisions to be served, the CIPP Model also includes four kinds of evaluation. Context evaluation serves planning decisions by identifying unmet needs, unused opportunities, and underlying problems which prevent the meeting of needs or the use of opportunities; input evaluation serves structuring decisions by projecting and analyzing alternative procedural designs; process evaluation serves implementing decisions by monitoring project operations; and product evaluation serves recycling decisions by determining the degree to which objectives have been achieved and by determining the cause of the obtained results. [156:268]

There are different approaches that might be followed to develop a group evaluation process. The group and evaluation processes must, however, be integrated into one process that provides an effective base for evaluating the advisory committee as well as all other aspects of the career and occupational program.

GUIDELINES FOR EVALUATING THE COMMITTEE

The evaluation of the advisory committee is not unlike the assessment or review procedures used in connection with other segments of the program. Evaluation must be integrated with the regular activities of the committee. It cannot be isolated from other committee actions. The complexity of the group evaluation process introduces a set of intertwining processes, theories, and components. The application of these concepts, however, need not be viewed as an arduous responsibility because through the application of some simple guidelines, the process can be made operative in a relatively easy manner.

Assignment to evaluate. The plans for evaluating the work of the committee should be established at the same time the committee is formed. This not only provides an opportunity for school personnel to demonstrate the importance of this activity to committee members but it also places emphasis on evaluation as an integral aspect of all committee action.

Practical application of the concepts. Using the evaluation process can provide committee members with firsthand experience in applying the techniques involved in evaluation. It can clarify the committee's understanding of its purposes by directly applying specific principles while at the same time providing an opportunity for committee self-assessment.

Scope and breadth. The plan used in evaluating the committee should be extensive and systematically developed. Narrow, vague, or poorly conceived evaluation efforts are often more detrimental than they are helpful. A well-organized plan normally includes one or more of the three types of committee evaluation: (1) *Pre- and post-studies* are a common technique employed by advisory committees to determine if their actions have had an impact on a particular program or program segment. To provide information about the current situation, the data may be collected through an initial needs study. Following the implementation of specific committee recommendations, a follow-up study can be undertaken to determine the impact of committee efforts. (2) *Formative assessments* are the most common type of evaluation utilized by advisory committees. These focus more directly on the tasks accomplished and activities of the committee. They may, for example, measure the effectiveness of the committee on a meeting by meeting basis, review committee actions in view of various group dynamics processes, evaluate committee progress toward specific goals, or measure the improvement in committee operating procedures. (3) *Annual or long-term evaluations* usually combine one or more of the elements identified in the first two types of committee evaluation. They are used as action items or discussion points in the last meeting of the year or at the culmination of a particular project. They may focus on committee self-criticism, planning an improved committee process, highlighting accomplishments and shortcomings, or completing a committee evaluation instrument.

Balance with other goals. The committee must maintain a proper perspective between its self-evaluation responsibilities and the performance of its other functions. An overemphasis on self-evaluation can detract from the primary mission of the committee. Also, the evaluation process can be frustrating for individuals on the committee, thereby increasing the possibility for internal strife.

Evaluation commitment. An advisory committee's commitment to evaluation can have a direct impact on how others associated with the program perceive evaluation. One of the common criticisms of advisory committees and administrators alike is that "they" are most willing to evaluate "us," but seldom review their own actions. While the committee's commitment to evaluate its own efforts extends beyond this concern, the committee must face this criticism.

Progress assessment. As part of a continuous review effort, committee self-evaluation can be used to reinforce accomplishments or reveal lack of progress. For example, a meeting devoted to a review of the year's work may indicate to the members that, in spite of frequent stalemates, a great deal was accomplished and may strengthen hope for greater future change. Where progress has been lacking, the assessment may also suggest areas of need and ways in which improvement might be fostered.

Levels of expectation. The results of a particular evaluative effort can frustrate committee members and school personnel alike. It is not uncommon to expect too much or too rapid results from a committee. In addition, many undertakings cannot be adequately evaluated at the end of the project. Change is usually slow, and committees may well spend long periods of time carrying out or fulfilling a single purpose. Also, the most meaningful evaluation may come months or years after the project was adopted.

How can evaluating the advisory committee improve committee actions? In an application of these guidelines to the state advisory councils, Robertson [145:4] identified eight ways in which an evaluative system could be used to enhance the actions taken by the group.

1. Assist the Council to develop a set of goals for vocational education that reflects the Council's expectations for accomplishments by vocational education.

2. Assist the Council to understand the state planning documents so that the Council knows the directions in which the state intends to move.

3. Increase the Council's knowledge of the present status of vocational education in the state in relation to Council goals and state plans.

4. Establish measures of progress toward goal attainment that are acceptable to the Council and to vocational educators.

5. Provide the framework and data for council responsibilities such as advising on the state plan, reporting, making recommendations and public relations activities.

6. Make maximum use of limited Council resources.

7. Assist the Council to maintain independence as the public's voice in shaping priorities in vocational education.

8. Maintain a set of long-range objectives and continuity of action with a Council membership that undergoes regular changes.

APPROACHES FOR EVALUATING THE COMMITTEE

How the committee evaluates the actual situation and itself may vary from a highly sophisticated systems analysis to an informal, unstructured approach. Normally, the efforts tend to be informal. Although no single plan can be applied to diverse settings, it is important that the basic principles involved in a group evaluation process be incorporated into the plan. It must be, for example, an integrated approach that is ongoing, objective, constructive, acceptable, and measurable.

Scope of evaluation

What procedures the committee uses to obtain the data necessary to evaluate itself may vary. Before determining to collect specific information, the committee should respond to the following basic questions:

- What is the purpose of the evaluation?
- How will the data be used to improve the committee or the occupational program?
- Is the evaluation only a self-assessment, or will information be collected from other sources?
- Is the evaluation part of a systemwide approach, or is it only a self-contained study?
- What types of evaluation are being considered?
- Is individual participation (frequency, flow, nature, and value) in the committee to be evaluated?
- Is the focus on individual/group action or on what impact these actions have on the program?
- What administrative procedures or leadership styles are to be reviewed?
- Is this a one-time effort, or will there be additional follow-up studies?

From these questions, it is readily apparent that the implications for evaluating the committee are great. This cannot, however, be viewed as an overburdening task, nor can the importance of the task be allowed to overshadow the primary purpose of the committee. The evaluation guidelines suggested in this chapter must remain at the forefront in order effectively to utilize the committee evaluation process as an integral part of the effort to improve the entire program.

Evaluation strategies

Committee evaluations may be grouped according to the particular person or group designated with the responsibility for collecting and analyzing the data, which is usually an individual in the administration, an outside observer/consultant, or an individual team member such as the chairperson or secretary. While each presents distinct advantages and disadvantages, the actual success of any effort depends on the skill demonstrated in collecting data and the manner in which it is collected.

The second, and most common, method of grouping evaluations is according to the type of data collected. The form of the data will depend on the intent of the review. For example, the assessment may focus on specific procedures, minutes, attendance records, or other reports made by the committee. The evaluation may be a review of the committee's operational format—the nature and extent of participation, the changes in attitudes, individual or group actions, or the postsession conversations.

Another alternative might be to assess the degree to which the goals, functions, and activities of the committee were attained. As the most prevalent form of committee evaluation, this third method of evaluation may be accomplished formally or informally.

A final type of evaluation might focus on outcomes of the committee and the impact that its actions have had on the program. While more difficult to obtain, information of this type is valuable and may have the greatest impact on the career and occupational-based programs. In any case, it must be pointed out that

1. No one method of evaluation should be used over and over. The effectiveness of any one will lessen after it has been used two or three times.

2. No technique of evaluation is effective unless it is applied by an observer who can translate the results into meaningful and specific suggestions for improving discussion procedure.

3. Reports of individual evaluations must be made, publicly or privately, in ways that will strengthen the group without making any member feel insecure.

4. Constant emphasis upon evaluations inclines some members to say nothing, rather than risk saying the wrong thing, and others to focus more upon procedures than products of discussion. [15:127]

The two main forms of committee evaluation are self-assessment, which may either be applied individually to each member or by the members to the entire committee, and evaluations made by individuals outside the formal committee structure, such as by a school administrator, a consultant, or other individuals in the community.

Committee self-assessment. In an informal sense, the group dynamics of the committee may be used as a measure of its effectiveness. It does not take an expert, for example, to determine if there is significant interaction in the committee, if there is a sharp focus on the issues being discussed, or if progress is being made by the committee. Members themselves can provide input as to how the meetings are progressing or whether they feel their services are being appreciated. Other factors that might be indicative are attendance records, the degree of follow-up on committee actions, the regularity of agenda and minutes, and the level of commitments made by committee members.

From a more formal perspective, the committee might utilize a self-assessment instrument, as illustrated in Figure 13–1, to provide some quantifiable measures. The vice-chairperson, secretary, and another member might serve as a subcommittee to collect and analyze such data. In addition, they might focus on the following:

1. Did the items on the agenda evoke interest and discussion by the committee?
   a. Were they understood by all members?
   b. Were they considered valid, within the committee's field of interest, and important?

2. Was the backup material sent out in time, and in proper form, to orient each member prior to the meeting?

3. Was the meeting room adequate for the meeting?

4. Are plans moving ahead on suggestions made at the meeting?
   a. Are the minutes ready to be mailed?
   b. Have all items needing special attention been identified? Who has this responsibility?
   c. Are there special tasks, reports, or assignments that call for immediate attention? [143:48]

Other approaches might be used to evaluate the committee in order to determine if the chairperson was fair to all members in the meeting, if all members were encouraged to participate, or if there are particular weaknesses in the committee structure. Regardless of the approach utilized, the individuals involved must try not to be overly sensitive to criticisms by the group. The goal is to identify concerns and problem areas in order to improve the effectiveness of the committee, thereby helping it to contribute to a sound student-oriented program.

Administrative or outside evaluation.   In addition to the committee itself, there are other formal and informal means to evaluate the effectiveness of the advisory committee. General perceptions in the community about the committee and its actions might be solicited through the following questions: What is the general impression of the actions of committee members in the community? What is the level of knowledge about the committee in the community? To what extent have committee members promoted the program? What has been the role of committee members in working with other agencies and organizations in the community? What is the general impression of personnel directors, supervisors, and others directly affected by the program about the committee? From a more specific perspective, information concerning the actual operation of

FIGURE 13-1. *Program advisory committee self-assessment instrument*

The local cooperative education advisory committee represents the communication link between the community and the school. The committee is important to the program through their efforts to review the curriculum, publicize and promote the program, secure training stations, advise on equipment, facilities, and instructional needs, and assist in vocational student organization activities.

Directions: The assessment is on a zero-to-five scale. Zero means the nonexistence and five means idea. Total and find the average.

Review Criteria:	Assessment	Comments
A. A local advisory committee has been organized to give guidance and direction to the program.	5 4 3 2 1 0	
B. The local advisory committee		
1. includes representatives of business, labor, students, and the public.	5 4 3 2 1 0	
2. includes members who also are utilized as on-site sponsors.	5 4 3 2 1 0	
3. is involved in determining community needs.	5 4 3 2 1 0	
4. is involved in publicizing and promoting the program.	5 4 3 2 1 0	
5. is involved in evaluating the program.	5 4 3 2 1 0	
6. is involved in developing employment opportunities.	5 4 3 2 1 0	
7. is involved in reviewing program objectives and course content.	5 4 3 2 1 0	
C. Duties and responsibilities of advisory committee members are outlined in writing and are being followed.	5 4 3 2 1 0	
D. The advisory committee meets on a regularly scheduled basis	5 4 3 2 1 0	
E. Minutes of advisory committee meetings are sent to the appropriate administrators.	5 4 3 2 1 0	

AVERAGE TOTAL ASSESSMENT _____

the committee might be collected. In such cases, the following questions might be included: Are the minutes and agenda sent out on a timely basis? Are the operational details (policies and procedures) spelled out and are they followed? What is the attendance record of the committee members? What actions were taken by the committee and what impact did these have? What is the interest level of committee members in respect to committee activity? What type of working relationship has been established in the committee? Are the meetings well planned and well operated? When an individual or group outside the committee structure attempts to answer questions of this type, the topic of evaluation must be introduced in a positive manner as a regular activity, and it must be applied consistently from committee to committee and from year to year. Usually the director of the program or another school administrator is responsible for this.

Administrators usually function informally, using information from several sources. They might review committee self-assessment materials, gain insights from faculty members on how much committee members contribute to the program, talk with committee members about their role and their perspectives of the committee, and might remain sensitive to comments made by individuals in the community. More formally the administrator should attend at least one meeting a year and actually observe the committee in action. In addition to serving as an evaluation tool, his or her attendance is also a means for demonstrating interest and support in the committee. Data collected in annual forms, as illustrated in Figures 13-2 and 13-3, can also serve as a valuable source of information. When direct contacts (via visits, questionnaires, conversations) are made with committee members, the administrator because of his/her position must maintain a high level of sensitivity to ensure that a false impression is not conveyed.

If a questionnaire is used, it will, of course, vary according to the type, purpose, intent, and scope of the review. Such instruments (or questionnaires) should be prepared carefully because their structure can significantly shape the data, information, and insights they solicit. Sources, both inside the school system and in the community, may be utilized to develop these instruments. Forms provided by committee members may also suggest additional criteria or procedures for obtaining the desired information. In this developmental process, the final appearance of the instrument should not be overlooked.

A final approach might be to use representatives from the community to evaluate the committee, which has the advantage of involving more individuals in the program and possibly gaining new insights or evaluative approaches used by these individuals in their own businesses. Reviews by members of the community, however, are limited to areas external to the committee itself, such as whether the committee has a balanced representation, open lines of communication, or close relationship with the appropriate segments of the community.

FIGURE 13–2. *A comprehensive checklist for an occupational advisory committee*

CHECKLISTS FOR PLANNING/ASSESSING ADVISORY COMMITTEES

TYPES OF COMMITTEES

	Yes	No	Need to Check
What types of Advisory Committees are serving your school?			
Vocational Education Advisory Committee for the District	☐	☐	☐
Regional Adult and Vocational Education Council.	☐	☐	☐
Vocational and Continuing Education Advisory Committee	☐	☐	☐
District or school Home Economics Advisory Committee serving *both* the CHE and HERO programs.	☐	☐	☐
District or school CHE Advisory Committee	☐	☐	☐
District or school HERO Advisory Committee.	☐	☐	☐

POLICIES AND PROCEDURES COVERING COMMITTEES

	Yes	No	Need to Check
Does the Board of Education have policies regulating Advisory Committees? If answer is yes do policies cover:			
Functions of a committee.	☐	☐	☐
Methods of selecting members.	☐	☐	☐
Number of members.	☐	☐	☐
Procedures for replacing members.	☐	☐	☐
Length of term a member serves.	☐	☐	☐
Continuity of committees by staggering terms of office.	☐	☐	☐
Provisions for members succeeding themselves.	☐	☐	☐
Relationship of committees to Board of Education, administrators, teachers and students.	☐	☐	☐
Methods of communication between the committee and school personnel.	☐	☐	☐
Representation of school personnel in an ex-officio capacity.	☐	☐	☐
Appointment or election of chairperson.	☐	☐	☐
Procedures for submitting committee recommendations.	☐	☐	☐

METHODS OF APPOINTING AND ORGANIZING COMMITTEES

	Yes	No	Need to Check
Is there a statement of need, goals and objectives established for the committee?	☐	☐	☐
Are committee members selected on the basis of:			
a. Interest in youth and education.	☐	☐	☐
b. Knowledge of community and/or occupation.	☐	☐	☐
c. Ability as a homemaker, business person or employer.	☐	☐	☐
d. Willingness to devote time to committee work.	☐	☐	☐
e. Representation of interest group or population segment.	☐	☐	☐
f. Character and integrity.	☐	☐	☐
Are committee members nominated by school staff?	☐	☐	☐

	Yes	No	Need to Check
Are committee appointments made by Board of Education?	☐	☐	☐
Can the principal appoint informal Advisory Committees?	☐	☐	☐
Are committee members notified of their appointment by letter?	☐	☐	☐
Are committee members contacted (prior to appointment) by phone or visit of a school representative?	☐	☐	☐
Are committee members provided with information on the specific purposes and the responsibilities of the committee?	☐	☐	☐
Is a school representative assigned as a liaison or ex-officio member of the committee?	☐	☐	☐
Are committee members informed of date and place of meeting three weeks in advance? Is a telephone or card follow-up made before the meetings?	☐	☐	☐
Are agendas prepared for each committee meeting?	☐	☐	☐
Is the chairperson elected by the committee?	☐	☐	☐
Are provisions made for a secretary?	☐	☐	☐
Are minutes of meetings and recommendations of the committee recorded and distributed to members and school authorities?	☐	☐	☐
Is suitable publicity given to committee activities?	☐	☐	☐
Are FHA/HERO activities coordinated with Advisory Committee work?	☐	☐	☐

WORKING WITH ADVISORY COMMITTEES

	Yes	No	Need to Check
Do you feel that services of an Advisory Committee are benefiting your CHE/HERO program?	☐	☐	☐
Have Advisory Committee activities for your school or program developed community understanding and support for Vocational Education?	☐	☐	☐
Do Advisory Committee members understand what is expected of them?	☐	☐	☐
Do committee members possess adequate knowledge of the philosophy and objectives of CHE/HERO programs?	☐	☐	☐
Are members provided information on developments in Vocational Education that affect CHE/HERO programs?	☐	☐	☐
Have committee members received sufficient orientation to the school, programs and vocational education to function effectively?	☐	☐	☐
Is the committee given sufficient information and an opportunity to study and discuss the issues before making recommendations?	☐	☐	☐
Does committee membership and representation reflect varying or opposing viewpoints which should be taken into consideration?	☐	☐	☐
Are committee members invited to attend school functions?	☐	☐	☐
Are committee meetings conducted in an impartial, parliamentary manner to allow all members to express opinions and give information?	☐	☐	☐
Is the importance of committee members' time recognized through keeping meetings on schedule and directed to an agenda?	☐	☐	☐
Are committee members presented the facts and consulted when changes are made in the CHE/HERO program?	☐	☐	☐

	Yes	No	Need to Check
Are committees presented with information on the value of FHA/HERO and asked for advice and suggestions on projects and activities for student organizations?	☐	☐	☐
Are committee functions selected with care, limited to a reasonable number and within the realm of accomplishment or measurable progress?	☐	☐	☐
Do committee members receive adequate advance notice of meetings and prompt reports of minutes?	☐	☐	☐
Are committee members involved in assignments based on their expertise?	☐	☐	☐
Does the committee chairperson maintain contact with school representatives in order to be familiar with school and program developments?	☐	☐	☐
Does the chairperson dominate or allow a school representative or committee member to dominate meetings?	☐	☐	☐
Does committee membership have adequate representation of ethnic minority and economically depressed area groups to reflect the community the school serves?	☐	☐	☐
Are committee members given recognition for contributions in school publications, news releases or by other methods?	☐	☐	☐
Are thank you letters, certificates or other methods used to express appreciation for services?	☐	☐	☐
Is there a reflection of positive support from administrators and teachers regarding the contribution advisory committees make to educational programs?	☐	☐	☐
Has the Advisory Committee been appointed simply to meet the requirements of legislation?	☐	☐	☐

California Bureau of Homemaking Education. *Advisory Committees: A Manual of Operation.* Sacramento: California State Department of Education, 1976, pp. 16–19. Used with permission.

FIGURE 13-3. *Sample format for annual self-evaluation of general vocational education advisory committee*

I.   Accomplishments

   A.   Contributed to the improvement of policies concerning vocational education. Specific contributions: _____

   B.   Contributed to the improvement of the vocational education program. Specific contributions: _____

   C.   Completed studies related to vocational education. Studies completed:
   _____

   D.   Contributed to better communication between school vocational education programs and the community. Examples: _____

II. Committee Morale and Relationships

   A.   Number of meetings held during year: _____

   B.   Average attendance at meetings: _____%

   C.   Members have acquired increased confidence in and liking for each other? (yes or no)   _____

   D.   Percentage of meetings attended by board representative: _____%

   E.   Percentage of meetings attended by representative of school administration: _____%

   F.   Percentage of meetings attended by teachers' representative: _____%

   G.   Number of joint meetings with school board: _____

   H.   Number of subcommittees used during year: _____

   I.   Total number of persons included as members of subcommittees: _____

   J.   Name or purpose of each subcommittee: _____
   _____

   K.   Number of persons involved in ground work other than as members of the committee and subcommittee (as consultants, resource persons, etc.):   _____

      1.   Number of these from the school staff: _____

      2.   Number from the community but not from the school staff: _____

      3.   Number from outside the community:
      Examples: _____

   L.   Number of contributions to community meetings: _____

      1.   Meetings of PTA units: _____

      2.   Other meetings:
      Examples: _____

   M.   Assistance in disseminating information about school policies:
   Examples: _____

   N.   Interest in the committee has increased or decreased during the year?

      1.   Interest of the members of the General Vocational Education Advisory Committee: _____

      2.   Interest of the members of subcommittees: _____

      3.   Interest of the members of the board: _____

4. Interest of the administrators: _____

5. Interest of the teachers: _____

6. Interest of community organizations: _____

7. Interest of the public: _____

O. Members of the committee have shared during the year with members of citizens committees in other communities in the discussion of common problems: _____

III. Committee Operation

A. Committee has kept in its proper sphere of operation? (yes or no) _____

B. Officers have functioned well? (yes or no) _____
Examples:_____

C. There was a satisfactory annual program of work? (yes or no) _____

D. Meetings were well planned? (yes or no) _____

E. The discussions at meetings were well conducted and fruitful? There was general participation in the discussion? (yes or no) _____

Examples of especially good or poor discussions:

_____

F. Subcommittees were well inducted into their responsibilities and given help with their assignments? (yes or no) _____

G. The progress reports and final reports of subcommittees were given adequate consideration? (yes or no) _____

H. There was occasional appraisals of the work of the committee leading to its improvement? (yes or no) _____

I. Magazines, journals, books and other published aids were used by the committee or individual members? (yes or no) _____

List: _____

_____

J. Consultants from outside the community were used? (yes or no) _____

Names and contributions: _____

K. A library of resource materials on schools and vocational education was available to the committee and improved during the year? (yes or no) _____

Indicate how it was improved and how its use was improved: _____

_____

L. Policies and procedures for the committee were reviewed by the committee and the board during the year? (yes or no) _____

Revision made: _____

_____

M. Committee rules were reviewed during the year? (yes or no) _____

Revision made: _____

_____

N. Committee objectives for the year were accomplished as follows:

Objectives	Statement of Accomplishment
1. _____	1. _____
2. _____	2. _____
3. _____	3. _____
4. _____	4. _____

Walter S. Ramey. *A Guide for the Organization and Operation of Local Advisory Committees for Vocational Education.* Richmond: Virginia State Department of Education, 1975, pp. 64–67. Used with permission.

SUGGESTED ACTIVITIES

1. Develop an outline for introducing the self-evaluation concept to the advisory committee.

2. Review evaluation procedures used by other committees in the school and community, and list ideas that may be used by an advisory committee or ways to improve current evaluation procedures.

3. Prepare a list of the key areas in which the committee will perform its self-evaluation.

4. Prepare a list of evaluation and group process concepts that would be helpful for a committee to use in evaluating itself.

5. Outline a procedure for incorporating the evaluations of individuals outside the committee into the committee's total evaluation process.

6. Develop a procedure to be used by a committee in conducting its own evaluation.

7. Develop an appropriate instrument to be used to measure the effectiveness of the committee in each of the key areas identified in item number 6.

8. Prepare a plan that will bring various committee evaluations together into one final report for the department, program, or schoolwide career and occupational education program.

9. Prepare a list of suggested hints and guides that may be used to integrate all forms of evaluation into the regular flow of committee action.

10. Contact the communications department or program at a nearby college and make arrangements for communications students to observe the committee in action at a regular meeting. Then have the observers report to the committee regarding their internal group processes.

SELECTED REFERENCES

Auer, J. Jeffery, and Ewbank, Henry Lee. *Handbook for Discussion Leaders.* New York: Harper & Row, 1954.

Bennett, James G. "Evaluation of Advisory Committees." *Business Education Forum* 28(1974):17-19.

Brilhart, John K. *Effective Group Discussion.* Dubuque, Iowa: William C. Brown Co., 1967.

Buontempo, Gregory, and Klavon, Michael. *Making the Most of Your Advisory Committee.* Trenton: New Jersey State Department of Education, undated.

Danenburg, William P.; Keene, T. Wayne; and Miller, Russell S. *An Evaluation of Advisory Committee Effectiveness.* Tallahassee: Florida State Department of Education, 1975.

Fisher, B. Aubrey. *Small Group Decision Making: Communication and the Group Process.* New York: McGraw-Hill Book Co., 1974.

Koontz, Harold. *Appraising Managers as Managers.* New York: McGraw-Hill Book Co., 1971.

National Center for Research in Vocational Education. *Kentucky Advisory Committee Evaluation System.* Columbus: The Ohio State University, 1976.

Reid, Richard A. "Guidelines for Evaluation Activities Conducted by State Advisory Councils for Vocational and Technical Education." Doctoral Dissertation, The Ohio State University, 1972.

Robertson, J. Marvin. *An Evaluation System for State Advisory Councils of Vocational Education.* Atlanta: Georgia State Advisory Council for Vocational Education, 1971.

Rogan, William B. "An Evaluation of Local Vocational Advisory Councils in Michigan." Doctoral Dissertation, Western Michigan University, 1973.

Steele, Sara M. *Contemporary Approaches to Program Evaluation: Implications for Evaluating Programs for Disadvantaged Adults.* Syracuse, N.Y.: ERIC Clearinghouse on Adult Education, 1973.

Stufflebeam, Daniel L. "The Use of Experimental Design in Educational Evaluation." *Journal of Educational Measurement,* 8 (Winter 1971):267–74.

Tirozzi, Gerald N. "An Assessment of the Expectations of School Administrators Concerning Advisory Councils in the Educational Decision-Making Process." Doctoral Dissertation, Michigan State University, 1973.

Wentling, Tim L., and Erickson, Richard C. *Measuring Student Growth: Techniques and Procedures for Occupational Education.* Boston: Allyn and Bacon, 1976.

APPENDIX A

PROGRAM STANDARDS OF QUALITY FOR ADVISORY COMMITTEES IN THE VOCATIONAL-TECHNICAL PROGRAMS IN MICHIGAN

Program Standard of Quality:

This Program Standard of Quality provides that local advisory councils be established and utilized.

Rationale:

A. Each eligible recipient (that is, each local educational agency or post-secondary educational institution which receives state or federal assistance for vocational-technical education programs) shall establish local advisory council(s) on vocational education.

B. The local advisory council(s) may be established for:

1. program areas,
2. schools,
3. the community, or
4. the CEPD in which the eligible recipient is located.

C. Local advisory council(s) shall be composed of representatives of the general public including at least a representative of (1) business, (2) industry; and (3) labor.

D. Representatives from several craft committees or representatives of several school councils within a local educational agency, having the requisite representatives in paragraph "C," may join together to form a general advisory council.

It should be noted that local educational agencies in Michigan which have met occupational advisory committee Program Standards of Quality in previous years are in full compliance with the above advisory council requirement. Agencies may, however, desire to modify their advisory structure to better meet local needs.

Vocational-Technical Education Service Role:

To maximize the potential of advisory councils, Vocational-Technical Education Service has contracted for the development of extensive in-service workshop materials which may be utilized upon request by educational agencies. In addition, a document entitled, *"A Guide for the Effective Utilization of Advisory Committees"* is provided by the Vocational-Technical Education Service. Individuals trained in conducting the workshops are also available. Finally, Section M, in the Administrative Guide, provides data relating to advisory councils. Procedures to be used and a suggested format in conducting an advisory committee review are provided to educational agencies by Vocational-Technical Education Service.

State Advisory Council Role:

The Michigan State Advisory Council will provide technical assistance to CEPD councils and selected local advisory councils upon request.

Enabling Activities:

Duties of local advisory councils.

A. Local advisory councils shall advise the eligible recipient on: (1) current job needs; and (2) the relevant of programs (courses) being offered by the LEA or postsecondary educational agency in meeting current job needs.

B. Local advisory councils shall assist the eligible recipient in developing its application(s) to the State Board.

C. Each local educational agency (LEA) will develop a plan describing how the district will utilize advisory councils or subcommittees to the advisory councils to:

1. develop written goals to be accomplished by advisory councils for each year;
2. advise in the adoption or revision of student level performance objectives for each vocational-technical education, program/courses(s) for the district;
3. make recommendations related to appropriate vocational-technical education equipment for each program operated by the district;
4. identify and recommend appropriate space utilization for all vocational-technical education programs;
5. assist educational agencies in articulating programs with other agencies and educational instructions;
6. advise and suggest to educational agencies safety standards for vocational programs;
7. assist with the development of articulation agreements with other educational agencies operating similar programs within the CEPD or region;
8. maintain a record of meetings through documented minutes which are forwarded to the program administrator.

D. Advisory councils will also be utilized to assist educational agencies in the planning, development and review of each vocational-technical education program.

Enabling Activities:

1. All approved vocational-technical education programs are subject to review by an advisory council *at least* once every three years using the Vocational-Technical Education Service format or an acceptable substitute.

2. All approved new and revised vocational-technical education programs are to be reviewed by an advisory council at the end of the first year of operation using the Vocational-Technical Education Service format or an acceptable substitute.

3. A suggested review questionnaire will be sent to each educational agency by

the Vocational-Technical Education Service. Results of the review procedure should be made available to the educational agency administrative personnel. The review report will be available to the Vocational-Technical Education Service upon request.

Additional tasks may be identified by educational agencies or by the Vocational-Technical Education Service. All of the above tasks should be reflected in the minutes or advisory council meetings and available to the Michigan Department of Education upon request.

Michigan Vocational-Technical Education Service. *Program Standards of Quality for Vocational-Technical Education Programs in Michigan for School Year 1977-78.* Lansing: Michigan Department of Education, 1977, pp. 5-7. Used with permission.

APPENDIX B

A COMPARISON OF EXISTING AND SUGGESTED MEANS AND RANKS FOR SECONDARY ADVISORY COMMITTEE INVOLVEMENT

| SUBACTIVITIES | SECONDARY | | | |
| | Existing | | Suggested | |
	Mean	Rank	Mean	Rank
Occupational Surveys				
Use of Michigan Manpower Development Handbook	31.5	33	29.3	32
Consultation with Michigan Employment Security Commission	24.0	20	27.9	30
Use of Occupational Outlook Handbook	24.2	22	27.3	26
Surveys Community Needs	10.8	12	12.0	12
Use of Community Survey Data	17.8	18	17.4	18
Course Content Advisement				
Identification of Occupational Competencies	5.6	2	6.4	3
Development of Program Goal Statements	6.1	4	9.7	7
Review of Topical Outlines	7.6	7	16.0	15
Review of Performance Objectives	6.0	3	7.7	5
Student Placement				
Organization of Employer/Student Conferences	23.8	19	17.2	17
Notification of Job Openings	9.2	9	5.3	1
Writing Recommendation Letters for Students	24.1	21	27.6	29
Employment of Graduates	9.4	10	13.3	14
Review of Follow-up Studies	24.5	23	20.0	21
Liaison with MESC	28.2	30	31.3	33
Community Public Relations				
Speaking to Civic Groups	33.9	35	31.7	34
Input at Program Funding Activities	34.0	36	27.3	26
Input at Public Hearings	36.6	40	26.9	25
Promoting the Program via the Media	26.7	27	16.4	16
Development of Promotional Materials	28.0	29	19.7	20
Equipment and Facilities				
Review of Equipment and Facilities	4.0	1	5.9	2
Survey of Equipment in Industry	7.0	6	11.2	9
Suggesting Equipment Replacement	8.1	8	12.1	13
Calculation of Depreciation Allowances	34.4	38	35.1	40
Suggesting Bid Solicitation Procedures	31.0	32	33.5	37
Soliciting Equipment Donations	29.9	31	28.9	31
Program Staffing				
Review of Teacher Selection Criteria	34.3	37	32.3	36
Suggesting Recruitment Policies	35.2	39	32.2	35
Recommending Potential Candidates	32.7	34	34.2	38
Review of Teaching Applicants	37.8	41	36.2	41
Program Review				
Evaluation of Student Performance	14.9	15	18.8	19
Evaluation of Teacher Performance	26.8	28	26.7	24
Use of Annual State Dept. Review Questionnaire	26.5	26	34.7	39
Suggestions for Program Improvement	6.4	5	6.6	4
Comparing Accomplishments with Stated Objectives	13.6	14	11.9	10
Making Periodic Reports to Administration	16.1	16	25.8	23
Obtaining Community Resources				
Arranging Field Trips	25.6	24	27.3	26
Recommending Potential Co-op Work Stations	9.6	11	9.2	6
Identifying Community Resources	11.8	13	11.9	10
Obtaining Personnel for Classroom Presentations	17.1	17	10.8	8
Obtaining Consultants for Teachers	25.8	25	25.0	22

Leslie H. Cochran, L. Allen Phelps, and Joseph F. Skupin. *Needs Assessment on the Use of Vocational Advisory Committees in Michigan.* Lansing: Michigan Department of Education, 1974, p. 33. Used with permission.

APPENDIX C

A COMPARISON OF EXISTING AND SUGGESTED MEANS AND RANKS FOR POSTSECONDARY ADVISORY COMMITTEE INVOLVEMENT

| | POSTSECONDARY | | | |
| | Existing | | Suggested | |
SUBACTIVITIES	Mean	Rank	Mean	Rank
Occupational Surveys				
Use of Michigan Manpower Development Handbook	30.5	37	28.1	32
Consultation with Michigan Employment Security Commission	22.7	22	21.7	21
Use of Occupational Outlook Handbook	28.5	32	27.6	29
Surveys Community Needs	9.5	5	11.1	6
Use of Community Survey Data	7.5	3	13.4	11
Course Content Advisement				
Identification of Occupational Competencies	13.7	9	6.0	1
Development of Program Goal Statements	17.9	15	15.4	14
Review of Topical Outlines	13.3	8	18.0	17
Review of Performance Objectives	16.2	12	15.6	15
Student Placement				
Organization of Employer/Student Conferences	20.5	20	11.7	8
Notification of Job Openings	6.6	2	9.4	3
Writing Recommendation Letters for Students	18.6	16	28.8	35
Employment of Graduates	8.6	4	11.0	5
Review of Follow-up Studies	20.1	19	14.9	12
Liaison with MESC	23.4	24	24.8	23
Community Public Relations				
Speaking to Civic Groups	28.7	33	32.1	38
Input at Program Funding Activities	32.5	40	26.4	27
Input at Public Hearings	27.5	28	28.7	34
Promoting the Program via the Media	28.1	30	18.7	18
Development of Promotional Materials	24.1	26	21.3	20
Equipment and Facilities				
Review of Equipment and Facilities	5.9	1	8.8	2
Survey of Equipment in Industry	11.1	7	15.6	15
Suggesting Equipment Replacement	14.7	10	14.9	13
Calculation of Depreciation Allowances	34.3	41	34.4	41
Suggesting Bid Solicitation Procedures	29.4	34	30.6	37
Soliciting Equipment Donations	24.0	25	28.5	33
Program Staffing				
Review of Teacher Selection Criteria	29.4	34	32.7	39
Suggesting Recruitment Policies	31.4	38	33.3	40
Recommending Potential Candidates	29.4	34	27.2	28
Review of Teaching Applicants	32.4	39	28.0	31
Program Review				
Evaluation of Student Performance	21.0	21	21.9	22
Evaluation of Teacher Performance	28.0	29	27.9	30
Use of Annual State Dept. Review Questionnaire	24.9	27	29.0	36
Suggestions for Program Improvement	10.8	6	9.6	4
Comparing Accomplishments with Stated Objectives	15.8	11	13.3	10
Making Periodic Reports to Administration	28.4	21	24.9	24
Obtaining Community Resources				
Arranging Field Trips	23.0	23	25.9	25
Recommending Potential Co-op Work Stations	17.2	13	12.8	9
Identifying Community Resources	17.2	13	11.3	7
Obtaining Personnel for Classroom Presentations	19.8	17	20.6	19
Obtaining Consultants for Teachers	19.8	17	26.0	26

Leslie H. Cochran, L. Allen Phelps, and Joseph F. Skupin. *Needs Assessment on the Use of Vocational Advisory Committees in Michigan.* Lansing: Michigan Department of Education, 1974, p. 35. Used with permission.

APPENDIX D

ADVISORY COMMITTEE INVOLVEMENT AND EFFECTIVENESS AS VIEWED BY ADMINISTRATORS AND BOARD MEMBERS OUTSIDE OF VOCATIONAL EDUCATION

EXTENT OF INVOLVEMENT		EFFECTIVENESS OF INVOLVEMENT	
Occupational Surveys	*Percent*	*Occupational Surveys*	*Percent*
Never	16.3	Ineffective	10.8
Not Usually	15.0	Slightly Effective	20.3
Moderately	43.7	Satisfactory	51.3
Greatly	25.0	Very Effective	17.6
Course Content Advisement	*Percent*	*Course Content Advisement*	*Percent*
Never	3.8	Ineffective	5.2
Not Usually	11.3	Slightly Effective	12.8
Moderately	45.6	Satisfactory	32.5
Greatly	39.3	Very Effective	30.5
Student Placement	*Percent*	*Student Placement*	*Percent*
Never	12.5	Ineffective	20.4
Not Usually	38.1	Slightly Effective	38.7
Moderately	34.2	Satisfactory	30.6
Greatly	15.2	Very Effective	10.7
Community Public Relations	*Percent*	*Community Public Relations*	*Percent*
Never	6.3	Ineffective	11.9
Not Usually	27.5	Slightly Effective	27.6
Moderately	46.2	Satisfactory	46.1
Greatly	20.0	Very Effective	14.4
Equipment and Facilities	*Percent*	*Equipment and Facilities*	*Percent*
Never	5.1	Ineffective	10.9
Not Usually	30.8	Slightly Effective	30.1
Moderately	33.3	Satisfactory	34.3
Greatly	30.8	Very Effective	24.7
Program Staffing	*Percent*	*Program Staffing*	*Percent*
Never	16.6	Ineffective	24.3
Not Usually	60.3	Slightly Effective	38.6
Moderately	19.2	Satisfactory	34.3
Greatly	3.9	Very Effective	2.8
Program Review	*Percent*	*Program Review*	*Percent*
Never	2.9	Ineffective	5.8
Not Usually	4.3	Slightly Effective	14.5
Moderately	60.0	Satisfactory	46.4
Greatly	32.8	Very Effective	33.3
Obtaining Community Resources	*Percent*	*Obtaining Community Resources*	*Percent*
Never	5.1	Ineffective	5.4
Not Usually	18.0	Slightly Effective	28.4
Moderately	42.3	Satisfactory	43.2
Greatly	34.6	Very Effective	23.0

Leslie H. Cochran, L. Allen Phelps, and Joseph F. Skupin. *Needs Assessment on the Use of Vocational Advisory Committees in Michigan.* Lansing: Michigan Department of Education, 1974, pp. 45–47. Used with permission.

APPENDIX E

IF YOU WANT ME TO SERVE ON A SCHOOL
ADVISORY COMMITTEE

Dear Educator:

I am pleased you have asked me to serve as an industry member of an advisory committee to our school system. I shall be delighted to accept your invitation—if you can assure me that I will be involved in an activity which is going to make some worthwhile and important contribution to the education of our youth. I want to be proud enough of this committee's work so that I may brag a little to my family, friends and associates that I was selected to participate—as you, yourself, stated—"because of my reputation as an outstanding member" of the field in which I am earning my living, "as well as for my interest in and understanding of the field of education."

To support my feelings about the importance of my service, I would like to have a letter appointing me on the committee signed by the highest possible school official. The letter should include some biographical information on the chairman and other members of the committee and also tell me exactly what is expected of me as a committee member in the way of advice, assistance, cooperation, money and time. Please note that if you tell me the committee will meet only two or three times a year, I will know that we really aren't going to do anything worthwhile!

On the other hand, if you seriously want help from the committee to improve our educational system, I need to be sure that I will be provided, initially and on a continuing basis, with information concerning educational developments within the school system, as well as at the state and national levels; be invited occasionally to attend local, state and national conventions of educators (you will be surprised by how many I will attend at my own or my company's expense); and that I will occasionally receive a special invitation to attend a school function, a board of education meeting, or a state board meeting. I would also like to be kept informed of special studies affecting the educational program of my school system, and if possible, receive copies.

In effect, what I am saying is that if you want me to advise you, I will feel much more comfortable if I know something about you and your environment. And while I am learning, hopefully I am becoming identified with you, the school, and the problems of the educational system. If you can get me to this point you can be assured of my active participation in the school program and on the committee. And beyond offering advice, I will actually cooperate with you to help you achieve your program goals.

How? In every way possible! I would be glad to help raise money for a scholarship fund; to help obtain needed school equipment on loan, as a gift, at special discount; to contribute expendable supplies, instructional and guidance materials; to provide work/study experiences; to employ graduates, to help counsel students; to assist teachers in enriching and expanding their instructional activities; and other services you may request. You name it! What I am really asking is that you, the professional educator, provide me, the interested layman, with counsel and leadership for my committee responsibilities.

I know there will be times when you will ask the committee for something you consider important that for some good reason we will not be able to provide. But we won't just be negative when this happens. We will tell you our problem and try to work things out with you. In the process, we will both learn more about industry and education, and together prove that industry-education cooperation can be a viable way of life for citizens and school people.

Sometimes I might want to do too much and try to get involved in administration. If I do, just point out that the best way I can help you is to give you advice and cooperation and leave the details of day-to-day school operations to you. In reality, I don't even have time to handle all my OWN day-to-day administrative problems, much less yours! But remember—as businessmen, we committee members are problem oriented and if you tell us about your problems we can help you with them, even if it takes time from our personal or business affairs. After all, we expected to spend time with you when we accepted service on the committee.

I would like to be welcomed in the schools as a friend and supporter—not seen as a meddlesome interloper. Naturally there are certain school regulations which I should observe when visiting and you should make them clear to me. But if I occasionally drop in for a visit, give me a few minutes of your time. Your courtesy will be well repaid. I wouldn't come if I weren't interested!

I would like to know what other schools and school systems are doing about the problems you present to my committee. I want to feel there is some linkage between our school system and others in the area. I would like to know what the private schools are doing and what MDTA educational and training programs are available in the community. I want to understand the relationships which exist between these programs, the State Employment Service, "war-on-poverty" programs, correctional institution training programs and any others that will be providing manpower for industry. I want to know the whole picture, and even get a chance to visit these other educational programs. Perhaps our advisory committees ought to meet together once or twice a year. I want to know about these other programs so that I will not have the nagging feeling that I am being "used" to support one program in opposition to another. I want to feel that I am helping to improve "MY" school's contribution to the total community effort—as a taxpayer, as an employer and as an interested citizen concerned with and involved in improving educational and manpower development programs in my community.

I would like to meet, more than on a token once-a-year basis, with the students in the school or program my committee was organized to serve. I want the students to know my committee exists. In the final analysis, our efforts are supposed to be directed at improving the education and training of students. I want them to tell me to what extent we are succeeding. As a matter of fact, I would like to have each graduating class elect one of its members to serve as an ex-officio member on our committee to tell us, in the first year after graduating, how relevant school really is in terms of real jobs.

I would like some expression of appreciation for my volunteered services and contributions. If this committee is as important as you tell me it is,

give it and its members some concrete form of recognition. For example, if
I donate a piece of equipment, put my nameplate on it. Send me a framed
certificate of appreciation for my services. Hold a special annual event
to recognize the services of all advisory committee members. Include our
names in the school catalog and annual reports. We all like to see our
names in print! Besides, when prospective students, their parents and
others see that your programs, as described in the catalog, are receiving
advice and assistance from industry people, the programs will gain in
stature and prestige. In addition, my company and the industry I represent
will be more than ever committed to support you.

When you ask me to attend a committee meeting, I want to know before
hand what will be on the agenda. I will want a brief background statement
of the problems to be discussed and several possible approaches to the
solution of each. Give me at least two weeks' notice of the meeting date.
Make it at a convenient time and preferably at a school. And don't hesitate
to remind me about it by letter or a phone call.

I want the meeting to be conducted informally and not to get tied up
in parliamentary rules of order. I will want the meeting to be held within
reasonable time limits. Don't let it drag on and on. I am used to crisp,
businesslike procedures. I will want something to happen as a result of
the meeting. I will want to know, as soon after the meeting is over as
possible, what did and will happen as a result of our advice and services.
I don't want to be asked to attend a meeting to approve something after it
has already happened. If I find out I am being used that way, don't be
surprised when I become your critic instead of your advisor!

I know I am asking a great deal of you. But I am willing to give a
great deal in return. And the more you get from the committee, the better
your program will be. The same is true for us, of course. All the committee
members, as well as the industries we represent, will be benefitted by
having a continuing source of qualified manpower available and by getting a
good return from our educational tax dollars. All kinds of benefits will
emerge if the committee is effectively used.

In the final analysis, this is exactly what I want—effective utilization of my expertise, my knowledge and my interest in serving one of the
most important components of my community—my schools and their students.
If you are prepared to tell me how, when and where, I will do my best to
help you and will appreciate the chance to serve—particularly if you get
me involved in an activity in which I have some special interest. This
means, of course, you and I will have to discuss what my special interests
are vis-a-vis education and young people.

If you think I speak for myself alone, you are very much mistaken.
Most industry representatives who agree to serve on school advisory committees feel as I do. However, too often and in too many situations, their
expectations have not materialized.

Why? Because in our experience, we have found that too few educators
and school administrators understand what motivates industry people to accept
service on a school advisory committee. Or, if they do understand, they have
not been able to provide the leadership, time and effort to effectively utilize

the committees. If you cannot provide the staff time needed to allow for the full range of interests and desires of your committee to serve the school program, you will be better advised not to establish the committee in the first place. A poorly used committee is worse than no committee at all—you would find that you had created your own Frankenstein. Disgruntled members of poorly used committees frequently become the most active critics of school officials and public education.

Well, that seems to cover everything I had to say. It's up to you now to decide whether you want me to serve on your committee. I look forward to hearing from you.

Sincerely,

_____

Signature

Samuel M. Burt. "If You Want Me to Serve on a School Advisory Committee." *News from NACVE*. National Advisory Council on Vocational Education, July, 1974. Used with permission.

Bibliography

1. Adams, Dewey A. "Significant Trends in Professional Development." *American Vocational Journal* (October 1965):22–26.

2. *Advisory Committees.* New York: Croft Educational Services, 1973.

3. "Advisory Committees in Cooperative Education Programs," A package of materials provided by Richard Campbell, Nebraska Department of Education, Lincoln, Nebr., April 1977.

4. "Advisory Council," A paper provided by Francine Kremsdorf, Career Development Systems, Parsippany, N.J. for Wayne Career Education Program, Wayne, N.J., April 1977.

5. Alabama Division of Vocational Education. *Guide for Organizing and Utilizing Local Vocational Education Advisory Councils.* Montgomery: Alabama State Department of Education, 1977.

6. Alexander, William M. "Citizen Advisory Committees on Curriculum." *Curriculum Trends,* Craft-NEI Publications (subscription series), (April 1975):1–4.

7. Allen, Fleet D. "Advisory Committee Organization, Role, and Utilization." Doctoral Dissertation, North Carolina State University at Raleigh, 1971.

8. Allen, Louis A. *Management and Organization.* New York: McGraw-Hill Book Co., 1958.

9. American Vocational Association. *The Advisory Committee and Vocational Education.* Washington, D.C.: American Vocational Association, 1969.

10. American Vocational Association. *Program Promotion Package.* Washington, D.C.: American Vocational Association, 1978.

11. American Vocational Association. *Promoting Vocational Education: A Public Relations Handbook for Vocational Educators.* Washington, D.C.: American Vocational Association, 1978.

12. Anderson, Sherry L. *Key Concepts in Vocational Education: Public Relations for Vocational Education.* Lansing: Michigan Department of Education, 1976.

13. "Annual Program of Work, 1975–76," A paper provided by Bobby G. Derryberry, Department of Education, Nashville, Tenn., March 1977.

14. Arizona Division of Vocational Education. *Advisory Committees.* Phoenix: Arizona State Department of Education, undated.

15. Auer, J. Jeffery, and Ewbank, Henry Lee. *Handbook for Discussion Leaders.* New York: Harper & Row, 1954.

16. Ayars, A. L., and Bovee, C. *How to Plan a Community Resources Workshop.* Buffalo, N.Y.: National Association for Industry-Education Cooperation, 1975.

17. Barrow, Connye M., et al. *Career Assistance and Placement Services Resource Manual, Report—Contract Number RDC–A5–225.* Springfield, Ill.: Department of Adult, Vocational and Technical Education, July 1976.

18. Basualdo, Eugenio A. *Advisory Committees in Vocational-Technical Programs.* Memphis: State Technical Institute at Memphis, 1976.

19. Behymer, Ruby J. "Vocational Advisory Committees and Perceptions of Members Regarding Selected Functions." Doctoral Dissertation, University of Missouri-Columbia, 1977.

20. Bennet, James G. "Evaluation of Advisory Committees." *Business Education Forum* 28 (1974):17–19.

21. Bergquist, William H., and Phillips, Steven R. "Components of an Effective Faculty Development Program," *Journal of Higher Education* 46 (March/April 1975):177–211.

22. Borgen, Joseph A., and Davis, Dwight E. *Planning, Implementing, and Evaluating Career Preparation Programs*. Bloomington, Ill.: McKnight Publishing Co., 1974.

23. Boyd, James E. *Organization and Effective Use of Representative Advisory Committees*. Cincinnati: Great Oaks Joint Vocational School District, 1975.

24. Brilhart, John K. *Effective Group Discussion*, Dubuque, Iowa: William C. Brown Co., 1967.

25. Brodinsky, Ben, ed. *Policies for Better Advisory Committees*. Waterford, Conn.: EPS/NSPA Policy Information Clearinghouse, 1972.

26. Buontempo, Gregory, and Klavon, Michael. *Making the Most of Your Advisory Committee*. Trenton: New Jersey State Department of Education, undated.

27. Burt, Samuel M. "If You Want Me to Serve on a School Advisory Committee." *News for NACVE* (July 1974).

28. Burt, Samuel M. *Industry and Community Teachers in Education*. Kalamazoo, Mich.: Upjohn Institute for Employment Research, 1969.

29. Burt, Samuel M. *Industry and Vocational-Technical Education*. New York: McGraw-Hill Book Co., 1967.

30. Burt, Samuel M., and Lessinger, Leon M. *Volunteer Industry Involvement in Public Education*. New York: Irvington Publishers, 1970.

31. "Bylaws for Barstow Regional Adult and Vocational Education Council," A paper provided by Mark J. Fabrizio, Barstow Unified School District, Barstow, Calif., undated.

32. California Bureau of Home Making. *Advisory Committees: A Manual of Operation*. Sacramento: California State Department of Education, 1976.

33. Carlisle, Howard M. *Situational Management*. New York: American Management Association, 1973.

34. Cartwright, Dorwin P. "Achieving Change in People: Some Applications of Group Dynamics Theory." In *Forces in Community Development*, edited by Dorothy and H. Curtis Mial. Washington, D.C.: National Education Association, 1961.

35. *Citizens Advisory Committees*. Arlington, Va.: National School Public Relations Association, 1973.

36. Cochran, Leslie H. *Key Concepts in Vocational Education: Advisory Committees*. Lansing: Michigan Department of Education, 1976.

37. Cochran, Leslie H.; Phelps, L. Allen; and Skupin, Joseph F. *A Guide for Effective Utilization of Advisory Committees*. Lansing: Michigan Department of Education, 1974.

38. Cochran, Leslie H.; Phelps, L. Allen; and Skupin, Joseph F. *Needs Assessment on the Use of Vocational Advisory Committees in Michigan*. Lansing: Michigan Department of Education, 1974.

39. "Community Advisory Involvement," A paper provided by Susan Brown, Mesa Verde High School, Citrus Heights, Calif., March 1977.

40. Comptroller General of the U.S., Report to Congress. *What Is the Role of Federal Assistance for Vocational Education?* Washington, D.C.: GPO, 1974.

41. Conrad, William R., Jr., and Glenn, William E. *The Effective Voluntary Board of Directors, What It Is and How It Works*. Chicago: The Swallow Press, 1976.

42. "Constitution for Lewis County Area Occupational Center," A paper provided by Myrle Bauer, Jefferson Vocational-Technical Center, Watertown, N.Y., undated.

43. Cook, Desmond L. *Program Evaluation and Review Technique: Applications to Education*. Washington, D.C.: GPO, 1966.

44. *Craft Committees*. Bath, Me.: Midcoast Educational Development Center, 1977.

45. Dakota County Area Vocational Technical Institute. A package of descriptive materials used by the Institute as provided by Marcella Lewis, West Saint Paul, Minn., April 1977.

46. Danenburg, William P.; Keene, T. Wayne; and Miller, Russell S. *An Evaluation of Advisory Committee Effectiveness.* Tallahassee: Florida State Department of Education, 1975.

47. Davies, Don; Stanton, Jim; Clasby, Miriam; Zerhykov, Ross; and Powers, Brian. *Sharing the Power?* Boston: Institute for Responsive Education, 1978.

48. Dellefield, Calvin. *Using Advisory Councils and Committees to Improve Vocational Programs for Rural Students.* Raleigh, N.C.: Center for Occupational Education, 1970.

49. Doty, Charles K., and Gepner, Ronald, eds. *Post-Secondary Personnel Development,* Vol. I. Trenton: New Jersey Department of Education, 1976.

50. Douglas, Cary L. "A Study to Determine the Perceived Effectiveness of Technical and Vocational Program Advisory Committees in Texas Community Colleges." Doctoral Dissertation, Texas A & M University, 1973.

51. Ely, Ron H. "How to Organize and Maintain a Productive Advisory Committee." *American Vocational Journal,* 52 (March 1977):37–39.

52. Evans, Rupert N., and Herr, Edwin L. *Foundations of Vocational Education,* Second Edition. Columbus, Ohio: Charles E. Merrill, 1978.

53. *Federal Register.* Vocational Education, State Programs and Commissioner's Discretionary Programs. 42 (3 October 1977).

54. Felstehausen, Joyce L. *If I Tell You, Will You Listen???* Charleston: Center for Educational Studies, Eastern Illinois University, 1974.

55. Felstehausen, Joyce L., and Lenihan, Genie O. *Followup Report on Illinois "Class of '73" Occupational Program Alumni.* Charleston: Center for Educational Studies, Eastern Illinois University, 1974.

56. Fisher, B. Aubrey. *Small Group Decision Making: Communication and the Group Process.* New York: McGraw-Hill Book Co., 1974.

57. Florida Department of Education. *Florida State Plan for Administration of Vocational Education,* Part I. Tallahassee: Department of Education, 1976.

58. Frantz, Nevin R., Jr. "Functional Specialists Needed in Four Critical Areas," *American Vocational Journal* (December 1976):24.

59. "General Policies Governing Specified Advisory Bodies," A paper provided by Michael B. Moon, State Advisory Council for Vocational and Technical Education, Baton Rouge, La., 1977.

60. Gill, William B., and Luke, Ann W. *Facilities Handbook for Career Education.* Washington, D.C.: National Institute of Education, 1976.

61. *Guide for Establishment and Conduct of Local Advisory Committees for Vocational Agriculture Departments.* San Luis Obispo: California State Polytechnic College, Vocational Education Productions, undated.

62. Haffner, Alden N. *Vocational Education: A Manual of Program Accessibility for the Physically Disabled Two-Year College Applicant.* New York: State University of New York, Coordinating Area #4, undated.

63. Hagmann, Larry A. "A Comparison of Selected Factors in the Operation of Craft/Occupational Advisory Committees." Doctoral Dissertation, University of California, Los Angeles, 1973.

64. Hamlin, Herbert M. *Citizens' Committees in the Public Schools.* Danville, Ill.: Interstate Printing Co., 1952.

65. Hawkins, Layton S.; Prosser, Charles A.; and Wright, John C. *Development of Vocational Education.* Chicago: American Technical Society, 1951.

66. Henning, Michael B. *PERT Applications: Formation of an Advisory Committee at the Community College.* Buffalo, N.Y.: Erie Community College, 1971.

67. Henning, Michael B. "Teaching Faculty and Advisory Committee Member Perceptions of the Role of the Advisory Committee in Curriculum Planning in New York State Community Colleges." Doctoral Dissertation, State University of New York at Buffalo, 1974.

68. Herrscher, Barton R., and Hartfield, Thomas M. *College-Community Relations.* Washington, D.C.: American Association of Junior Colleges, 1969.

69. Hofstrand, Richard K., and Phipps, Lloyd J. *Advisory Councils for Education: A Handbook.* Urbana: Rurban Educational Development Laboratory, University of Illinois, 1971.

70. Hoyt, Kenneth B. *A Primer for Career Education.* Washington, D.C.: GPO, 1977.

71. Illinois Board of Vocational Education and Rehabilitation. *Advisory Council Member.* Springfield: State of Illinois Board of Vocational Education and Rehabilitation, undated.

72. Illinois Board of Vocational Education and Rehabilitation. *Three Phase System for Statewide Evaluation of Occupational Educational Programs.* Springfield: State of Illinois Board of Vocational Education and Rehabilitation, undated.

73. Illinois Division of Vocational and Technical Education. *Area Secondary Vocational Center Planning Guide.* Springfield: Illinois Office of Education, 1971.

74. Illinois Office of Education. *Composite Evaluation Report for Occupational Education in the State of Illinois,* FY 1975. Springfield: Illinois Office of Education, 1976.

75. Indiana State Advisory Council on Vocational Education. *Local Advisory Committee Handbook.* Indianapolis: Indiana State Advisory Council on Vocational Education, 1976.

76. *Industry-Education Councils: A Handbook.* Buffalo, N.Y.: National Association for Industry Education Cooperation, undated.

77. *Involving the Public in Adult, Vocational and Manpower Programs.* Washington, D.C.: Bureau of Adult, Vocational and Technical Education, U.S. Office of Education, 1970.

78. Jobe, Max E. "Administrative Aspects of State Advisory Councils on Vocational Education." Doctoral Dissertation, University of Georgia, 1972.

79. Kansas State Advisory Council for Vocational Education. *The Advisory Committee Organization and Function in Vocational Education.* Topeka: Kansas State Advisory Council for Vocational Education, undated.

80. Kentucky State Board of Education. *Vocational-Technical Education Regional Advisory Committees in Kentucky.* Frankfort: State Department of Education, 1976.

81. King, Sam W. *Organization and Effective Use of Advisory Committees.* Washington, D.C.: GPO, 1960.

82. Koontz, Harold. *Appraising Managers as Managers.* New York: McGraw-Hill Book Co., 1971.

83. Korb, August W. "A Study of Selected Practices in the Use of Advisory Committees, Community Surveys, and Placement Services in Trade and Industrial Education Programs in Ohio." Doctoral Dissertation, The Ohio State University, 1972.

84. Kruger, Daniel H. *Occupational Preparation Programs: Implications for Vocational Education R & D.* Columbus: The Center for Vocational Education, The Ohio State University, 1977.

85. Lahren, James A. "An Examination of the Role of Occupational Advisory Committees in State University of New York Agricultural and Technical Colleges as Perceived by the Committee Members." Doctoral Dissertation, State University of New York at Buffalo, 1970.

86. Land, Ming H. "The Status of Advisory Committees for Vocational and Technical Education in Utah with Comparison of the Structures and Functions to a Theoretical Model." Doctoral Dissertation, Utah State University, 1971.

87. Learning Services Division, Vocational-Technical Education. *Guidelines Cooperative Vocational Education in Vermont.* Montpelier: Vermont Department of Education, 1972.

88. Link, Dwight E. "Occupational Advisory Council Interactions: Their Relationship to Council Age and to Perceptions of Effectiveness as Reported by Participants." Doctoral Dissertation, University of Illinois, 1973.

89. Lippett, Gordon L., ed. *Leadership in Action.* Washington, D.C.: National Education Association, 1961.

90. Lund, Duane. "Some Effects from the National Advisory Council Effort." *AVA Convention Proceedings.* Washington, D.C.: American Vocational Association (1973): 365.

91. Marburger, Carl L. "The Role of the Citizen in Education." *Journal of Teacher Education* 26 (1975): 24–29.

92. Martin, Loren. "A Project to Develop An Instructional Packet for Advisory Committees in Vocational Education To Be Used in the Orientation of School Personnel and Committee Members." Salt Lake City: Utah State Board of Education, 1972.

93. Mason, Emmett E. *Industrial Arts Curriculum Improvements: A Change Agent's Guide.* Columbus: The Center for Vocational and Technical Education, 1971.

94. Mason, Ralph E., and Haines, Peter G. *Cooperative Occupational Education.* Danville, Illinois: Interstate Publishers and Printers, 1972.

95. McCurdy, John, and Johnson, Tommy. *Key Concepts in Vocational Education: Placement.* Lansing: Michigan Department of Education, 1976.

96. McInnis, Douglas W. "An Appraisal of the Organization and Function of Advisory Committees in Community College Occupational Education in the State of Washington." Doctoral Dissertation, Washington State University, 1971.

97. Mial, Dorothy, and Mial, H. Curtis., eds. *Forces in Community Development.* Washington, D.C.: National Education Association, 1961.

98. Michigan Vocational-Technical Education Service. *Administrative Guide for Vocational Education.* Lansing: Michigan Department of Education, 1974.

99. Michigan Vocational-Technical Education Service. *Program Standards of Quality for Vocational-Technical Educational Programs in Michigan for School Year 1977-78.* Lansing: Michigan Department of Education, 1977.

100. Missouri Advisory Council on Vocational Education. *Handbook for Local Advisory Committees.* Jefferson City: Missouri Advisory Council on Vocational Education, 1977.

101. Moe, Edward O. "Consulting with a Community System: A Case Study." In *Forces in Community Development,* edited by Dorothy and H. Curtis Mial. Washington, D.C.: National Education Association, 1961.

102. Morgan, Samuel D. *Proceedings of National Leadership Development Seminar for State and National Advisory Councils on Vocational Education,* Blacksburg: Virginia Polytechnic Institute and State University, June 1976.

103. Nagel, James E. "Characteristics of Effective Vocational Education Occupational Advisory Committees in Secondary Schools of the United States." Doctoral Dissertation, The University of North Dakota, 1973.

104. Nance, Everette E. *The Community Council: Its Organization and Function.* Midland, Mich.: Pendell Publishing Co., 1975.

105. National Center for Research in Vocational Education. *Kentucky Advisory Committee Evaluation System.* Columbus: The Ohio State University, 1976.

106. National Center for Research in Vocational Education. *Professional Vocational Teacher Education Module: Conduct a Student Follow-up Study,* Module A–10. Columbus: The Ohio State University, 1976.

107. National Center for Research in Vocational Education. *Professional Vocational Teacher Education Module: Conduct an Open House,* Module G–7. Columbus: The Ohio State University, 1976.

108. National Center for Research in Vocational Education. *Professional Vocational Teacher Education Module: Develop a Plan for School Community Relations.* Module G–1. Columbus: The Ohio State University, 1976.

109. National Center for Research in Vocational Education. *Professional Vocational Teacher Education Module: Give Presentations to School and Community Groups About the Vocational Education Program,* Module G–2. Columbus: The Ohio State University, 1976.

110. National Center for Research in Vocational Education. *Professional Vocational Teacher Education Module: Maintain an Occupational Advisory Committee*, Module A–5. Columbus: The Ohio State University, 1975.

111. National Center for Research in Vocational Education. *Professional Vocational Teacher Education Module: Organize or Reorganize an Occupational Advisory Committee*, Module A–4. Columbus: The Ohio State University, 1975.

112. National Center for Research in Vocational Education. *Professional Vocational Teacher Education Module: Provide Brochures to Inform the School and Community About the Vocational Education Program*, Module G–3. Columbus: The Ohio State University, 1976.

113. National Center for Research in Vocational Education. *Professional Vocational Teacher Education Module: Provide Displays in the School and Community on the Vocational Education Program*, Module G–4. Columbus: The Ohio State University, 1976.

114. National Center for Research in Vocational Education. *Staff Development Program for the Implementation of Career Education (Teacher's Guide): A Group Approach.* Columbus: The Ohio State University, 1975.

115. National Center for Research in Vocational Education. *Staff Development Program for the Implementation of Career Education (Teacher's Guide): An Individual Approach.* Columbus: The Ohio State University, 1975.

116. National Center for Research in Vocational Education. *Staff Development Guidelines and Procedures for Career Education.* Columbus: The Ohio State University, 1975.

117. National Center for Research in Vocational Education. *Staff Development Program for Promoting More Effective Use of Community Resources in Career Education.* Columbus: The Ohio State University, 1975.

118. Nerden, Joseph T. "Advisory Committees in Vocational Education." *American Vocational Journal* 52 (January 1977):27–29.

119. Nerden, Joseph T. *Vocational-Technical Facilities for Secondary Schools: A Planning Guide.* Columbus, Ohio: Council of Educational Facility Planners, undated.

120. Nevada Department of Education. *Vocational Education Local Advisory Committee Handbook.* Carson City: Nevada Department of Education, 1977.

121. New Hampshire Division of Vocational-Technical Education. *Making the Most of Your Advisory Committee.* Concord: New Hampshire Department of Education, undated.

122. Newman, William H.; Summer, Charles E.; and Warren, E. Kirby. *The Process of Management: Concepts, Behavior, and Practice*, Third Edition. Englewood Cliffs, N.J.: Prentice-Hall, 1972.

123. North Carolina Department of Community Colleges. *Organization, Function, and Operation of Advisory Committees.* Raleigh, N.C.: Department of Community Colleges, 1972.

124. North Carolina State Advisory Council on Vocational Education. *Citizen Participation in Vocational Education Programs: A Handbook.* Raleigh, N.C.: State Advisory Council on Vocational Education, 1976.

125. North Dakota Board for Vocational Education. *The Vocational Education Advisory Committee.* Fargo: North Dakota State Advisory Council for Vocational Education, undated.

126. "Occupational Education Advisory Councils," A paper provided by Robert C. Cervak, Rich Township High Schools, Olympia Fields, Ill., March 1977.

127. Office of Occupational and Continuing Education. *A Handbook for Members of Consultant Committees for Occupations.* Albany: New York State Department of Education, undated.

128. Olson, Herbert A. "The Development and Comparison of a Model Industrial Advisory Council for the Technical-Vocational Program of the Community College." Doctoral Dissertation, University of Houston, 1970.

129. Pennsylvania Bureau of Vocational Education. *Pennsylvania VICA Advisor's Handbook.* Harrisburg: Pennsylvania Department of Education, 1977.

130. Pennsylvania State Advisory Council on Vocational Education. *Effective Uses of Vocational Education Advisory Groups.* Harrisburg: Pennsylvania Department of Education, undated.

131. Peterson, O.F. "Leadership and Group Behavior." In *Leadership in Action,* edited by Gordon L. Lippett. Washington, D.C.: National Education Association, 1961.

132. Phelps, L. Allen, and Lutz, Ronald J. *Career Exploration and Preparation for the Special Needs Learner.* Boston: Allyn and Bacon, 1977.

133. Phillips, Linda. "Mentors and Protégés: A Study of the Career Development of Women Managers and Executives in Business and Industry." Doctoral Dissertation, University of California, Los Angeles, 1977.

134. Phipps, Lloyd J. *Worshops on Developing and Using Vocational and Technical Education Citizens' Advisory Councils.* Springfield: Illinois State Office of Superintendent of Public Instruction, 1971.

135. Phipps, Lloyd J.; Jackson, Franklin D.; and Shores, Lee F. *Activities of Citizens' Advisory Councils and Committees.* Urbana: Rurban Educational Development Laboratory, University of Illinois, 1973.

136. Phipps, Lloyd J.; Hofstrand, Richard K.; and Shipley, W. E. *Course of Study: Citizens' Advisory Councils in Education.* Urbana: Rurban Educational Development Laboratory, University of Illinois, 1972.

137. Phipps, Lloyd J., et al. *CRU System: A Manual for Community Resource Utilization.* Springfield: Illinois Office of Education, Division of Vocational and Technical Education, 1976.

138. Pitale, Anthony J. "An Analysis and Comparison of Selected Roles for State Advisory Councils on Vocational Education." Doctoral Dissertation, University of California—Los Angeles, 1973.

139. Pophorn, Estelle L.; Schrag, Adele Frisbie; and Blockhus, Wanda. *A Teaching Learning System for Business Education.* New York: McGraw-Hill Book Co, 1975.

140. Pucinski, Roman. *The Role of State and Local Advisory Councils in Vocational Education.* Columbus: The National Center for Research in Vocational Education, The Ohio State University, February 1978.

141. Ramey, Walter S. *A Guide for the Organization and Operation of Local Advisory Committees for Vocational Education.* Richmond: Virginia State Department of Education, 1975.

142. Reid, Richard A. "Guidelines for Evaluation Activities Conducted by State Advisory Councils for Vocational and Technical Education." Doctoral Dissertation, The Ohio State University, 1972.

143. Riendeau, Albert J. *Advisory Committees for Occupational Education: A Guide to Organization and Operation.* New York: McGraw-Hill Book Co., 1977.

144. Riendeau, Albert J. *The Role of the Advisory Committee in Occupational Education in the Junior College.* Washington, D.C.: American Association of Junior Colleges, 1967.

145. Robertson, J. Marvin. *An Evaluation System for State Advisory Councils of Vocational Education.* Atlanta: Georgia State Advisory Council for Vocational Education, 1971.

146. Rogan, William B. "An Evaluation of Local Vocational Advisory Councils in Michigan." Doctoral Dissertation, Western Michigan University, 1973.

147. Russell, Earl B. "Career Education in the Middle School: Where Specialists and Generalists Meet." *American Vocation Journal* (December 1976):27.

148. San Diego County Department of Education. *A Guide for Community School Advisory Councils.* San Diego: San Diego County Department of Education, 1975.

149. School District of the City of Royal Oak. *Career Awareness—Grades K-6: Guide for Implementation,* Second Edition. Royal Oak, Mich.: School District of the City of Royal Oak, 1974.

150. Shinn, Larry. "Is an Advisory Committee Necessary?" *The Balance Sheet* 56 (March 1975):252–253, 278.

151. Sorensen, Robert P. "Perceived Priorities and Achievements of Occupational Advisory Committee Functions in the Wisconsin Vocational, Technical and Adult Education System." Doctoral Dissertation, University of Wisconsin at Madison, 1974.

152. Stadt, Ronald W., and Gooch, Bill G. *Cooperative Education: Vocational-Occupational-Career.* Indianapolis: The Bobbs-Merrill Co., 1977.

153. *State Plan for Professional Development of School Staffs.* Lansing: Michigan Department of Education, 1978.

154. Steele, Sara M. *Contemporary Approaches to Program Evaluation: Implications for Evaluating Programs for Disadvantaged Adults.* Syracuse, N.Y.: ERIC Clearinghouse on Adult Education, 1973.

155. Storm, George. *Managing the Occupational Education Laboratory.* Belmont, Calif.: Wadsworth Publishing Co., 1976.

156. Stufflebeam, Daniel L. "The Use of Experimental Design in Educational Evaluation." *Journal of Educational Measurement* 8 (Winter 1971):267–74.

157. Sumption, Merle R., and Engstrom, Yvonne. *School-Community Relations.* New York: McGraw-Hill Book Co., 1966.

158. *Technical Handbook for Facilities—Section 4.12: Design of Barrier-Free Facilities.* Washington, D.C.: Department of Health, Education, and Welfare, Office of Facilities Engineering, November 1977.

159. Tirozzi, Gerald N. "An Assessment of the Expectations of School Administrators Concerning Advisory Councils in the Educational Decision-Making Process." Doctoral Dissertation, Michigan State University, 1973.

160. Touche Ross and Company. *Vocational Education Local Manpower Planning Handbook.* Lansing: Michigan Department of Education, 1972.

161. U.S. Congress, Public Law 88–210. *Vocational Education Act of 1963.* 88th Congress, 1963.

162. U.S. Congress, Public Law 90–576. *The Vocational Education Amendments of 1968.* 90th Congress, 1968.

163. U.S. Congress, Public Law 92–148. *Education for All Handicapped Children Act.* 92nd Congress, 1975.

164. U.S. Congress, Public Law 93–203. *Comprehensive Employment and Training Act of 1973.* 93rd Congress, 1973.

165. U.S. Congress, Public Law 94–482. *Education Amendments of 1976.* 94th Congress, 1976.

166. U.S. Congress, Public Law 95–207. *Career Education Incentive Act.* 95th Congress, 1977.

167. U.S. Congress, Public Law 95–524. *Comprehensive Employment and Training Act Amendments of 1978.* 95th Congress, 1978.

168. U.S. Office of Education. *Education for a Changing World of Work.* Washington, D.C.: GPO, 1963.

169. U.S. Office of Education. *A How-to-Do Handbook for Coordinators of Volunteers in Education.* Washington, D.C.: GPO, 1971.

170. *Vocational Education: The Bridge Between Man and His Work.* Washington, D.C.: GPO, 1968.

171. Vogler, Daniel E. "Relationship of Operational Techniques Used by Junior College Agricultural Advisory Committees to College Personnel Attitude and Program Evaluation Criteria." Doctoral Dissertation, University of Illinois, 1971.

172. Wentling, Tim L. *Locally Directed Evaluation Guide 2: Student Follow-up Survey.* Springfield: Illinois Office of Education, 1976.

173. Wentling, Tim L. *Locally Directed Evaluation Guide 3: Employer Follow-up Survey.* Springfield: Illinois Office of Education, 1976.

174. Wentling, Tim L. *Locally Directed Evaluation Guide 5: Assessment of Student Services.* Springfield: Illinois Office of Education, 1976.

175. Wentling, Tim L. *Locally Directed Evaluation Guide 8: Evaluation of Facilities.* Springfield: Illinois Office of Education, 1976.

176. Wentling, Tim L. *Locally Directed Evaluation Guide 16: Analysis of Community Resources.* Springfield: Illinois Office of Education, 1976.

177. Wentling, Tim L., and Erickson, Richard C. *Measuring Student Growth: Techniques and Procedures for Occupational Education.* Boston: Allyn and Bacon, 1976.

178. Wentling, Tim L., and Lawson, Tom E. *Evaluating Occupational Education and Training Programs.* Boston: Allyn and Bacon, 1975.

179. West, B. R. "PBVE Calls for Orderly Transition." *American Vocational Journal* (December 1976):25.

180. Whitten, Benjamin, et al. "The Effective Functioning of Local Advisory Committees." *American Vocational Journal* 52 (January 1977):30–35.

181. *World of Work: Resource Units for Elementary School Teachers.* Dekalb: ABLE Model Program, Northern Illinois University, undated.

Index